Talking about Writing

Talking about Writing

A Guide for Tutor and Teacher Conferences

Beverly Lyon Clark

Ann Arbor   The University of Michigan Press

For Roger

Library of Congress Cataloging in Publication Data

Clark, Beverly Lyon.
  Talking about writing.

  Bibliography: p.
    1. English language—Rhetoric—Study and teaching.
2. English language—Composition and exercises—Study
and teaching.   3. Tutors and tutoring.   I. Title.
PE1404.C52   1985   808'.042'071073   85-1136
ISBN 0-472-08062-8 (pbk. : alk. paper)

Preface

In the last decade, writing teachers have increasingly turned to one-on-one instruction, reviving a tradition that is as old as Socrates but that was largely neglected earlier in the twentieth century. Partly the revival reflects an increased emphasis on writing as a process rather than a product—on teaching the full process of writing, not just a few editing skills. Since each individual's process is so different, and is different for different tasks, it's necessary to individualize instruction—to help one person expand on and develop abstractions, to help another to rethink sequencing. No longer do classroom drills on "who" and "whom" suffice.

One way to provide such individualized instruction is for the teacher to hold individual conferences, either outside class or instead of regular classes. Lester A. Fisher and Donald M. Murray advocated such an approach more than a decade ago, in "Perhaps the Professor Should Cut Class," *College English* 35 (1973): 169–73. Regular class meetings can even be restructured to allow the teacher to hold brief conferences with each student in a workshop setting, as Roger H. Garrison advocated in his influential "One-to-One: Tutorial Instruction in Freshman Composition," *New Directions for Community Colleges* 2, no. 1 (1974): 55–84. Thomas A. Carnicelli has further explored the rationale and the procedures, in "The Writing Conference: A One-to-One Conversation," in *Eight Approaches to Teaching Composition,* edited by Timothy R. Donovan and Ben W. McClelland (Urbana, Ill.: National Council of Teachers of English, 1980), pp. 101–31. And Charles W. Dawe and Edward A. Dornan have put Garrison's ideas into practice in their highly successful textbook, *One to One: Resources for Conference-Centered Writing* (Boston: Little, Brown, 1984), now in its second edition. More and more, teachers are discovering that working one-on-one can produce dramatic improvement in students' writing and that it humanizes teaching and energizes the teacher.

Another method for individualizing instruction is peer or professional tutoring: students can tutor one another or can work with professional tutors. Tutoring has received a powerful impetus from Kenneth A. Bruffee, whose influential program is described in "The Brooklyn Plan: Attaining Intellectual Growth through Peer-Group Tutoring," *Liberal Education* 64 (1978): 447–68. Many other articles describe successful tutoring programs, including Paula Beck, Thom Hawkins, and Marcia Silver's "Training and Using Peer Tutors," *College English* 40 (1978): 432–49. Like conferences between teacher and student, those between tutor and tutee benefit both the tutee and the tutor. Perhaps the best place to turn for a discussion of the value of peer tutoring is to a peer tutor.

> I have been giving some thought to the advantages and disadvantages of having a peer tutoring program. Even though the writing tutors appear to be having a lot of success, I wonder if there are students who feel wary about coming to a student tutor? As I am a preceptor [peer academic advisor], the advantages and disadvantages of having peer counselors are an issue that I have often thought about and discussed. For my preceptor class I read an article . . . that stated that researchers found that student advisors are as effective as professional advisors and that student advisors have a greater client acceptance. It appears to me that the writing tutor program has a "strong clientele," judging from my own tutee load and the load of my fellow tutors in the class. Another advantage I see in using student tutors is that it is an economical means for providing services. Having professional tutors would be costly, and the tutoring program has a difficult enough time getting its minimal funding.
>
> I also feel that a student advising program provides the tutors themselves with a meaningful learning experience, especially for those students (like myself) who are interested in careers in the helping fields. Exposure to interpersonal skills training and constant interaction with other students provide tutors with meaningful work experience.
>
> One thing that may be considered a disadvantage in using students as tutors is that there is not much continuity. Qualified tutors are available for no more than three years, and usually when their skills are most developed, they have to graduate. Another disadvantage may be that familiarity with students may inhibit effective counseling and tutoring. I have found this to be a problem when trying to tutor my friends.
>
> All in all, however, I have found the advantages to outweigh the disadvantages both for myself as a tutor and for those that utilize the tutoring program. (Diane Ciarletta)

As Diane suggests, peer tutors can have "greater client acceptance"—students can find them less intimidating than other instructors, allies rather than adversaries. In addition, if the tutor is a peer, he is closer to the student's experiences and may be more sympathetic than a teacher, and a student may feel less embarrassed about asking "stupid" questions.

This volume is intended for both teachers and tutors—for anyone who teaches writing through conferences with individuals. Throughout I will use "tutoring" to refer not only to conferences between tutors and tutees but also to conferences between teachers and students. And I will often use the terms "tutor" and "instructor" to refer to both tutors and teachers. For one thing, we teachers need to remind ourselves to behave more like peers in conferences—to share the conference with the student and to listen more and preach less.

My own experiences, as a teacher conferring individually with students and as a trainer of peer tutors, suggest that both of these individualized approaches to teaching writing are highly effective. Certainly students have consistently singled out the conference approach, whether used in addition to or instead of class meetings, as the most effective part of my courses.

I've learned a lot too—especially from the peer tutors I presumably train. Since spring 1978, when we stumbled through a course for training writing tutors, Richard Dollase and I have realized that the students could teach other tutors and teachers a lot too. Thus we began asking experienced tutors to share their discoveries, in person and in writing, with new tutors. Over the years we accumulated excerpts from the tutors' journals, the tutors themselves sorting and sifting them. And as we graduated from the purple ink of dittos to the black ink of multilith, I started to supply narrative links. The current embodiment of this collaborative effort is *Talking about Writing*.

Like the book, the tutoring course has always emphasized both the content of tutoring and tutoring itself, both the writing and the tutoring processes; and like the book, the tutoring program has continued to evolve. Currently, Wheaton faculty members nominate sophomores, juniors, and seniors from all disciplines to become writing tutors. These students take "Introduction to Tutoring Writing," Education 025, a half-credit course (1.5 semester hours). After the first five hours of class (and practice in tutoring one another), the students start tutoring. (For more details about the course see Beverly Lyon Clark and Richard Dollase's "Whose Tower Is It? Training Peer Tutors of Writing," forthcoming as a Service Bulletin of the Wisconsin Council of Teachers of English.) After students complete the course they are paid for tutoring. And both old and new tutors staff a writing room during the day and have hours in the dorms at night.

Without the efforts of these Wheaton writing tutors, many of whose journals I quote, this book would not be possible. The quoted excerpts, it should be stressed, are from journals and thus contain errors and infelicities that the tutors would have corrected if they had been writing formal essays. Throughout the book I have given the real names of the tutors but have changed the names of the students they were tutoring. The tutors whose journals I quote and to whom I am especially grateful are Julie Along, Leslie Aubin, Jacqui Belleville, Beth Brown, Caroline Brown, Dawn Carroll, Mary Carroll, Jen Ciaburri, Diane Ciarletta, Nancy Cicco, Janine Clarke, Celeste Cobb, Cathy Coffin, Liz Como, Tina Cunningham, Karen Curry, Barbara Emerson, Sarah Ettman, Cynthia Fulton, Laura Guadagno, Sue Haberberger, Cathy Halgas, Amy Halpern, Sydney Herman, Dianne Holcomb, Sarah Hutcheon, Karen Kielar, Ann Kohler, Kris Leary, Stacy Lee, Robin McAlear, Ellen McVeigh, Pauline Meehan, Sue Moore, Jane O'Sullivan, Penny Penn, Sandra Prouty, Abbie Reponen, Anne Rice, Susan Rich, Barb Rose, Ann Rowan, Eileen Salathé, Ann Schipani, Barbara Shea, Nancy Solaas, Gayle Tangney, Mary Alice Taylor, Melinda Wadman, Pam Webster, Deborah Williams, M. F. Withum, and Terry Wood. I am also grateful to Pat Farrell, Mary Spence, and Amy Sweetnam.

Others have likewise contributed to whatever strengths this book has. I am especially grateful to Richard Dollase (now of Middlebury College), who first came up with the main idea and many of the concepts for this book, and who helped revise early drafts. Cathy Coffin, now of Dartmouth College, also helped to revise early drafts. Linda Flower, of Carnegie-Mellon University; Frances Shirley, of Wheaton College; and Joan Moscovitch Webb have read drafts and offered invaluable advice. Susan Clark, of Wheaton College, and Ten-Broeck Heussler, of Peoples Academy, have offered useful suggestions too, as has Roger Clark, of Rhode Island College. He has likewise provided many other kinds of support, moral and otherwise.

I'd like further to thank Alice Peterson for help with typing and running off drafts. Financial support for an early version of the handbook came from the Fund for the Improvement of Post-Secondary Education and from Wheaton College.

I am also grateful for permission to reprint material that has appeared in somewhat different form elsewhere. Part of "Evaluating Writing" appeared as "Ranking Writing," in *Structuring for Success in the English Classroom: Classroom Practices in Teaching English,* edited by Candy Carter (Urbana, Ill.: National Council of Teachers of English, 1982), pp. 126–28. It is reprinted with the permission of the National Council of Teachers of English. I am indebted to A. D. Van Nostrand for the assignment on which this ranking exercise is based, a supplemental assignment for an early version of *Functional Writing* (Boston: Houghton Mifflin, 1978), now called *The Process of Writing* in a revised edition (Boston: Houghton Mifflin, 1982). The exercise is published with the permission of A. D. Van Nostrand and Houghton Mifflin. Some of the ideas in "Getting Started" and elsewhere appeared as "Tutoring, Within Limits," in *College Composition and Communication* 35 (1984): 238–40. This material is reprinted with the permission of the National Council of Teachers of English. Thom Hawkins has generously given permission to reprint a modified version of his "Personal Checklist of Tutoring Skills."

Contents

Introduction

Myth number 1, about writing: a person is either a born writer or a born nonwriter—and hence no tutoring help can overcome a basic inability to write. Is that true? Can writing be taught? Or is inspiration a mystical state that descends upon the lucky few? Does it make sense to attempt to tutor someone in writing? One tutor responds,

> Those for whom writing is difficult think there is no solution. Either one can write, or one can't. This is not true. One person may be able to write better or more easily than another, but this does not mean writing problems can't be lessened, or even solved. Many times, the writing problems are specific ones, which may be relevant only to a particular assignment. (Caroline Brown)

It is indeed possible to learn how to write.

Myth number 2, about tutoring: a tutor or teacher is an authority who corrects a student's errors and tells her what she did wrong. Is that true? Is such an approach an effective way for the student to learn to improve her writing? Caroline again offers a response.

> The beauty of the tutoring program is the fact that the tutor helps a student to help herself. When a problem of verb tense exists, the tutor can refer a student to exercises to correct the problem. When a student's problem is organizational, the tutor depends upon the student to help solve the problem, and when the problem is solved, when that paper is rewritten and reorganized, the student can say she did it.

After all, did you learn to ride a bicycle by hearing the principles of balance explained? Of course not. A student learns more if she is active rather than passive, doing rather than simply listening. Thus a tutor or teacher should not be dictating but helping a student to discover how to improve herself. Tutoring means sharing and guiding. It means coaching, catalyzing, collaborating.

Why Be Afraid?

Whether you are a sophomore about to tutor your peers, a master's candidate about to tutor undergraduates, or a teacher about to use the conference method of teaching writing, it can be frightening to face that first conference. Everyone is a little scared at first. You may think you don't know enough.

> Sometimes I don't feel as if I have all of the qualifications to be a tutor. For example, a girl came in the other day wanting to know how to do a character analysis. I had no idea how to do one. Luckily I found a chapter on them in one of the tutoring books. Sometimes I find that when I'm looking over a paper or making suggestions I'm afraid I'll miss something major or I'm not making the right suggestions. I know I can't know everything but people seem to think that if you are a tutor you *have* to know all the answers, which I don't always have. I want to be looked at as just someone who is there to read their papers objectively and make suggestions, someone who may not always have all the answers. (Melinda Wadman)

In the process of writing about her anxiety Melinda reminded herself of what a tutor actually does. And tutors and teachers certainly don't need to know all the answers. In fact, you can set a good example for the student if you look up spelling in a dictionary or punctuation in a handbook or character analysis in a literary guide.

Another tutor's anxiety leads her to imagine a student returning in anger.

> Here I sit. It is the close of another week and . . . I sit on my bed anticipating the student who will charge through my door raging and sputtering about a grade that she received on a paper she is wildly waving around. The student will look vaguely familiar and a cold sweat will break out on my brow as the sudden realization dawns on me that this was the first tutee I ever had. She will accuse me of misinforming her and because of my poor guidance and suggestions she received a very low mark. I see myself lamely making excuses and stuttering phrases regarding the honor code and how tutees are re-

sponsible for the work they produce, but my attempts are to no avail. The girl storms about my room accusing me of incompetence and vowing she will ruin any hope of a reputation I had ever dreamed of acquiring as an English tutor on campus. She leaves my room and the resounding smack of the door awakens me. The wind has slammed the door closed and my nightmare is over; the fictitious tutee is no longer with me, yet her accusations still haunt me. . . .

Here I sit. (Abbie Reponen)

Abbie's nightmare never did come true. Students come because they want help. They have confidence in you—so relax and have confidence in yourself. You'd be surprised how much you do know about writing.

What is more, some of your "weaknesses" are actually strengths: if you've ever had trouble writing, you can relate better to struggling writers who come for help. As M. F. Withum admits,

> I used to hate writing. It was the first class that I ever got a D in. Needless to say, becoming a writing tutor makes me somewhat nervous. However, I think that with such miserable memories about my first attempts in high school at serious paper writing, I can be a very sympathetic tutor. I can relate to the anguish and mental gymnastics nearly every person goes through while attempting to write a paper.

What many students need most is a sympathetic listener, someone who can be understanding, who can listen as they talk about a paper. In fact, it's always best to let the student do most of the work herself. That way she doesn't simply get her paper cosmetically fixed but actually learns something. And that's easy enough to do—you don't need special knowledge in order to listen to her. Paradoxically you're often most helpful when you feel as though you're doing least.

Of course, tutoring can have its frustrations. Improving one's writing takes time, and you or the student may feel the progress is too slow. But look for small successes and don't expect too much. Watch for the smile of understanding and appreciation. Watch for a reduction in spelling errors, for better use of supporting detail, even for greater facility in handwriting. And sometimes successes may be more dramatic: the student who rushes up to you in the dining hall to tell you excitedly that he has finally received a C on his paper; the instructor who tells you how much your creativity and compassion have helped her student; the student who starts writing B instead of D papers.

Who Comes for Tutoring Help?

If you're part of a drop-in tutoring program, you may get a lot of students seeking help once only, with particular assignments. You need to learn what you can about the student and the assignment quickly; then you work on the most basic difficulties.

Or students may be assigned to come regularly: they may be sent by an instructor; they may receive course credit for being tutored; you may be grading them on their performance. Sometimes you can also persuade a drop-in student to come regularly. With some of these regular students you may need to work on overcoming resistance to being tutored, even anger. But you'll be able to develop a long-term working relationship—and you'll be able to watch the student improve.

Some students may be continuing education students, older students, many of whom need to regain confidence and fluency in writing. Some may be traditional college or high school students, many of whom need to refine skills they already have some control over. Some may be learning English as a second language or may be basic writers, many of whom can benefit from techniques discussed in Mina P. Shaughnessy's *Errors and Expectations* (1977), in Christina Bratt Paulston and Mary Newton Bruder's *Teaching English as a Second Language* (1976), and in Marian Arkin's *Tutoring ESL Students* (1982).

You'll soon learn a variety of approaches for working with these students. The trick is to be flexible. Not every technique works with every student. But that's what makes tutoring exciting.

How Far Should a Tutor or Teacher Go?

Some beginning tutors and teachers—and many tutees—think that a tutor is an authority figure, someone who knows the answers and loftily corrects those who venture to come for help. But the tutor and the tutee are partners in learning about writing. Or, better still, the tutee should be the senior partner: the tutee should do most of the work. Tutors and teachers are like Peace Corps volunteers, who seek to make themselves dispensable, by helping their hosts to help themselves.

Sometimes letting the student do the work is difficult. It's easy to be the authority, fun to be in charge. But it's important to know when to stop taking over. Certainly you should not write a student's paper for her. The student wouldn't learn anything, wouldn't learn skills that she could use the next time she writes.

Then there's the matter of ethics. Tutors and teachers need to be responsible to the student and to the academic community (including any instructor for whom the student may be writing). Writing a student's paper for her would, of course, be unethical—it would violate your responsibility to the student and to the academic community. Even if she is writing a paper that you will grade, it's unethical to do too much for her, but ethics are particularly salient when a student is writing for another instructor.

So, given that you don't write the student's paper, how much can you do? One tutor turned to her school's honor code, which states that

> "all work for which a student receives credit be solely the result of her own efforts," and that "each student shall acknowledge her dependence on the scholarship of others where appropriate." Pretty vague, if one considers these rules as guidelines for the tutoring program. No one really knows the answer to our problem. . . . The chairwoman of the Wheaton Judicial Board told me that she is unsure how the honor code affects the tutoring program, other than her feeling that tutees could not directly use the *ideas* of tutors. But then what can be considered "ideas" and what cannot? (Cathy Coffin)

In particular, should you even read an ungraded paper being submitted to another instructor? If so, what kinds of help should you offer? Should you proofread the paper? Should you ever correct an error on it? What can you do instead? Should you make general comments about the organization or content of a paper? Should you tutor take-home exams?

Here are one tutor's conclusions:

> The tutor can find the tutee's mistakes, but she should use examples not related to the paper for demonstrating the student's prob-

lems. The tutor cannot suggest words or phrases to replace those the tutee has used.

Another case is the student who comes with a paper that has already been graded. In that case, help can be unlimited. (Karen Kielar)

I'd agree with Karen: it's a good idea not to make corrections on a paper to be turned in to another instructor, unless it has been graded, to avoid the specter of plagiarism. You may, however, notice a difficulty in an ungraded paper and then do exercises on correcting the difficulty and ask the student to apply what she has learned to the paper. Or possibly in some cases you may indicate where there are errors, without correcting them.

> Lately I've taken to proofreading my roommate's essays. I know that a tutor's job is not really to proofread, but she usually asks me to look them over quickly to see if I spot any errors she had overlooked. (By errors I mean punctuation, spelling, etc.) I usually spot a few slight mechanical errors, and simply designate them with a pencil mark at the end of the line. In this way she can go back and correct them herself. They usually turn out to be stupid errors, errors that she usually doesn't make. They're mostly "typos" committed in the flurry of typing the essay at 7:00 A.M. so she can finish it by her 9:30 class. (Leslie Aubin)

Leslie's approach would be less effective, however, with other students, especially those who make more than careless mistakes and might try to push you to make corrections. Usually I'd advise against proofreading a student's paper. But you need to develop guidelines that are suitable for your own circumstances.

Whatever your guidelines, you can avoid possible misunderstandings by telling students right away what you can and cannot do and also by encouraging them to acknowledge your help in their papers.

> First of all, I let students know how much I can and can't do for them. I can't . . . correct all of their mistakes or proofread a final draft. What I can do is . . . see if they have a strong organizing idea. I can also ask tutees what their strong and weak points are. . . .
>
> During a tutoring session I encourage students to indicate on their papers that they have received help from a tutor. I think this saves the tutor and the student a lot of hassles that might be encountered otherwise. Some think that a professor will downgrade them because they had to see a tutor, but I tell them that it shows a professor that they are concerned about doing well on their paper. (Sarah Ettman)

Once you've decided whether you may or may not proofread an ungraded paper, may or may not correct errors, may or may not suggest organizing principles, don't be discouraged to discover that it can be difficult to follow your guidelines.

> I know from my own experience that it is hard to adhere to what the honor code says (or is supposed to say) when I'm helping a tutee. It was suggested that we should not give specific help to a student who brings in a paper that has not yet been graded. However, this is easier said than done. I have found it very difficult to sit down with a student and help her only by giving her hints about where her mistakes are. For one thing, she probably won't be able to find them and probably needs more specific help on the problem. (Gayle Tangney)

It's hard to draw the line, and it's important to discuss your experiences with others. (Techniques for coping, for getting the student to take control, are discussed in Part 2.) Integrity and honesty and responsibility to the academic community require adhering as closely to your guidelines as possible. And responsibility to the student requires trying to stay within the guidelines too, so that she will get the most out of the session.

There are other ethical issues to consider as well—other questions of how far you should go. For one thing, your responsibility to a student's instructor, if the student is writing for someone else, requires more than avoiding plagiarism. What do you do if, for instance, you disagree with the instructor's advice or tone or grade? Do you talk with the instructor? Do you tell the student that you disagree? I'd encourage talking with the instructor. Yet I would not tell a student that I disagreed with his teacher's grade. I'd be wary of mentioning other disagreements too—and certainly would not do so in a disparaging way. That would be unprofessional (it can also create poor public relations, once the student tells the instructor what "my tutor" said). Instead, maybe you can redirect the student's distress and focus on how to improve the paper, as Sue Moore did with Maria.

> When she walked into the room she was nearly in tears because she had received a D on a history paper. She is a sophomore and has never received anything less than a B+ on a paper since she entered college. . . .
>
> The main problem that she complained about was that the professor had made no comments, or very few, on what she had to say in this

paper (actually a book analysis). Instead, all he did was remark on her style of writing. . . . Also Maria was discouraged because of the way in which the comments were written. They were actually very rude. One comment said—or rather was written like this: "What *can* this sentence *possibly* mean." I felt it rather rude to underline those two words for stress. The professor did not make any suggestions on how to help Maria but rather just shattered her confidence. Of course, I could not sit there and say how I thought the professor was rude, as that would have given Maria the idea that nothing was wrong with her paper, but instead we looked at the paper, discussed his comments, and tried to see how we could improve her writing.

One problem Maria had was that her book analysis was supposed to be her own opinion and therefore written from the first-person point of view. Maria, in writing from this view, used very weak words or phrases—like "maybe," "possibly," "I think," "perhaps," etc. I saw that, through the professor's comments, he felt this made the paper weak, so Maria and I worked on picking up stronger words. I explained to her that she was a smart girl, which she is, and that she can say "this is so" . . . —this I explained, however, must be backed up by facts or concrete evidence. She immediately caught on and proceeded to go through her whole paper telling me how she could have made her argument appear stronger to the reader. This was done with great enthusiasm, which made me see that Maria was emotionally being picked up by realizing what she had done wrong.

Next we worked on run-ons. These Maria easily picked up and said with a smile, "Sue, I'm no dummy. I know these are run-ons, but I didn't bother to really proofread before I typed so I guess I just overlooked them." Thus she realized her own mistake and promised to go over her final draft more thoroughly before typing.

In the end, after working on some comma problems which solved themselves, Maria said she felt much better. She was still upset about the grade but said that now that she knows what's wrong she would calmly discuss it with the professor.

You should be discreet not only about the instructor but also about the student. How would you like it if your doctor talked about your hemorrhoids or acne with your friends? Or if your social worker talked about your debts, or your minister about your marital problems? Doctors, social workers, and ministers should keep such information confidential—unless they have the permission of the person involved. The same goes for tutoring. Your tutoring work is confidential, unless the student gives you permission to mention his name. No "You wouldn't believe who came for tutoring yesterday!" No "Jerry writes such garbage."

Should such confidentiality hold even if you want to talk to the student's instructor or your own supervisor? If the instructor requires the student to be tutored, and it's clear to the student that you are reporting to the instructor—fine, go ahead and talk. Otherwise, with a drop-in student, I'd get his permission before talking to his instructor. As for talking with your supervisor, it's tricky. Sometimes you have to talk about a case in order to get advice. One approach is not to mention names.

A final area of responsibility to the student has to do with possible role conflicts, which are especially acute if you are a peer tutor. One issue is dating. For no matter how egalitarian you try to be, a tutor is nonetheless in a position of power. Even if you try to make the tutee the senior partner, it's still you who establishes the ground rules. Thus you must be careful not to take advantage of the student's vulnerability to your power—not to use the vulnerability to gain, for instance, sexual leverage. It may not seem as if you have sexual leverage if you start dating a tutee, but think about it. If tutoring is important to him, he might agree to a date in order not to weaken the tutoring relationship. And if you have any direct influence on a grade, the possibility of sexual leverage is even greater. Social workers, in fact, are barred from dating clients. Tutors and teachers should certainly think twice before doing so. One solution, if you decide to date, would be to ask the student to see another tutor. Another is to put off dating until an extended tutoring relationship ends, as it may at the end of a semester.

What do you do if you're already dating someone and he asks to be tutored? Yes, you can tutor him. But tutoring anyone who is a friend can be difficult: while it's often easier for a tutee to seek a friend to tutor him, someone with whom he'll feel comfortable, tutoring a friend is often hard on the tutor. For you don't want to offend your friend and you may be especially reluctant to offer criticism, even if it's constructive. You might therefore start by saying that you're going to be honestly critical—and give the friend a chance to leave if that's not what he has in mind.

Another kind of role conflict can occur if a classmate asks for help on an assignment that you're doing too. You may have the advantage of understanding the assignment and material well. But there are potential difficulties. You may find yourself holding back on your tutoring.

> I was subconsciously thinking of my own paper while reading hers. I don't think I gave her paper all the attention I could have. (Cynthia Fulton)

Or you may be tempted to give too much help. Or to receive too much help, unintentionally plagiarizing—it's hard to ignore a useful idea that hadn't occurred to you before. Should you therefore refuse to tutor a classmate? Some tutors do.

> I would ask the tutee to see another tutor, for that one decision/action could avoid many complications and problems later on. It is one thing to tell a tutee you may get ideas from her paper or she may get some ideas from yours, but I really do not feel it would be ethical. . . . I would ask the tutee, for her benefit as well as my own peace of mind, to see another tutor. I would also let her know I would be more than happy to help her with any other work for another class. . . . If it were the same class but different topics, perhaps I would help, but I would still feel uneasy about the possibility of supplying ideas which she had not thought to include in her paper. (Susan Rich)

You don't necessarily have to decline to tutor a classmate. But if you do tutor him be sure that you know what you're getting into and that he understands potential dangers too.

Why Tutor Anyway?

Through tutoring you help someone learn a valuable skill: writing. Writing is useful not only because a person will often need to write—as a marketing executive or civil engineer, for instance—but also because writing is, as researcher Janet Emig points out, a mode of learning. We learn in the process of writing: we learn how to interpret, how to analyze. When we write we also integrate new material with what we already know, and therefore writing enables us to absorb new information. Thus tutoring someone in writing not only helps her to communicate but also to think better.

Tutoring is a particularly effective way to help a student with writing since you work with her individually. For writing is complex. It requires much more than rote learning of the principal parts of verbs. It's a process that requires skill in generating ideas, relating them, organizing them, developing them, not to mention imagining the needs of the reader, choosing effective words, clarifying one's logic, even making the pen shape recognizable strokes as it sweeps across the page. Effectively teaching such a complex process requires individualized attention.

Do students find this individualized attention—this tutoring—helpful?

> I had a very new experience last week and this was I went to a tutor. Before I had always gone to friends with problems about homework. Any English papers I wrote were just proofread and I fixed small mistakes but was never satisfied by my final product. I went to my tutor with no idea what to expect. We sat down and I just said "What should I do with this paper?" She looked over the paper and just asked me some questions about it. These questions got me thinking in a new direction and I could finally see what was lacking in my paper.
>
> From just my first experience with a tutor I can see how much help they can be. It is nice to have someone who doesn't say "this is awful" or "write this instead of that." I found that by just talking with her about the paper I could see my weak points and knew how I wanted to fix them. I know if I had just sat back and tried to rewrite my paper without any outside help I would have never gotten the paper so I was satisfied. I would recommend getting a tutor to anyone. (Amy Sweetnam)

Tutees benefit because they learn new approaches to writing and also because the personal attention humanizes the learning process.

The tutor or teacher benefits too. One tutor found an improvement in her interpersonal skills.

> I am a bit more sympathetic towards those who don't speak and write clearly. I often, in the past, used to "write off" people who could not express themselves well. I believe this was due to the fact, not that I did not want to waste my time, but rather that I didn't know how to listen or read. I find I am more patient and ask questions when I don't understand. (Ann Schipani)

Another tutor found that her own writing had improved.

> I am able to analyze my writing more critically. . . . Before this course rewriting was much more difficult because criticizing my own writing seemed so self-destructive. I feel that I am now able to analyze my papers more objectively. . . . I am able to part with the unnecessary, redraft, and add. Before this course I wasn't that thrilled about writing multiple drafts but I have now started to do so and find it to be a great advantage. My papers are much better and I like them more.

> This ability to extricate myself from my writing has been a positive result from this class, a result which I had not expected. (Ann Kohler)

Still another enjoys learning about other courses, enjoys

> the extra knowledge I gain from reading papers on various subjects. I ask my tutees for some background material on their paper subject before I begin to read the paper so I can better understand what I am reading. It is very interesting to read about Mozart's techniques or the employment outlook for women or the themes of Melville's works. (Sue Haberberger)

Tutoring can also help in developing career skills.

> For those who see a possible teaching career ahead of them, they can see how very difficult it can be to try to help someone understand something. If indeed I do end up teaching, I'm sure lots of what I've learned in tutoring will be helpful. . . .
>
> Tutoring could also help one to think more clearly herself. Having to explain to someone else tends to clear things up in one's own mind. The practice of being confronted with having to explain things without warning, such as when asked to read a paper over and comment on it, is good because it helps to prepare one for spontaneous explanation. This is also something that is important for a teacher to learn—she might be hit with spontaneous questions for which she must have an answer at her fingertips. What a scary thought!
>
> Also, I think a side-benefit from tutoring might be that one gets lots of practice in dealing with people who are generally afraid, nervous, and may feel inhibited by a tutor in many ways. This is very good practice in learning how to relax people and . . . how to make them feel more comfortable with you as well as confident about themselves. It's kind of a neat feeling to have transformed (or at least taken part in the transformation of) someone from a nervous and anxious being to one who has confidence and direction and feels more comfortable with others. (Pam Webster)

But the helping professions are not all that tutoring prepares one for.

> The experience of working on a one-to-one basis has been an exciting part of tutoring. I have become more assured that I have something to offer, and now I am a lot less nervous. I feel this ability is an essential one to possess in the business world, and tutoring is really the only practice I have gotten. (Sydney Herman)

Finally, tutoring can give one a sense of fulfillment.

> It has been very fulfilling to see a student's work continually improve, and realize that I had a part in that improvement. When a student who has struggled over a paper comes to me thrilled with her grade, I share in her sense of achievement. (Sydney Herman)

Tutoring can, in fact, humanize the teaching of writing. Grading papers alone at one's desk, while drinking cup after cup of coffee to stay awake, can sap a teacher's energy and become dehumanizing drudgery. One starts lashing out with the red pen if only in self-defense. But conferring with student writers—tutoring them—both energizes the instructor and humanizes the process.

As for how to go about tutoring someone in writing, that is the subject of the rest of this book.

Part 1 addresses the writing process. Chapter 1 will help you in setting priorities: what you should work on first. Then chapter 2 focuses on generating ideas; chapter 3, on organizing, drafting, and reworking; chapter 4, on grammar, mechanics, usage, and style. Chapter 5 will help you to approach special writing tasks like essay exams and book reviews. And chapter 6 gives you practice in evaluating writing.

Part 2 addresses the tutoring process. Chapter 7 asks what your basic stance should be: coach or dictator? Chapter 8 suggests techniques for starting a conference; chapter 9, strategies for the middle and end. Chapter 10 discusses external constraints imposed by time and grading, while chapter 11 discusses other problems you may encounter, such as anxiety or hostility. The last chapter in this section, chapter 12, offers ways of evaluating your effectiveness so that you can continue to grow as a tutor or teacher.

Finally, Part 3 takes us beyond tutoring. Chapter 13 encourages you to keep a journal, both to reflect on tutoring and to practice writing. Chapter 14 investigates some of the unexpected perils of tutoring, such as expecting too much of your own writing. And chapter 15 suggests ways of reaching a broader audience, both locally and nationally.

Part 1
What to Tutor

Many first-time tutors and teachers feel nervous about whether they know enough—when to use "who" and "whom," what an ablative absolute is, whether the titles of poems should be underlined. But these worries are unnecessary. For one thing, if you're not sure about rules you can look them up in a handbook (and provide a role model for your tutee). Furthermore, what you need to know about writing is not so much the rules of mechanics and usage and the definitions of grammatical terms (though some knowledge helps—better still is some familiarity with a handbook, so that you know where to turn for help). It's more important to know strategies for thinking, writing, revising. And at least as important as knowledge about writing are interpersonal skills, including setting people at ease and listening well.

Tutoring thus requires two kinds of skills: not only knowledge about the writing process but also the ability to interact with another person so that he learns to write better. Part 1 focuses on the first skill, the content of tutoring, while Part 2 focuses on the second, the tutoring itself. In particular, Part 1 suggests ways of generating ideas; of organizing, drafting, and reworking; of working on grammar, mechanics, usage, and style; of approaching special writing tasks; of evaluating writing. But before discussing writing strategies, we should consider priorities.

1 Setting Priorities

Sometimes a student will ask for help on a particular problem: she may want drills on recognizing sentence fragments. Or she may come in to talk about a paper before writing it. Or an instructor may have told her to work with a tutor on eliminating wordiness. But often she will arrive clutching a crossed-out, crumpled draft and expecting you to tell her what to do. Then you need to read through the paper, decide what she needs to work on, and set priorities.

What should she work on first? Generating ideas and thinking about their relationships, if she has had trouble coming up with ideas or details or else her ideas seem confused or ambiguous. Then focus and organization. These are fundamental, and if they need work no amount of sentence doctoring will significantly improve the paper. Furthermore, some sentence-level errors will disappear after a student has restructured the paper and figured out exactly what she wants to say—especially problems caused by vagueness and awkwardness.

Sometimes, though, if you're embarking on an extended tutoring relationship—if you know that you'll be working with a student throughout the semester—you might like to start with something easy, to boost her confidence before she attacks more complex problems. So you think about what's easy for you. You gauge how much time and effort you would spend on reorganizing her paper. And you gauge how much easier it would be to run through the paper and correct grammar, usage, mechanics. So you decide to work on an easy sentence-level error.

But it may well not be so easy for the student. True, correcting some errors may be easy for her. Sometimes a student will readily see how she can attach each free-floating "this" to a noun, changing "They considered this for awhile" to "They considered this new angle for awhile." But many sentence-level errors are deeply in-grained and difficult to explain. You may be able to avoid inappropriate sentence fragments seemingly by instinct. But how do you explain to a student how to recognize and avoid fragments? A sentence is a complete thought, you say? But what is a complete thought? And even if you can explain what fragments are, the student who doesn't recognize them needs much practice and vigilance. Her problem will not be cured by your fifteen-minute lecture, no matter how lucid and entertaining it is.

On the other hand, a "difficult" organizational problem may be relatively easy to explain. And some students will learn from your explanation very quickly. A student who simply hadn't realized the expected structure for a paper may understand your explanation of what to include in an introduction, how to group similar topics together in the body of a paper, and what to include in a conclusion. Or she may merely need the reminder that she should spend as much time organizing a paper for anthropology as one for English.

I remember a discussion with a senior. She'd had a problem with paragraphing, and I stumbled about explaining how she could revise particular passages. She then turned to me and said, "You mean that a paragraph should contain one idea?" I suppose I'd assumed she knew that already. But apparently she didn't. And that sentence was all she needed to hear (though perhaps making the generalization herself helped to fix it in her mind). Improving her paragraphing turned out to be surprisingly easy: she didn't have a problem with it afterward.

Tutoring such students on organization can be one of the most gratifying experiences you have, for the improvement is often dramatic. And the improvement is often dramatically reflected in grades: students suddenly find themselves writing B rather than C papers or, in one case I know of, B+ instead of D.

Let me mention two more advantages of starting with ideas and organization rather than sentence-level errors. One is that some students may be so nauseated by the sight of yet another workbook exercise on restrictive and nonrestrictive clauses that they'll be overjoyed, by comparison, to think about organization.

The other advantage is the subtle message you're communicating: that ideas and organization are more important. And they are.

Sentence-level errors may be annoying, but organizational confusion can more seriously impede communication and imply confused thinking. Such problems may force the reader to conclude that the writer really has nothing to say.

2 *Generating Ideas*

When a student presents you with a paper it's easy to overlook so-called prewriting skills, skills in generating ideas, and to focus instead on tangible problems with paragraphing or spelling. But a student's more tangible problems may reflect a failure in thinking and planning—and even daydreaming—about his paper. A good paper requires good ideas. And prewriting strategies can help a student generate ideas, whether he comes to talk about his paper before he starts writing, or he shows you a draft full of clichés and abstractions ungrounded in detail. Prewriting does not always precede writing—we often come up with new ideas as we write—but we usually need to do some preliminary thinking before we start drafting a paper. I'm going to suggest some advice you can give students—and some ways you can help them—as they explore their topics and generate ideas. Try the strategies yourself, so that your advice will be meaningful.

Allowing Enough Time

One of the first requirements for coming up with ideas to write about is time. A student should find a topic and do some analysis and research early so that her mind will have time to play with the topic—and suddenly up pops an idea just before she falls asleep or while she's in the shower. (And she should note the idea when it occurs to her or she may forget it.) A tutor can urge a student to plan ahead, not just so that she will have time to complete everything before the deadline but so that she'll come up with more ideas (although she shouldn't assume that time alone will solve her problems). Occasionally a student will bring a paper that needs more thinking, and merely looking at it with you will give her new ideas:

since she wrote the first draft she has had time to do some more unconscious thinking.

Relaxing

Now for a counter-example to my advice about allowing sufficient time—to make a point about the need to be relaxed. Sometimes students don't give themselves enough time because of anxiety about writing (or they may convince themselves that they write better with the pressure of an imminent deadline). Yet they also need to control their anxiety, once the deadline looms, to prevent it from producing writer's block. One tutor tells how she delayed writing a history paper until the night before but found an effective way of relaxing.

> The paper was due the Friday after spring break. It was on a colony, and I was supposed to have read an entire book before I wrote the paper. It was 7 P.M. and the paper was due at 8:30 A.M. I had read 50 pages out of 300 and I was sitting in a friend's room, looking at pictures from our vacation, eating pizza, and drinking beer. I stayed up all night, using the book's index to find the details on what I was to write about.
>
> Can you see me telling a tutee to have a couple of beers before writing a paper? I just thought of something, though. The fun I had before writing made me very relaxed. That I could tell a tutee. Relax, do something you enjoy, and then write the paper. It just might make the entire process easier. (Ann Rowan)

Other ways of relaxing, of controlling anxiety, include the strategies for unstructured and structured exploring discussed in the next sections. Simply getting something down on paper can help a lot.

Unstructured Exploring

Both unstructured and structured exploring enable a student to realize how much he does know about his topic: they give him confidence as well as ideas. The unstructured strategies described here are all relatively simple and don't require much practice in order to be effective. They are good ones to start with, whether a student has recurring or temporary problems with prewriting. And they can be valuable not just in writing personal essays, which obviously draw on the writer's feelings and attitudes, but in writing expository essays. For expository essays should plumb the writer's thoughts and feelings. And these thoughts and feelings can give a writer focus while doing research and analysis.

In general, a student needs at this point to turn off his internal censor, that inner voice that keeps saying that his ideas are lousy, that a particular idea is dumb. How can he venture to come up with a new idea if he knows he will immediately shoot it down? What he needs to do is separate the two processes, separate the generating of ideas from the judging of them. He should start by simply generating ideas and delay judging them.

Listing

The student might begin by making a list, a list of all the ideas the topic brings to mind. Or all the concrete details. Only after he's generated a sizable list—he can set a goal of fifty items, or a time limit of ten minutes—does he go through the list to decide which items are workable and which are not. You can help by praising the student for the quantity of his ideas, encouraging him to come up with as many as possible. Listing is particularly effective with students who tend to be too abstract and to include too little detail— you can ask them to come up with details, whether for the paper as a whole or for particular subtopics.

A student could also list questions about his topic. What does he want to learn? What puzzles him? Has he found anything that's unusual or unexpected?

Brainstorming

A special kind of listing—possible with a group of students—is brainstorming, which James L. Adams describes in *Conceptual Blockbusting* (1980), along with many other techniques for overcoming creative blocks. Within ten minutes the group comes up with as many ideas as possible, building on one another's ideas, someone jotting down each one. The goal here is quantity, not quality, and each idea should be recorded, no matter how crazy it seems at first.

(Sometimes these crazy ideas are not so crazy after all, and sometimes they suggest other valuable ideas.) To get the group in the right mood you might do a practice brainstorming first, such as generating as many uses as possible for a brick. Creative brainstormers will think not only of its uses as a building material or weapon or doorstop but also of its potential as, say, an article of clothing (the shoulder pad guaranteed to mow down the opposing team?) and its potential when smashed into pieces (a new source of vitamins and minerals?). Then you can turn to the issue at hand, such as possible paper topics or possible causes of the Crusades or possible interpretations of *The Turn of the Screw*. As with other prewriting strategies, the object is to come up with ideas first. Then, later, one can go through the list and sift and sort.

Freewriting

Another way to generate ideas is freewriting, one of many invaluable techniques described by Peter Elbow in *Writing Without Teachers* (1973) and *Writing with Power* (1981). The object is to write without stopping for ten minutes (or twenty or whatever), getting down ideas and not worrying about grammar, mechanics, usage. A student can choose a topic and then write—and discover ideas, which she later uses in a more formal paper. Freewriting becomes a way of helping her to think. She may be able to mine ideas and even phrases for a formal paper, but freewriting should not usually be incorporated into the formal paper. It is prewriting, not writing, and you might want to emphasize that a student should not turn in raw freewriting as formal writing. (And a way of telling a student that her paper is not yet suitable for turning in as a formal paper is to tell her that she has done a fine job of freewriting—of coming up with ideas—but now she needs to shape it so that it will be easy for a reader to follow. In other words, instead of telling her that her paper is a mess, you can tell her that she has done some good freewriting.)

Like listing, freewriting can help a student who needs more detail. But it can also help a student to ferret out connections among details: students whose writing includes lots of unrelated details and lacks generalizations can freewrite in order to find connections and significance. A student may even be able to narrow her focus through freewriting.

> In the last series of journal entries I handed in there was one in which I started writing about how I write a paper. . . . Although I started out following my plan (to talk about my writing process), I ended up talking about a particular problem I have in writing. Somehow I had unconsciously shifted the focus of the entry. It wasn't until I reread what I had written that I discovered this twist.
>
> After considering what had happened, I realized what an effective technique this could be to narrow a topic. That is, the writer could start off broad and just keep writing to see what develops. Through continual writing the writer could discover what really interested her and what direction a paper could take. (Sarah Hutcheon)

Freewriting can also be valuable with students who are experiencing writer's block—who are feeling so much anxiety about writing that they can't begin, who stare blankly at a blank sheet of paper, who spend two hours writing their first sentence. These students could start by freewriting about something other than their paper topic: about their immediate environment, about their problems with a roommate, about their problems with writing, about anything that comes to mind. Then they can try freewriting on their paper topic. Freewriting allows one temporarily to turn off the internal censor that demands attention to spelling, punctuation, pronoun reference, audience, paragraphing, wording, wordiness. . . . One can attend to those issues later.

One tutor chose the topic of cars and freewrote about it, to see what she could come up with.

> With the advent of the Model T, the automobile has become a common commodity in this society. The appearance is as important today as the utility. The auto manufacturers spend great amounts of time and money just deciding on the color and shape of a car. Names are also important. Animals have been used, because of their similarity to the type of auto. Rabbit, mustang, pinto, etc. Using the name of an animal makes advertising, slogans, etc., easier. For example, the commercials advertising the mustang showed the car in some canyons surrounded by wild mustang horses. This type of ad not only helps the viewer to remember the car, but also appeals to the type of person who sees himself as sporty, free, wild, etc. Many people buy cars that are a reflection of their lifestyle. Ex.—The station wagon for the suburban family with four kids and a dog. However, with the gas situation as it is, many people are looking for gas-savers, no longer caring for the extras. That seems to be the trend in auto designing today. Utility,

basics, etc. More depends on use, instead of appearance. Fewer people are concerned with spoked wheels, sunroofs, etc. They just want to get where they're going, and cheaply.

Ten minutes is a long time to write, even when one has a subject in mind. I occasionally found myself stopping to think about the structure of my next sentence. It's hard to break old habits. However, I can see how freewriting would help a tutee. It gets her thinking, and in the case of my subject, cars, it allows a number of possibilities to write about. Ex., the advertising aspect of automobiles, the changes in autos over time, the appeals of car manufacturers to potential buyers, etc. (Penny Penn)

Another tutor loosened up even more and focused less on a particular topic, freewriting loosely about freewriting.

freewriting, mental tangents, one of the best ways to get ideas out on paper, how to clear them out from your mind and keep them flowing. I do this best when I am writing letters or writing in my journal, I'd never really thought about using it for my papers until I got to Wheaton but you can get a lot of ideas from free association and ideas about how to organize your thoughts in your papers. What are some of the connections that you find yourself making between topics? And what relevance does this have to your major topic, or do you find your mind blank. Then try reading a children's book or take a shower, a walk, or make a list of what you need to do, clean your room but don't let procrastination take hold of you or you might be trapped, trapped in circles from which you can't escape. . . . I feel like I'm not writing as much or the caliber of journal writing that I want to. Is this because I can't force my thoughts out or is force the key, I'm trying to force the ideas out when I should be letting them come, flow freely the way I want them to, the way I talk about wanting to let them out. Right now there are so many thoughts crowding in, perhaps this is another reason why I am having problems with this, too many thoughts of such a diverse nature, too many tangents, like geometry or the Platonic Symposium, where we all spoke on Love, Madness and Intoxication, what a place to get ideas out. If you can talk about a paper the ideas can be brought out verbally. Perhaps a tutor can be considered a sounding board, someone whom you can bounce ideas off of. Could this be a way to advertise the tutoring to students? (Liz Como)

Liz also notes,

my best ideas will creep into my mind when I am rambling. I still keep journals and some of my thoughts have been helpful in papers later on.

Freetalking

The student can also generate ideas by doing what could be called freetalking. He can talk into a tape recorder. But talking with you gives him a real audience, someone who nods in interest and asks questions. You might ask some questions—asking for clarification and amplification—but mostly you just listen as the student talks about the course and the assignment and possible paper topics and ideas for his topic. Then he should jot down his ideas before he forgets them.

As with freewriting, freetalking can be either focused or unfocused. One tutor worked with a student who, having been told that she needed to develop her ideas more, said that she

> was in such a hurry to put these brilliant ideas down on paper that she wasn't bothering to analyze them; rather she put them all in one paragraph, almost listing them. To start, we chose one of her "brilliant ideas," one the professor really liked, and worked with that. I had her write the point she was trying to make in one clear, coherent sentence. That was no problem. Next, we talked about how she came to this belief, why she thought it was significant. I told her we were going to take this *one* idea, this one specific thesis, and develop it into a whole paragraph. Once we established her reasons for thinking why this point was so important we set about trying to back it up. She was able to pick out a few relevant quotes from the story which supported her thesis and incorporate them into her paragraph. She finally constructed a cohesive paragraph. It started with her thesis, followed by how she came to believe its significance, and several statements in support of it. The quotes from the story itself helped, too. In the end, she had put together a clear paragraph—a *whole* paragraph from *one* statement of her opinion. (Leslie Aubin)

Leslie shows how talking—in this case, focused talking—can help a student to come up with ideas.

Stacy Lee, herself a tutor, found it useful to freetalk with another instructor about a short story, exploring one of her characters.

> The worst, or rather the hardest, part about writing stories is developing the characters. There are so many different aspects to consider. Does he/she appeal to the audience? To me? Is he/she an individual? Is it someone I could relate to? Is the character too typical? Too boring? Is he/she realistic or only an ideal image? I really enjoyed talking my character out, because it opened up so many possibilities and

showed me that a character can have many facets, not only those which are typical of the character's basic image. By discovering such different perspectives I realize, now when I think about it, that every individual is a complex character.

Another tutor worked with a student who was having trouble writing an introduction. Even after freetalking, the student couldn't seem to write. But a combination of talking and writing worked.

> I knew from our talk that she knew what she wanted to say. I explained to her that the first draft didn't have to be 100 percent perfect. I told her to freewrite the introduction. She tried this but was still having troubles. I asked her to verbalize her ideas again. She then proceeded to finish writing the paragraph while talking out loud. By thinking out loud she was able to write. (Sarah Hutcheon)

Freetalking can also be less focused. For instance, a student may come for help in finding a thesis. Maybe he wants to write something about Korea. He can freetalk about Korea until he decides he wants to focus on its economy. He can freetalk about its economy until he narrows his topic to the causes of recent economic growth. Sometimes too you can pretend to play a role to help him generate ideas. Perhaps you could be the president of a country that wants to emulate Korea's growth but doesn't know how. Or perhaps he could explain his ideas to you as he would explain them to his little sister, his best friend, his economics instructor.

In addition, much as freewriting allows you to stress how it differs from writing for a reader, freetalking allows you to discuss how talking differs from writing. Sometimes a writer relies too much on talking techniques. You can then explain that writing requires more context, since the context is not immediately apparent, and writing requires more explanation and attention to transition, since the writer can't rely on nonverbal cues to tell him when the audience doesn't follow.

Freedrawing

Analogous to freewriting and freetalking is freedrawing. Some people can think by doodling or sketching. And diagrams can help enormously when writing a description. In describing an internal combustion engine or explaining how it works, a diagram can help one remember all the parts or steps—whether or not one includes the diagram with the paper.

In addition, when thinking about a list, you may find lines and circles and arrows—and other nonverbal markings—invaluable. More generally, as one tutor notes,

> It only seems logical to me to draw a flow chart to illustrate the causes of something or to diagram an argument. . . . I guess I like to be able to see things visually and clearly. (Cathy Halgas)

Changing Perspective

As Lil Brannon and her coauthors suggest in *Writers Writing* (1982), a writer can try changing perspective to discover ideas. Suppose a student has completed a draft that he's not altogether happy with. He could try writing a new draft in which he argues for an opposing point of view, or creates a dialogue between himself and an opponent, or recasts his essay as a letter or story or popular magazine article, or develops a subtopic that didn't fit into the original essay. Such a revision may not be better than the original one—may not replace the original—but it will give the student a fresh view of his topic and may well generate new ideas. I know that even writing an abstract of a paper or a version suitable for oral presentation often gives me new insights. Such experimentation with perspective is particularly valuable when writing a persuasive essay, for the writer needs to be closely attuned to the arguments of the opposition. And this technique can also encourage a student who thinks revising is simply rephrasing to try rethinking—gaining perspective on—the paper as a whole.

On the other hand, instead of writing an alternate version the student could try talking it. How would a pro-life supporter argue against the writer's thesis that abortions should be available on demand during the first trimester? Or how would he present his insights into homophobia to a high school audience?

Sometimes you can help a student to appreciate alternative perspectives by adopting one yourself.

> The assignment dwelt on Elizabethan drama and stage, so the first thing I talked about with her was what my perspective of the Eliz-

abethan stage was, preconceptions I have embedded in my brain—stereotypes of that period. She confirmed some of my ideas. . . . I talked a great deal about this (we hadn't even begun to tackle the specific assignment at this point), trying to offer alternatives to her point of view. Next we talked about organizing a thesis. In the end, this student admitted that my point of view . . . was totally different from hers and that our talking cleared her head and opened her eyes to alternative routes. (Mary Carroll)

Reviewing Old Work

Another springboard for ideas is one's previous work: reviewing her earlier work may give a student new ideas (and may also give a blocked student confidence that she can write, since she has before). Maybe she touched on an idea that she'd like to explore further. Or maybe, if she keeps a journal, she can mine it for ideas.

I remember having to write a paper on Emerson on the idea of supporting one's beliefs strongly and the next day changing one's mind but supporting this change as strongly. I couldn't get my paper started and what I did write down sounded lame. I finally went to my journals from high school and as I was reading the first journal I realized that I could agree with Emerson. I had written two papers at the beginning of the course. They were both on the question, "Does God create Man or does Man create God?" . . . Here was an example of my being able to argue both sides. So I started off on my paper with a fresh view. At the end, though, I found myself wondering if I really did believe Emerson so I added a little Emersonian twist stating that I didn't really believe his philosophy on the subject. (Liz Como)

And More

Here are still other prewriting strategies, generated while a tutor did some freewriting:

One idea is something like a word association exercise. Anyway, one could think of a simple list of words that might provoke an idea for the writer. Present her with a word and have her respond with the first thing that comes to her mind, given a general topic heading. Write your words and her responses down and see if they have generated any ideas for her to begin writing with. . . .

Another idea might be to read a paragraph or excerpt about the subject and write about the paragraph in a freewriting way. This may provoke some ideas, some style—anything that may spark a beginning for the writer.

Another idea which may not be as productive as the others may be to think of a one-word title for the paper, given the subject, and then begin making a list of synonyms and opposites for that word—seeing if that sparks anything. I guess I'm thinking that this may spark some ideas and give the writer a chance to discover what she does and does not want to cover in her paper. This idea may also be used to help someone limit herself after she has many ideas, but is lost as to where to begin and what to cover. (Pam Webster)

Structured Exploring

If the techniques for unstructured exploring don't seem to work, you may want to help the student do more structured exploring. The following techniques can generate oral responses, with you asking the student questions, or else written ones, with the student writing responses in a chart. I'm going to give just a brief overview of each technique and tell you where you can learn more about the more complex ones. (Note: these are primarily strategies for coming up with ideas, not for organizing the paper. Papers should usually *not* be organized around these questions. Nor should the student expect to include all the answers she comes up with.)

The student could respond to the journalist's questions: who? what? when? where? why? how? This technique is particularly useful for descriptive and factual essays, but it can also start a writer thinking about more abstract issues as well.

On the other hand, the student could compare her topic to something else, to make an analogy with something familiar to her: e.g., how was the Vietnam War like a tennis match? Or how is *David Copperfield* like a fairy tale?

The student could also use a scheme described by Richard E. Young, Alton L. Becker, and Kenneth L. Pike in *Rhetoric: Discovery and Change* (1970). Consider the topic in terms of the following:

1. Static particle: What is it like in itself? What makes it distinctive? What parts comprise it? What are possible attitudes toward it?
2. Dynamic wave: What process does it fit into? How does it change? How do attitudes toward it change?
3. Relational field: How does it relate to other topics? How would it be classified? How is it similar to and different from other topics? What are possible analogies for the topic?

For example, (1) how many calories and vitamins are you consuming in today's lunch? (2) How has your diet changed during the past week or month? (3) What else are you doing to control your weight and stay healthy? (For more details about the scheme see chapter 6 of *Rhetoric: Discovery and Change*.)

Still another model is Kenneth Burke's pentad, as modified and developed by William F. Irmscher in *The Holt Guide to English* (1981). Consider the topic in terms of the following five features:

1. Action: What happened or is happening? What will happen or could happen? What is it?
2. Actors/agents: Who or what did or is doing it? What is causing it? What kind of agent is it?
3. Scene: When and where did it happen or is it happening or will it happen? What is the background?
4. Means: How did the agent do it? By what means?
5. Purpose: Why? Why not?

For example, suppose that the action is dieting. The actor could be you, or chubby toddlers, or anorexics. Then, with regard to scene, how does atmosphere affect appetite? With regard to means, how can you suppress appetite? Is exercise effective? Is binge and purge? Finally, why is it so important to be thin—is fat a feminist issue?

One tutor tried the pentad and came up with the following:

I think I'll try the "actor" method for a topic I've been thinking about for my sociology class. The topic is gender inequality in the Catholic church. I haven't researched much on this yet, so it's just going to be very basic.

action—discrimination against women in the church

actors—priests, nuns, parishioners, the Pope, women who want to be priests, women who disagree with church rulings on birth control, abortion, and divorce

scene—present time, mostly in America, the church struggling to keep parishioners when their values are changing quicker than the church's, older Catholics who are still devout in their customs

means—women are turning away from the church more (?), church is quickly changing some rules in order not to lose parishioners

purpose—all these issues are related to efforts of women to gain equality in the church. (Cathy Halgas)

Another kind of structured exploring is library or observational or experimental research. Before beginning the research the student should usually do some unstructured and/or structured exploring, to find a tentative thesis or question or hypothesis to focus her research. Then, while doing the research, she can bounce her preliminary ideas off whatever she finds.

In general, during work on prewriting the tutor or teacher should be passive. The student should do virtually all the work, while the tutor simply listens. Or explains the ground rules for freewriting. Or shares how he generates ideas and plans for writing. Or possibly jots down the student's ideas to free her creativity.

3 Organizing, Drafting, and Reworking

Writing is a process. It requires preparing, recording, revising—approximately in that order, but one often rethinks while writing, revises as one rethinks. So the stages are not entirely distinct. Chapter 2, on generating ideas, was largely concerned with preparation before writing. But its strategies are also useful after a student has written a draft, especially if she needs to clarify her ideas or come up with more supporting details. Now it's time to turn to strategies for organizing one's thoughts, planning the organization of a paper, or revising the organization after writing a draft.

Tutoring a student in organization can be particularly gratifying—for she can make dramatic improvement. Eradicating errors in word choice may require protracted diligence and constant vigilance. But to improve organization, sometimes a student simply needs to hear a basic principle explained.

A month ago I helped a girl in my dorm with a paper that had been returned to her with comments relating to "poor organization" and diction. Today she came to see me again. Since the time I had helped her she had written and received back another paper written for the same course and professor as the first paper. She showed me the grade (B+) and the comments relating to how much her organization, especially, had improved since the first paper. This student had come to thank me for the help I had given her. Not only did it make me feel good about helping her in the first place . . . but it gave me a better feeling about something that had been bothering me about tutoring. My concern had been that I did not think that helping a student for a short time and only for that one time would really make any difference in improving her writing—it seemed that a half hour of help wouldn't prove very helpful. However, today I felt better about this. What proves to me even more that any small amount of time spent tutoring can make a real contribution towards helping someone is that the paper she did well on was not one I helped her with. . . . She had taken the ideas we discussed the first time and applied them on her own in a new situation. (Cathy Coffin)

Initial Planning

Once a student has some idea of his topic, he can find it extremely valuable to sort out his ideas by talking to someone. You can be most useful here if you're simply a sounding board. You can listen and ask questions: "Why?" "How do you know?" "What connects those ideas?" "What idea would tie the whole paper together?" These questions are also valuable when discussing a paper full of details and examples but without clear indications of their interrelationships or of what they're supposed to illustrate. And you can introduce the student to some of the following strategies.

Sorting

To begin with, the student may draw arrows between items on her list, or circle words in her freewriting and draw lines between them. She may then find it useful to build an issue tree, as described by Linda Flower in *Problem-Solving Strategies for Writing* (1985). It is more flexible than an outline and gives a visual idea of a paper's structure. To write an outline you need to know what your organization is, but an issue tree allows you to decide on your organization as you sketch it. And an issue tree can help you to come up with categories (to build up) or to generate ideas (to build down). The tree shown as an example here demonstrates not only how miscellaneous ideas can be grouped into categories but also how the categories can help generate ideas. Suppose a whimsical freshman English teacher has asked a student to write a paper on breeding spiders in the dorm. It's probably a little hard to come up with ideas immediately. But if the student has some major categories in mind, generating ideas is much easier.

For a cause-and-effect paper her major categories might be a series of "why"'s—for instance, political, social, economic causes. For a descriptive paper she might (like a journalist) answer who, what, when, where, why, and how. For a persuasive paper she might think of advantages and disadvantages. And that could be how she

starts thinking through the spider paper. As she jots down ideas—
"look repulsive," "may cause visiting relatives to scold"—she can
group like ideas together and further subdivide her major headings
into aesthetic and practical. Her tree could grow to look like the
example (and could keep on growing).

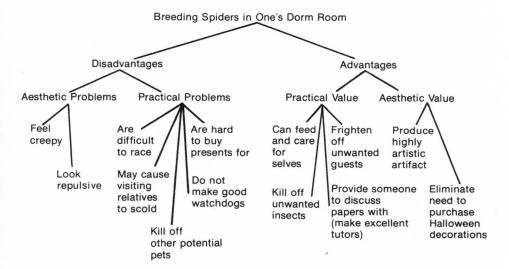

A technique like the issue tree might not seem helpful till you
try it, as one tutor acknowledges. She remembered

> the branching type outline, which I thought was kind of silly at first,
> but a girl in my hall just asked in passing if I had any other ideas on
> how to do organization, and she liked that and apparently used it. I've
> found that it works better for me—not on a whole paper—but on
> sections of longer papers when I don't want to lose my train of thought
> or lose the whole point of the paper. (Julie Along)

Try ideas like the issue tree yourself and feel free to adapt them.

Focusing

In the process of building the issue tree, or even before it, the student should decide on a central focus. What question does she want
to answer? What problem does she want to solve? And perhaps she
should find a focus before she generates too many ideas or does too

much research—for she may find focusing increasingly difficult as she does more research.

> My friend had vast research materials around her—she was going in many directions. Basically, she did most of the talking. I would repeat . . . what she had said, asking her is that what she meant. I felt it was my job to help her restrict her topic, which we kept paring down. I suggested the particle, wave, and field means of analyzing the problem: black, single-parent, head-of-household women in urban environments. I questioned her about what aspects of this she is interested in. This was difficult for her because of the dabbling in so many areas she had done. I suggested that maybe she could forget about all the information, focus on her interest and *then* do a literature sweep. She needed to focus. I suggested she think of the paper as three five-page papers, dividing it up into three subtopics to develop. She kept wanting to have everything in her paper. She would talk—I would listen, then ask her if she thought maybe the general topic could again be narrowed—it seemed, listening to her, that what she was really interested in was the cause and effect on the children of black single-parent head-of-household urban families. I asked if this was so and she said yes. Phew! This was really all she needed me for—we talked a little about how to approach the topic, but she seemed set with that project. (Dianne Holcomb)

Like Dianne, you can keep asking such a student her focus. Or you can ask her to do what researcher Linda Flower calls nutshelling: stating the gist of her topic in a couple of sentences. Stating ideas in a nutshell helps her to focus on major points and to see their relationship to one another.

Then the student can work on developing a thesis or a central question: for example, "Although the methodology in Emile Durkheim's nineteenth-century study of suicide has been criticized, subsequent research largely substantiates his conclusions" or "Are the conclusions of Emile Durkheim's nineteenth-century study of suicide still considered valid?" The best theses generally try to make an argument—such as that Durkheim's insights have stood the test of time. And they make parts of the argument modify one another, unlike a laundry list. "Although the methodology in Emile Durkheim's nineteenth-century study of suicide has been criticized, subsequent research largely substantiates his conclusions" is a more focused thesis than "There are strengths and weaknesses in Emile Durkheim's nineteenth-century study of suicide." A good writer might be able to write a good paper using the second thesis, but the first thesis provides better guidance for most students. In *Teaching Students to Write* (1980), Beth Neman argues the virtues of building a thesis with an "although"-clause or its equivalent; certainly such a thesis is likely to have an argumentative focus. Thus if a student has trouble coming up with a focused thesis, you can ask her to rephrase her sentence so that she uses "although." Neman also suggests two questions for evaluating a tentative thesis: Is it worth proving? Is there enough evidence? Then, once the student has decided on an organizing idea, she can sift through the ideas she has generated to decide what's relevant.

One way to help a student to focus may be to remind her of her reader. True, she may want to write an initial draft simply to get her ideas straight, without worrying about the reader. But somewhere in the process—before or after the first draft—she must remind herself that she is not writing just for herself: it's important that a writer not only organize her own thoughts and get them down on paper but also present them so that a reader will be receptive and will understand them. It may be okay in a diary to write simply to express oneself, but when writing for a course she is writing to someone else. And, sometimes, focusing on the reader will give the writer needed focus for writing the first draft. Or, if she finds her reader intimidating, she might write her first draft in the form of a letter to a friend. Then, once she has thrashed out her ideas, she can focus on her ultimate reader.

Often you can help a student to improve her focus not just by remembering the reader but by revising her concept of the reader. Why does she plod through causes chronologically, without sorting them and stating their significance? Or why does she include so much plot summary? She may think that she has to provide all this background for the reader. On the other hand, when writing for her teacher, she may think there's no sense in including what the teacher already knows. And pretty soon she wonders why she's writing in the first place. How can she possibly tell the teacher something new? In *Writing in the Arts and Sciences* (1981), Elaine Maimon and her coauthors suggest that the writer imagine a somewhat larger audience: her instructor and classmates. Then the writer will have a better idea of what she needs to include and how clearly she must explain it. This audience will have some familiarity with the student's general topic but not with her thesis. And thus instead of retelling all the factual or fictional events, in chronological order, she needs to argue her thesis, drawing on the details of history or of the story only when they help to prove her points.

After working on an issue tree and deciding on an organizing idea, a student can write an outline. Outlines can be valuable for longer papers, yet they are not always necessary. The organization sketched in an issue tree may be sufficient, especially for a short paper of a few pages.

The organizing strategies suggested here may be useful before a person starts writing. But the strategies can also be useful after she has written a draft. For one thing, many people must write multiple drafts: they don't know what they want to say until they've written a discovery draft or done exploratory freewriting. These people may not know enough about their topics to be able to build issue trees or outlines before writing. (I'd bet that when we were in high school most of us wrote our obligatory outlines after we'd drafted our papers.) Then there are the people who don't realize that their first drafts are actually discovery drafts, which need substantial revision. Some students will bring you drafts that need to be reorganized, and you can work out this reorganization with them by building issue trees and coming up with a focused thesis.

The Structure of the Academic Essay

Because a student is writing for a reader, structure and arrangement are important. Not all courses require the same structure for papers, but the one I suggest here would be appropriate for most subjects. This structure describes what an American academic paper should end up looking like, what a writer should aim for, not the process whereby one gets there: I've discussed the process some already and will discuss it more later. But you can nonetheless help the student to decide whether a paper adequately fulfills the expectations enumerated here. Some students may not have figured out the structure expected in an academic essay, and your brief explanation may be a revelation. Some students too may come from cultures with different expectations of essay form: they may consider the directness of an American academic essay, with its transitions that make connections obvious, insulting to the reader. So you may want to spend some time with such a student explaining American essay structure.

The structure described here is useful not only in academic essays but also in other contexts, such as oral reports.

> Yesterday I attended a conference on bioethics at Brown University. . . . The conference was a totally undergraduate one, with students from various colleges and universities . . . presenting papers on such topics as the treatment of defective newborn infants, the allocation of scarce medical resources, etc. . . . The papers which included the organizing idea early and forecasted well at the beginning, and continued to refer back to the organizing idea throughout the paper, made the better presentations. Hearing someone read aloud a lengthy piece of writing, without the listener having a copy of the paper in front of him, really makes the listener aware of the paper's organization. I think it also determines how much of the paper's content a listener will remember. (Cathy Coffin)

Understanding the structure can also help a student understand and absorb a textbook or lecture better. If he notices forecasting in an introduction, for instance, he'll be better prepared for what follows.

But the suggested format is not suitable for everything. It is not suitable for creative writing. Nor is it exactly suitable for writing such pieces as lab reports or business letters (although general principles still apply). And advanced writers may well want to violate some of the suggested principles in order to achieve particular effects. Yet the format is useful for novice writers—and it will work in most academic essays that students have to write.

Introduction

The introduction is the most important place for accommodating the reader, for if the reader is bored or confused, why should he continue reading? An introduction may start by providing a larger context for the paper (many good term papers start this way) or by whetting the reader's appetite with an intriguing fact or statistic or quotation (popular articles often start this way). Or, in a persuasive paper, an introduction may start by acknowledging some understanding of the opposition, some sympathy for a different point of view (so as not to alienate the reader right off). Then, usually at the end of the introduction should come a forecast of what follows—at least the organizing idea or thesis or central question of the paper. It's important for the reader to know the focus, to know the whole into which each of the parts fits, as A. D. Van Nostrand and his coauthors urge in *The Process of Writing* (1982). And it can be helpful to the reader if, in addition, the introduction previews the structure of the paper, indicating the sequence of the main topics to be discussed: for example, "The main ways of getting peanut butter off the roof of one's mouth—the shaking, the blowing, and the finger-wiping methods— are all ineffective." The reader would expect to find a discussion of the shaking, blowing, and finger-wiping methods, in that order. Such a preview is especially helpful in long papers.

Body

The body of the paper should consist of developed paragraphs, each with its own organizing idea or thesis, supported by relevant evidence. Often the thesis of a paragraph is stated in its first or last sentence. The remaining sentences should all be related to the thesis and follow smoothly from one another. Most paragraphs should be shorter than a page—long paragraphs can be broken into shorter units. Most paragraphs should also be longer than a sentence or two—short paragraphs can be combined or their ideas developed more. While tutoring one student, Nancy Solaas came up with the following checklist of ingredients (not necessarily in order) for each paragraph of the body of a paper analyzing literature:

- An organizing idea.
- An example (if possible) from the literature—e.g., a character who portrays this idea.
- A clear introduction for any quote she wishes to use.
- A development of the relationship between this paragraph and her thesis.
- And finally, good transitions.

The most effective sequencing of paragraphs usually derives from a student's categorizing of ideas, not from chronology. True, when describing a process, such as how to prepare a microscope slide, it's necessary to go through the steps in chronological order.

But in analytic papers, reliance on chronological order suggests laziness. Instead of narrating the events that led to World War II in chronological order, it's more effective to group them in categories, such as political, economic, and social causes. And an effective principle for ordering these causes might be to go from least to most important.

In writing a comparison it's often effective not to write the first half of a paper about one book (or whatever you're comparing) and the second half about the other; instead, you can discuss both books under each of your major points. Such a procedure forces the writer to focus on analytic points rather than chronology (unlike the practice of the author of sample essay 1, "Aliosha and Miranda," in chapter 6, "Evaluating Writing"), although when the points overlap a great deal such segmenting may not be feasible. In comparing Huck Finn and Tom Sawyer, one could go from Huck's and Tom's family backgrounds, to the ways in which Huck and Tom accommodate to their families and to society (such as the distinctive kinds of lies they tell), to whether Huck and Tom function primarily inside or outside society.

   I. Family background
     A. Huck
     B. Tom
  II. Accommodation to family
     A. Huck
     B. Tom
 III. Accommodation to society
     A. Huck
     B. Tom
 IV. Inside or outside society
     A. Huck
     B. Tom

Notice too how the sequencing of the points follows a principle, in this case going from small unit (family) to large (society).

In writing a persuasive paper it's often a good idea to dispose of opposing arguments first, then to work through arguments favoring your position, ending with the strongest argument. Suppose that a student wants to argue that Humbert loves Lolita selflessly. Instead of simply retelling Humbert's adventures with her, it's more effective first to refute evidence for the insensitivity of his passion, then to give evidence for his emerging selflessness.

To highlight the sequencing of a paper, there should also be effective transitions: the reader needs guidance in seeing the sequence. In the first sentence of a paragraph writers often clarify the relationship of the paragraph to what has gone before. Sometimes a single word like "also" or "another" or "however" will clarify the relationship. Sometimes a sentence can briefly recapitulate what has already been discussed and then indicate what will follow; a crucial transition in the *Lolita* paper described earlier, bridging the discussions of insensitivity and selflessness, could be something like the following: "Yet although Humbert's passion sometimes made him insensitive, it eventually turns into selfless love."

Conclusion

The conclusion should follow from the rest of the paper and usually comprises both a summary and something more. The summary may, in a short paper of a couple of pages, be simply a restatement of the thesis. Or it may, in a longer paper, include some recapitulation of major points. The something more can hint at the solution to a problem, or issue a call to action, or develop implications, or provide an expanded context. Sometimes one can achieve a sense of closure by reiterating images and themes that opened the paper.

Exercises

Sometimes you can reinforce your explanation of, say, paragraph structure or introductions by giving the student an exercise. You may be able to find a relevant one in a textbook, or you may need to create your own.

Suppose a student has trouble writing coherent paragraphs. As a first step, you could give him an exercise in which you've taken a coherent paragraph and scrambled sentences or thrown in irrelevant ones. Or you could, as Pauline Meehan has, do both in one exercise—but notice how difficult that makes the exercise for the student (you wouldn't want to make this the first exercise you give him).

Exercise: Paragraph Organization (Pauline Meehan)

Reorganize the sentences in this paragraph so that they follow a logical and coherent pattern. Omit any unnecessary sentences.

1. French became the language of the court, the language of the nobility, the language of polite society, the language of literature.
2. Great numbers of Normans came to England, but they came as rulers and landlords.
3. The Normans were a hearty, warlike people.
4. One might wonder why, after the Norman Conquest, French did not become the national language, replacing English entirely.
5. The feudal system had not yet begun in England.
6. There must always have been hundreds of towns and villages in which French was never heard except when visitors of high station passed through.
7. The reason is that the Conquest was not a national migration, as the earlier Anglo-Saxon invasion had been.
8. But it did not replace English as the language of the people.

(Answers for this exercise and the following one are in Appendix B.) Then you and the student could work on his own paragraphs. If you scrambled his sentences, would a stranger be able to unscramble them? Why are the sentences in the order the student has chosen? Can you diagram the structure of each paragraph with an issue tree? How do transitions, pronouns, and repetitions clarify the structure?

Or suppose the student has trouble writing introductions. After going over what is desirable in an introduction (and whether an introduction has to be written first), you could give him an exercise like the following:

Exercise: Introductory Paragraphs (Nancy Solaas)

From the following lists, choose the group of words or sentences that should be included in an introductory paragraph about the given topic. Then write a well-organized paragraph with the information you have selected.

I. The History of Music
1. The terms in music history are often borrowed from art and literature.

2. Music began with the Gregorian chant in the early Middle Ages.
3. Claude Debussy is a composer from the Impressionistic period.
4. Louis XIV and court music.
5. Adagio is a tempo marking between andante and largo.
6. Even the Expressionistic and Electronic music of our period have their roots in the tonal music of the earlier periods.
7. Both the flute and the clarinet are wind instruments.

II. Strategies for Exam Preparation
1. The most important preparation is the attendance of all the class meetings for your course.
2. Don't wait until the night before to begin your studying.
3. Don't diet during exam periods. Be sure to eat properly.
4. Get a good night's sleep before your exam.
5. Physical preparation and your own healthiness are as important as intellectual preparation.
6. Review for exams using both your text and your lecture notes.

Then the student could rewrite the introductions of some of his previous papers, perhaps even writing three or four alternative versions. And he could bring you the introductions of future papers for close scrutiny.

The Process

Loosening Up

While the structure outlined in the preceding sections describes what the final draft should be like, it does not indicate how the paper gets there. Many students assume that they should write the paper sentence by sentence in the order in which it will finally appear. But they're wrong. True, some people work best if they plan everything ahead of time and then write it down in the final order. But most do not.

I used to write that way, sentence by painful sentence, when I was in college. As a result, writing was excruciating. I also found it hard to revise—I felt that I would disrupt the organic flow of a paper if I tried to insert a new paragraph or sentence or tried to change the sequence. (I'd also invested so much energy and concentration in each sentence that lopping it off was like lopping off a finger.)

Since then, though, I don't try to do as much at one time. I often start with some idea of the overall structure and then start writing the section I think will be easiest. By the time I've worked through that section I have a better idea of what to include in the other sections—and they become easier. I revise and cut and paste a lot (revising is easier with computer word processing). And the last things I write are usually the introduction and conclusion, although I have been known to write the conclusion first.

Students are sometimes shocked to hear that it's okay to write in scrambled order—to postpone, say, writing the introduction. Yet if the introduction predicts what follows and if you learn as you write, how can you predict what you haven't learned yet? Furthermore, introductions can be exceedingly difficult to write—it's always hard to overcome the blankness of an empty page, and introductions require even more planning than other parts of a paper. Some students say that as soon as they have written the introduction the rest of the paper follows easily. If that approach works—fine. But most people who use it confront writer's block at some time or other. They would find it useful, at the very least, not to insist on coming up with a perfect introduction before they write anything else. It may be enough to start with a sentence or two, stating the paper's tentative thesis. Eventually the introduction may include some version of that sentence, but the introduction can later be developed to fit the paper. Here is one tutor's advice to students struggling with the opening paragraph:

> So many times I have had students come in after hours of struggling to produce an opening paragraph. Yet they have no idea of what they are going to write about, or how. They all seem to expect that to magically evolve from their opening. Some even felt they couldn't create an outline until they had developed that first paragraph. Thus, when I had them sit down and write ideas, they were relieved to find that their writing block had been only temporary, and they proceeded to write down ideas. Later, one girl told me she never realized how much easier it is to decide what to write about, and how to organize everything, when your thoughts are down on paper. Even if they're just sentence fragments, the notes seem to be just what some people need. . . . I try to explain that the first draft opening paragraph is not sacred and can be altered. I relate how I have often changed my beginning once the paper was finished and I realized I had shifted my focus a bit. It's even possible to write the beginning last, and it's sometimes much easier! (Sydney Herman)

Some writers do more than just postpone the introduction. They know, when they sit down to write, that they are writing a discovery draft, simply getting down ideas in no particular order (rather like freewriting). Sometimes they know they will discard this draft, after mining it for ideas. Sometimes they chop it up, add pieces, discard others, and tape the whole thing together again. They know that they have to do drastic revision, if not complete rewriting, after writing a discovery draft.

Some writers write a modified discovery draft. The first draft has much of the final structure but still needs considerable revision.

> While I'm writing a paper, I don't pay too much attention to having it come out perfectly. When I write a paragraph on one idea, I just try to get down everything I'm thinking about it right away. If I can't find the right word, I leave a set of parentheses and keep going. I can always go back later. By writing this way, my paper is finished before I know it, or at least the basics are down. Then I usually let it sit for a while, even if it's just for half a day. When I come back I look at it more objectively, and I can notice areas for improvement much easier. Then I go back and do a lot of revising. I change awkward words, sentence structure, or add ideas that I left out. Sometimes I change the order of whole paragraphs. I always feel free to mark up my draft as much as I want, though, until satisfied with the finished product. (Cathy Halgas)

In an unpublished handbook for writing history papers (*Writing About History*), Richard Dollase, Paul Helmreich, and Roberta Dollase suggest that one may be a Method A or a Method B writer (or a combination). The Method A writer follows the traditional textbook pattern, planning everything before writing. The Method B writer, however, needs to write in order to plan, and then revise extensively. Traditional texts do not allow for Method B, and writers who incline toward this method can become frustrated. It's important to encourage a student to experiment, especially when running into difficulties, and to find what works best for her. She may also find that different approaches are useful for different writing tasks.

You should experiment too. You may be a Method A writer right now, if you've had traditional training in writing. If the structured approach works for you—fine. But if you find yourself running into difficulties, or if you find writing more painful than joyous, try loosening up with Method B. You may indeed find you really are a Method A writer. But you may find that Method B opens up a new world to you, as it did for me. Diane Ciarletta tried experimenting with Method B and concluded that she needs a synthesis of the two approaches.

> I just had a paper due and had a pretty hard time getting started writing. Not because I didn't know what I was writing about, but because everything I wrote didn't seem satisfactory to me. I picked apart everything I wrote and became my own worst enemy. However, I recalled some of the methods of writing that Dollase and Helmreich outlined in their *Writing About History* during the course of my struggles, and found their examples helpful. I am accustomed to writing in the type A approach—that is, I write one sentence at a time, perfecting my words as I write. Letting my pen flow with incoherent, unstructured ideas is like blasphemy! With this paper I was writing I figured that, since I was having such a bad time writing my old way, I should try the type B approach—"letting my thoughts loose." It seemed to be helpful to other students in class and I thought it wouldn't hurt to try my luck. Well I did—and it really worked! I found that my ideas increased in number and ease because flow wasn't being interrupted by my correcting grammatical errors or word choice. Once I started I couldn't stop! I wrote a whole three pages practically without stopping to breathe. After, I went back and reread what I had written, and I realized I didn't have to do too much revision. Patch up a few sentences here and there, but for the most part I had expressed my ideas better and faster without the pains of writing word for word. I think the type B approach will take a little getting used to, but I feel it is really useful in getting me out of that writer's block. I'm sure I'll use this technique more in the future.

Coping with Distractions

Other strategies can also help with the process of writing and are worth sharing with tutees. One is to be sure to write in a comfortable environment. You can ask the student what his ideal writing conditions would be. And then he should decide how he can make his actual conditions more ideal. If his most important requirements are quietness and freedom from interruptions, perhaps he should write not in his room with his roommates but in a secluded nook in the library. If sitting in an easy chair puts him to sleep, perhaps he should write in a straight-backed chair. On the other hand, if he gets nervous when he writes and needs to relax more, the easy chair might be preferable.

> Among other things, I might suggest sitting under a tree rather than laboring for four unsuccessful hours at one's desk. Two girls on my floor actually locked themselves in the phone booth to write their papers, placing a sign on the door which read, "Dare to be different." (Beth Brown)

Similarly, a student can decide whether he writes best early in the morning, late at night, after running two miles, after washing his hair. Nancy Solaas thought about her best environment after she tried to write a paper while home for Thanksgiving.

> Half way through your first paragraph the phone rings; then your mom asks you to walk the dog. By the second paragraph dinner is ready and it's time to leave the paper again. What can you do about all these distractions and what really does constitute a good writing atmosphere? I think everyone would agree that the distractions described above are unfavorable, but beyond that, personal tastes really vary—just as some people will study with music on and others will not. I think it is important to find your own best writing atmosphere (or even best place to write) and try to duplicate that when you write. For some people the best spot may be the library; for others it may be under their favorite desk lamp with some classical music on. This second choice happens to be my favorite because it relieves some of the pressures of paper writing.

A student might also feel that he writes best after he's disposed of various distractions, chores he needs to do. That may be true. But one can keep inventing chores just to avoid writing.

> Everyone has some trick to postpone actually sitting down to write. My roommate prefers washing her face and repeatedly brushing her teeth throughout the evening. I, on the other hand, adjust the temperature in the room or open a window, unconsciously giving myself an excuse to change my clothes. (Beth Brown)

A student needs to draw the line somewhere—perhaps set a time limit, give himself half an hour to dispose of preliminaries. Then he must get to work and write. If stray thoughts still keep intruding he can note them on a scrap of paper, to attend to later. He can jot down a reminder to wash a dress shirt for Friday or to buy some more disposable razors. Or jot down an idea that just occurred to him for another section of the paper. Or any other stray thoughts that he wants to remember but that are cluttering his mind as he tries to write.

One kind of distraction that may bother a student as he prepares a research paper is particularly insidious: it's the research itself. He may spend so much time doing research—tracking down just one more book, just one more piece of information—that he doesn't have enough time to write and revise the paper. He tells himself that he's making the paper better. And he may be. But not if he slights the writing and revising. Here too it's important for a student to set limits—to tell himself that the treasure hunt in the library will end on Saturday and on Sunday he will start writing with whatever information he has.

A final kind of distraction is a time gap in the process of writing a draft. Often a student can't finish a paper at one sitting—he has to go to dinner, to class, to sleep. When he stops he should be sure to leave himself clear directions for what he wants to write when he returns to it again. Some people find it helpful to write the first sentence of the next paragraph. Some work from a detailed outline, so that the next section is already mapped out. Some at least jot down the next two points they want to make, or the three examples they want to use in the next paragraph. Then, when returning, it helps for a writer to reread what he has already written, to get back in the swing. (Rereading is also a good idea before writing a conclusion.)

Imagining a Reader

To help gauge a reader's response (and to work out her own ideas as well) a student might carry on an imaginary dialogue with a reader. She could imagine, for instance, that she has an appointment with her instructor or an interview with her prospective employer and has to explain her ideas in ten minutes. Or that she has read her paper to her class or colleagues and must respond to questions. Or that, in a persuasive paper, she is carrying on a debate with someone who disagrees with her. One can carry on these imaginary dialogues in one's head, but it's often more effective to talk out loud. If talking makes the student self-conscious, she can talk into a tape recorder. Or to a tutor. (Sometimes just explaining her ideas to a tutor gives a student new perspectives and ideas.) Such techniques enable a student not only to express and clarify her ideas but also to imagine her audience's reaction.

A similar idea, a modification of one suggested by Ann E. Berthoff in *Forming/Thinking/Writing* (1982), can help a student who finds a topic boring. The student can imagine someone who would care about the condition of serfs in pre-Revolutionary Russia or about Keynes's contribution to economic theory. Why not pretend to carry on a dialogue with a serf or the czar? Or with Keynes?

Focusing on the reader can also help a student understand why she should bother attending to sequence or transitions or anything else that makes the reader's job easier. The student may feel that as long as her ideas are good the presentation doesn't matter, that the reader should be intelligent enough to supply transitions or to figure out that some scattered paragraphs describe causes and others effects. Ask her to visualize a teacher who has ten—twenty—fifty—papers to grade. And he wants to get through them quickly—not to spend two hours analyzing each essay with the care he might devote to analyzing an essay by Woolf or Wolfe. It's therefore important to make the reader's job as easy as possible. Furthermore, whether or not a teacher consciously marks a paper down for lack of clarity, he will unconsciously do so: if he has to work to piece together a student's ideas, he'll have less energy to appreciate them.

Revising: Timing, Distancing, Questioning

A student should set aside time to revise—and she should think of revision not as patching up, changing a word here and there, but as rethinking the paper. In fact, knowing that she'll have time to revise can make writing the first draft much easier. She doesn't have to craft each sentence perfectly the first time through—she can leave a squiggle where she can't think of the right word or example and go on to capture her ideas before they vanish. She can put off revising till later so that it doesn't impede the composing process.

You can encourage a student to set aside enough time to write and revise a paper by helping her to plan her schedule.

For our next meeting she is going to bring a large calendar so that we can map out when her papers are due and when she will start them, and when we will work on them and so on. (Liz Como)

I strongly believe in the value of writing an early draft. But some students tell me they write best under pressure; they feel they do their best work when they wait until the last minute, until they know they can't procrastinate any longer.

> I think I'm a hypocrite. I've been sitting here in a panic because I have a 5–7 page paper due tomorrow and I haven't even picked a topic yet. Granted, if this happened every now and then it would be O.K. but it happens every single time I have a paper due. Since I entered college I have had *one* paper done in advance. Now here comes the weird part—I like doing papers this way as I do better under pressure. If I know that paper has to be in tomorrow and there's no more time to procrastinate I do better. Thoughts flow faster and easier and, well, everything just comes together quicker and better.
>
> Now, why I'm a hypocrite. If anyone ever asked me how to begin or write a paper I could never tell them this. What would I do? Say, "Wait till the last moment when panic sets in and then just pray you get a brainstorm?" *No*—I would have to tell them about outlines, starting early, formulating an hypothesis, doing a rough draft, final draft, and then typing. All things which I find to be a complete waste of time. I write one draft, go over it and make corrections on that draft and then type.
>
> Oh well. . . . They will have to find, as I have, their own way to write a paper no matter how wacky or weird it may be. (Sue Moore)

True, to some extent—a student needs to find what works best for her. And some may write pretty well if they create the pressure cooker of waiting till the deadline. But if such students could somehow set themselves an earlier deadline, an artificial one—and then take the trouble to revise—I bet they'd write even better. One tutor, Deborah Williams, records the wrong due dates for papers in her calendar—she hoodwinks herself into believing that papers are due a week earlier than they actually are and thus has plenty of time to revise. Another tutor, after working with a student for a number of weeks, gave an ultimatum: if you don't show me your Friday paper on Wednesday, I won't tutor you again.

These tutors know that the best way to gain distance and perspective on a paper is to let it sit awhile—ideally a week or longer.

But even a day is better than nothing. (I've seen writing improve dramatically when the student finally forces herself to draft a paper one day early.) The student is then better able to distance herself from the paper, to come to it fresh. Such distancing enables her to rethink the paper as a whole, instead of limiting her revising to changing a word here and there, as many novice writers do.

A student can also gain some distance from a paper if she tries reading it aloud, perhaps reading into a tape recorder and then listening.

> Several weeks ago, I tried a strategy with a paper I had written for a psychology class. I tape-recorded the paper and played it back so I could hear how it sounded out loud.
>
> This technique is useful because I got to hear the paper aloud twice: once when I read it into the recorder, and again when I played the tape back. I believe writing seems different when you read it silently than when you read it aloud.
>
> Unfortunately, this method of proofreading is only useful, for me anyway, for finding errors in sentence structure and mechanics (spelling, punctuation, etc.). I have little trouble with these problems. My biggest obstacle is the content of my papers: Do I have enough of the right ideas? Are they described clearly? Do I elaborate on and give evidence for my ideas and opinions?
>
> I have found the use of the tape recorder somewhat useful in finding small errors that don't constantly plague me. But when it comes to style, this method may not be reliable. I would recommend, instead, reading the paper aloud to someone else to see if he/she can follow and understand your ideas and logic. (Kris Leary)

Or a student can try having a friend read the paper aloud. Or she can ask a friend to read it and comment, someone who can be both sympathetic and critical—a good writing tutor, in other words.

Still another way of gaining distance and making revision easier is by typing a draft—I find it easier to see problems in a typed copy than in a handwritten one. Or better yet, by using computer text editing or word processing. As schools acquire and expand computer facilities, they usually acquire some kind of text-editing program. Some students may even have their own microcomputers. Tutors can encourage students to take advantage of such computer facilities. Typing an initial draft at a terminal takes as long as typing a draft on a typewriter. But then revising becomes much,

much easier. Moving a paragraph, for instance, may require typing a command like the following, where the numbers are line numbers in the text: "m 1100:1180 % to 320." On videoscreens the commands are often even easier. Then one has moved the paragraph, without retyping it, and can quickly and easily get a clean copy of the revised paper. The first paper that a student types on the computer will take extra time, as she learns the procedures, but subsequent papers will not. And revision becomes so easy and magical that students may even enjoy reworking a paper.

In any case, if the student brings a draft of a paper to you and needs to revise her organization, you can ask the following questions:

- Do you have a clear organizing idea or thesis? Is it a good one?
- Is it clear from the beginning?
- If, without looking at the paper, you tell me the gist of what you have tried to communicate, is it what I find in the paper?
- Is each paragraph relevant? Or have you thrown in something because it's interesting, not because it's relevant?
- Does each paragraph contain a central idea? Is each sentence relevant to this idea?
- What is your strongest point? What makes it strong? Can you use similar techniques elsewhere in the paper?
- What is your weakest point? How could you make it strong?
- Are there enough details or examples? Is there enough explanation of them?
- Have you left out any important information? Have you oversimplified complex issues?
- Have you devoted the most space to discussing the most important points?
- Does the paper have a suitable introduction? A suitable conclusion?
- If you jot down the central idea of each paragraph in a word or two, and then go through the list, does the sequencing make sense?
- Does each paragraph follow smoothly from the preceding one, with appropriate transitional words or other cues?
- Pretend you're the audience to whom the paper is directed. What do you find unconvincing or distressing?
- If you're using outside sources, do you reveal your own thinking, not just that of the experts? Do you use your own organizational scheme, rather than relying on that of a source? (For instance, when writing about a character in a novel it's generally better to develop paragraphs on character traits, such as willfulness and insensitivity, than to retell the story and note incidentally that the character is willful here, insensitive there.)

In the process of rethinking, the student will probably find it necessary to leave something out, yet it can be hard to amputate a limb of one's brainchild. It can help a little to approach the paper expecting to discard something. And the student can try a strategy suggested by Karin Mack and Eric Skjei in *Overcoming Writing Blocks* (1979): to keep an archives box or file, where she stashes discarded nuggets. Throwing away then feels like saving (and—who knows?—maybe these nuggets will prove useful for future papers).

All of these strategies for organizing a paper are worth sharing with students, as the need arises, and each student can decide which ones work for her and when they work for her—though you may want to encourage a student to try a strategy that she initially resists. If in discussing her paper the student mentions that she's a last-minute writer, you may want to encourage her to get started earlier. If she complains about how noisy her roommates are, you may want to encourage her to write in the library. The process of writing is, in short, different from the product. The suggested structure for a paper indicates only what the paper should end up looking like. How one gets there is another matter.

4 Improving Grammar, Mechanics, Usage, Style

When students go to a writing tutor or teacher, they're likely to expect her to correct their spelling, change a pronoun, delete a word, add a semicolon. They're likely to think that one improves one's writing by tinkering with sentences—by adjusting grammar, mechanics, usage, perhaps style. They think so because many teachers have limited comments on papers to these issues: "awk," "sp," "ref," in angry red ink. Usually you should disappoint these students.

True, a student may insist that apostrophes are his worst problem and that's what he wants to work on. Or the instructor for whom he's writing may so insist. Or a paper may be so good in content and organization that all the writer really needs to work on is sentence combining. Or you may be working with a student regularly and you eventually get around to working on pronoun reference. In all these cases you and the student may decide to focus on sentence-level skills rather than global ones.

But usually you should focus on more global matters like having enough ideas and relating them logically and setting them out with a clear organization that is easy for the reader to follow. After dealing with these global matters you can turn to sentence-level ones. For one thing, once a student has worked out focus and approach, some of the sentence-level errors may disappear. Sometimes, too, when a student writes frequently for an appreciative reader who doesn't demolish the papers, some errors will disappear by themselves.

Of course, even if you do decide to focus on sentence-level errors, you'll disappoint some students in another respect: you won't simply correct their errors for them. If the instructor has already seen the paper, or if you are the instructor who grades the paper, you can get away with making a few corrections. But you should try to get the student to come up with corrections himself. And you should usually avoid writing anything down: if the student writes down corrections himself he can reinforce his learning.

On the other hand, you may get a student who doesn't want to be bothered with sentence-level errors. After all, he argues, the reader can still figure out what he wants to say. . . . Possibly— though the reader may not always be able to puzzle out the writer's meaning. And even if she could, she doesn't want to spend the time: an instructor, like any reader, wants to be able to read the paper quickly and easily, without having to reread passages. She may find the errors annoying, an annoyance that she's likely to express in her grading. And errors may lead her to believe that the writer is careless about details, doesn't care about his reader, or is too stupid to learn some simple rules.

Once you decide to work on sentence-level problems, you need to distinguish between two kinds: outright errors and stylistic infelicities. The former should clearly take precedence over the latter. But many tutors have trouble distinguishing between the two. A tutor may read a sentence, feel uncomfortable with it, know that she would express herself differently, but be unsure whether she's noticing an error or just awkwardness. Look, for instance, at the opening words of a sample paragraph: "Being picked on throughout my childhood by my older brother I often aspired . . . ." Something seems awkward about that opening. Something about "Being." Maybe if you'd been writing the sentence you'd have begun with "Because I was picked on throughout my childhood by my older brother . . . ." But you may hesitate to impose your style on the student. Is there an outright error there? Yes, an error in the verb. Instead of "Being" the student should have written "Having been." You may thus have noticed a problem but not gauged exactly what it was, an error or an infelicity. With time, you'll learn to recognize the difference. But you can also find it helpful to review grammar, to learn why a certain phrase makes you uncomfortable.

To help you decide what to review, read the following paragraph. It contains at least twenty-five different constructions (including "Being") that could be considered errors—not just stylistic infelicities but outright errors. Some are like those made by basic writers, some like those made by students for whom English is a second language, and some like those made by traditional college students. In other words, the paragraph is an artificial hodgepodge.

> Being picked on throughout my childhood by my older brother I often aspired I was a male, however now that he and I have grown out of this stage I'm very glad I am female. If I was living in an earlyer century I'm not sure I would feel this. Having to unendingly cook, clean, and caring for childs, womens' lives were very difficult. Men force women too work hard than anyone should. But now in late twentieth century decades hopefully women have the ability in outdoing men, which is why I'm glad I am the female.

Once you find the "errors," you can group them into the following categories:

1. Most important to work on
2. Important
3. Less important
4. Of marginal importance—not necessarily an error, becoming increasingly acceptable in contemporary prose

Then you can read the discussion in Appendix A. Did you find all the "errors"? What do you need to review? You can also give this paragraph to a tutee for correction, to gauge what grammatical problems he has and what you and he might work on first.

Diagnosing the Problem

The first step, here as elsewhere, is diagnosing the problem and deciding what to work on first. The most valuable resource for diagnosis is the student's own writing. You could also ask her to take diagnostic tests, often available in handbooks (many exercises can serve as diagnostic tests, whether or not they're so labeled). But it's better to start by examining her papers and looking for patterns. A paper may, for example, seem to be filled with errors. But if you can figure out patterns in the errors then neither you nor the student will feel quite so intimidated. Maybe you quickly see that the most frequent errors are with pronoun reference, apostrophes, and run-ons. Or maybe, after puzzling over the seemingly random punctuation, you finally realize that the student is using commas and periods interchangeably.

Then you need to focus on causes. Whether you discover frequent run-ons in a paper that the student has written or she comes to you with a mandate to work on run-ons, you need to decide what exactly her problems with run-ons are. Perhaps she uses "however" and "therefore" as conjunctions. Or perhaps she gets entangled in complex sentences with many subordinate clauses and forgets that she already has main clauses for her sentences. Or perhaps she needs to learn systematically that a sentence requires a subject and predicate and needs to be followed by a period. Be sure to ask her what rules she follows. Sometimes her answers will surprise you.

> She explained to me that she had a problem with commas. Then she took out two drafts of a paper from her freshman writing class. The first was her original final draft. The paper had good ideas and was well organized, but there were no commas where they were needed. The teacher's note read "paper needs commas." Her grade was lowered for her lack of commas. She told me that she went back to her room and rewrote it, putting in the commas where she thought they should be. She showed me the second draft, which the professor had torn apart with red pen. The poor girl had gone back and . . . inserted commas after every sixth or seventh word! She said she didn't really know how commas should be used but the things that she had read "always have a lot of commas." She thought she had done what her teacher wanted. I asked if she had ever studied the comma, to which she replied yes, but she never could remember when to use them in one of her pieces of writing. I then asked her to tell me what she thought commas were used for. She said to separate words in a series. I wrote this down and asked if they had any other uses. She said no. I then asked what she meant by a series, to which she replied that when you have a lot of words in a sentence you divide them so the sentence doesn't sound so long. This explained to me her use of commas. She was inserting them so her sentences wouldn't sound long instead of using them in a grammatical manner. (Jen Ciaburri)

Sometimes errors result from the interference of another language or dialect. Students whose first language is not English may have trouble with articles and prepositions. Students who speak a dialect like Black English may use different endings for singular and plural nouns and verbs. Although many of the techniques described in the following pages and in the previous discussions of generating and organizing ideas can be useful with such students, you'll find it helpful to turn to a specialized source. Mina P. Shaughnessy's *Errors and Expectations* (1977) continues to be the best general guide to work with basic writers, including those whose writing is influenced by Black English. Christina Bratt Paulston and Mary

Newton Bruder's *Teaching English as a Second Language* (1976) provides many ideas for working with students for whom English is a second language (ESL). Marian Arkin's *Tutoring ESL Students* (1982) also offers some insights. In any case, as Mina Shaughnessy points out, remember that errors are not signs of a student's stupidity but guides to her attempts to learn.

Overcoming Carelessness

After you've narrowed your focus to a particular problem, you need to decide whether it's an entrenched error or just a slip: you need to decide whether the student doesn't know how to correct the error or was just careless. (Or perhaps he was not so much careless as concentrating on difficult intellectual content and made mistakes he otherwise wouldn't have. Or perhaps he isn't exactly careless but hasn't learned how to proofread—how to read with the right kind of attention.) One clue is whether the error recurs consistently in the paper: if not, the student may just be careless. You can also give him a chance to look at his paper from a slightly new perspective. You can ask him to read it aloud—and he may notice or silently correct some of his errors. You can read it to him—and he may be able to hear that something doesn't sound right or notice when you stumble. His responses will help you to decide if his problem is proofreading or an entrenched error.

Sometimes a student may have some understanding of a difficulty but needs goading to act on it. Why should I bother proofreading a biology paper, he may ask. Or why are you always so picky? And you can explain that even if a teacher doesn't seem to mark down for carelessness, the student can show courtesy by taking care over the paper. He not only makes it easier for the teacher, though, but also for himself: a teacher who has to struggle with making sense of individual words and sentences (silently correcting errors) will have less patience for struggling with the student's ideas—and will probably mark the paper down, either consciously or unconsciously.

Sometimes leading questions can help both in overcoming a problem and in determining whether the student needs more than a reminder. For example: What does an apostrophe indicate? What is possessing what here? What's another way of saying "the hand of

Jose"? What's another way of saying "Maria's face"? Can you replace this phrase here, where you use an apostrophe, with one in
which you use an "of"? If you can't, is the word possessive? Should
you use an apostrophe? Did you use the apostrophe correctly here on
page 2? Can you explain why? How can you correct this use of the
apostrophe on page 3? Now can you go through the rest of the paper
and correct the rest of your possessives?

You can also suggest that a student learn some techniques to
help him check his own papers. If he writes his first drafts by hand,
for instance, he might type a second draft before the final copy—it's
often easier to spot errors in typescript than in handwriting. And he
should learn techniques for coping with his most common problems.
If he has trouble with pronoun reference, he could underline all his
pronouns and draw arrows back to the referents, to make sure his
reference is clear. If he has trouble with spelling, he could underline
words whose spelling he's unsure of or read his paper backward,
word by word, so that he'll focus on individual words.

Another technique similarly entails going through the paper
and underlining or otherwise marking particular words. Then to
decide whether the word is correct the student tries a substitution.
For instance, if he has trouble distinguishing between "its" and
"it's" he can try substituting "his" and "he's." When "he's" fits the
structure of the sentence (ignoring the meaning of sentences like
"He's raining out today"), he should use "it's." Both require apostrophes. And when "his" fits, he should use "its." Neither requires
an apostrophe. Similarly, students often write run-on sentences, or
comma splices, because they think "however" and "therefore" behave like conjunctions. To help him decide whether he has written a
run-on sentence, a student could substitute an adverb like "slowly."
If the sentence containing "slowly" would be a run-on, then so would
the sentence containing "however" or "therefore." Another test is to
see whether the word connecting two independent clauses is, like an
adverb, movable within the sentence or else, like a conjunction,
stationary. If it's movable, as "therefore" is—I can write either "She
was hungry; therefore she went to work" or "She was hungry; she
therefore went to work"—the sentence requires a semicolon or the
equivalent. If the connecting word is stationary, as "and" is, the
clauses can be joined with just a comma: "She was hungry, and she
went to work."

Overcoming Entrenched Errors

Let's suppose you find not a careless but an entrenched error in a student's paper, or she comes seeking (or is sent to seek) help on that error. With luck, she'll work with you more than once. Let me give an example of how to approach such problems. But rather than give exhaustive treatment of all the possible errors you could work on, I'll discuss spelling in some detail. You can then be creative in coming up with comparable strategies when working on other errors.

Mary Alice Taylor recounts her initial meetings with a student who had spelling problems.

> My second night on tutor duty I actually tutored someone! And her problem was not an easy one to deal with. Spelling. The tutee, Linda, informed me she had a learning disability because she learned to read very late and she thought she had whipped the problem until she received her first (freshman) paper back. It was full of spelling errors. Her professor's final comment was "Your spelling is unusually poor. Perhaps you should see a tutor about a diagnostic test." Well, Linda asked me to get her one as she handed me her paper. I told her the diagnostic test wasn't going to prove extremely helpful, but I would certainly get her one. Then I suggested putting our heads together on some methods to improve her spelling. Her biggest problems were words that sound the same but are spelled differently, changing the *y* to *i* before adding suffixes and *i* before *e* except after *c*. She also could not sound words out to spell them.
>
> So, I suggested a few things after looking over her corrected paper:
>
> 1. Making a list of words she misspells.
> 2. Adding definitions after the ones that sound like others—for example, "week" and "weak"—so she could learn the difference and use them correctly.
> 3. I explained the *i*-before-*e* rule because she was interpreting it backwards.
> 4. I explained my method for learning the differences among "to," "too," and "two."
>
> I then looked over a paper she was about to turn in. The poor girl had looked up every single word she had used in the dictionary before typing. Naturally there were still several errors because of those darn words that have several spellings!!! So what I did when I found a misspelled word was to put an "X" next to the line that contained it and told her there was a misspelled word in that line. (I didn't know

how far I could go without breaking the honor code.) I did *not* want to send that girl back to her dictionary without some clue! I kept reassuring her that she was not alone in her problem with those words. I told her her errors were quite common and that with the learning and practicing of some rules and memorization of some of those similar words it would be cleared up. The more she referred to her list the easier it would be because a lot of it would sink in before she knew it.

I also informed her that she was going to have to do it herself and that the only things I could do would be help her understand the spelling rules and help her compile a list. The rest was up to her. She understood without my saying so . . . and is very willing to put forth the effort.

I told her to come by the next night because I would get some stuff together for her.

Rummaging through the tutoring file cabinets, I found some helpful exercises. I got that diagnostic test since her professor suggested it. And I also found two good sources for her. One of which contained a complete list of those words that have several spellings and meanings. I xeroxed it for her (she paid me) and that left her only the definitions to look up and fill in. I was glad it didn't provide them because I think looking them up will help it to sink in.

I then suggested, to help enforce the definitions and separate spellings, that she make flash cards for herself and practice with them. I figured if it works for multiplication tables it will work for spelling. For example, "Thursday is a day of the _____" on the front. And on the back she could print "week." Coming up with sentences and writing out the cards would help a lot too, I thought. And I told her to use the books in the tutoring room.

After I showed her what I had for her and told her my ideas I told her to do the exercise sheets and lists and come back to me with questions, etc., and I would be glad to help in any way in explaining rules and helping explain anything in the books that she didn't understand. I also loaned her my Warriner's *Grammar and Spelling Book* from junior high. . . .

So I'm going to see her Tuesday night during my tutoring hours. I've got my fingers crossed. I've tried to think of anything else I can do and I really don't think there is anything. It's all really up to her.

Notice how Mary Alice starts with diagnosis and then plans a multifaceted attack: the student makes lists, checks spellings in the dictionary, finds definitions, makes flashcards, completes exercises.

As Mary Alice suggests, the best place to start the diagnosis is with the student's own writing. But you may want to supplement the student's writing with a diagnostic test, either one that you find or one that you create, as M. F. Withum has. M. F. found a list of commonly misspelled words and created sentences for them. Then she asked the student to choose between plausible alternative spellings.

Exercise: Spelling (M. F. Withum)

Choose the correct spelling.

1. Her (absence, absance) was inexcusable.
2. She had a guilty (concience, conscience).
3. Many (criticized, criticised) him for his beliefs.
4. He became a (desperate, desparate) man.
5. You are (eligable, eligible) to take this (exellent, excellent) (exersize, exercise).
6. The (goverment, government) was overthrown by the guerrillas.
7. (Grammer, Grammar) can be difficult.
8. Every social system has its (hierarchy, heirarchy).
9. The (instructer, instructor) voiced many (grievances, greivances) about the educational system.
10. You need a special (lisence, license) to work in that (labratory, laboratory).
11. I spent my (leisure, liesure) time applying for a (mortgage, morgage).
12. My (neighbor, nieghbor) is (niether, neither) (noticable, noticeable) nor likable.
13. Only the bubonic plague is worse than (pnuemonia, pneumonia).
14. The (professer, professor) was a (priviledged, privileged) member of the faculty.
15. The (questionaire, questionnaire) asked for our most convenient (rehersal, rehearsal) time.
16. The (restaraunt, restaurant) had two (seperate, separate) lounges.
17. My (schedual, schedule) conflicted with theirs.
18. Today is (Teusday, Tuesday) and tomorrow is (Wednesday, Wenesday).

(Answers for this exercise and the following one are in Appendix B.)

Once the student has completed the exercise, you look for patterns. Mary Alice's student might misspell "hierarchy," "grievances," "leisure," "neighbor," and "neither" since she has a problem with *i*-before-*e*. In addition to the strategies Mary Alice suggests, you could, after going over the rule and its exceptions, arrange to give the student a quiz the next week. After the quiz, to reinforce her learning and to start bridging between the exercise and her own writing, you might ask her to proofread the following nonsensical paragraph that you have prepared.

Exercise: Spelling: I-before-E

> Upon hearing me shreik, my neighbor's niece presented me with a wierd lei. I then lay siege to a freight van driver, who had failed to give me a reciept for the new chandeleir that now hung from my cieling. Niether his hieght nor his weight deterred me, as I siezed a piece of his shirt. He said that he had to check with his feild chief but did not want to deceive me.

You could even ask the student to prepare her own nonsensical paragraph that, say, uses fifteen "ie" or "ei" words correctly. Finally, though, you want the student to be able to proofread her own writing. She could, for instance, start by underlining all words that contain "ie" or "ei," then check each one, and finally bring the paper to you to see if she's missed any.

She could also use other strategies suggested by tutors.

> Spelling has always been a problem for me—and the way it looks now it may always be that way. Fortuntelly [see what she means?] I have found a few ways to help me along when writing papers, letters, essays, etc. Here are the helpful hints I use which maybe can also help others:
>
> 1. The most basic—use a dictionary or a speller dictionary. I personally prefer the speller dictionary because it is specifically for that purpose. It is small, compact, and has words only spelled and syllabified—there are no definitions and such to contend with. The speller is much quicker and easier to use than a regular dictionary.
> 2. The second trick . . . is, when writing a paper, to have a piece of scrap paper on your desk right beside where you are working. Whenever a word has to be looked up in the speller I write it down on this piece of paper. Often in a paper words are used more than once so then you have the word right there rather than always having to look it up. Also by constantly looking at this paper with hard-to-spell words on it, the words eventually stick in your mind, forming a kind of mental picture. (Sue Moore)

Jen Ciaburri keeps her own dictionary.

> I keep a notebook called "Jen's Dictionary." Every page is labeled
> with a letter. In it I have a list of words and their definitions (just to
> keep the format of a dictionary) that I commonly misspell. I find that
> when I am writing it is so much less frustrating to pick up my diction-
> ary, which is much smaller than Webster's. I know exactly what part
> of the page a word is on. I also find that after a few weeks of having a
> word in it I don't have to use my dictionary any longer. Looking it up
> and seeing it in my own handwriting helps me to learn it. But it's nice
> to know it's still there if I should blank out.

In general, when working with a student on an entrenched
error, whether it's spelling or pronoun reference or dangling modifiers or word endings, you can be inventive and try lots of approaches. Different approaches may be effective with different students. And different approaches can keep a student's interest and
provide multiple perspectives on a weakness.

Still, the following general sequence is good to keep in mind:

1. You should start with a diagnosis of exactly what the problem is:
   you can examine the student's writing and give her a diagnostic
   test.
2. Then, if she needs more than an admonition, you and she can look
   up relevant rules and work on exercises (more on that in the next
   section), progressing from sentence and paragraph exercises to controlled writing exercises.
3. And then you can both go over her writing for these errors and
   think up ways to avoid them.

Using Exercises

As part of your program for overcoming entrenched errors, you may
look for exercises, like M. F. Withum's in the preceding discussion of
spelling. Be sure, though, that the exercises are suitable for your
student and are part of a multipronged program.

Handbook Exercises

Handbooks on grammar and mechanics commonly provide fill-in-
the-blank and sentence exercises. These can be a useful starting

place, but a student also needs to transfer what he learns in exercises to his writing practice.

To begin with, you might familiarize yourself with a handbook—perhaps invest in your own copy and then keep it with you when you work with students. Know how to find pertinent sections in it easily, and try some of the exercises so that you know how well they work. Then if you suddenly need an exercise while you're tutoring, or want to consult a rule, this book can be the first place you turn.

If you have more time, though—if a student will be returning to work with you—you might explore other books in the library or the writing center. What you look for depends on the student's needs, but here are some general principles.

Explanation. Is the explanation of the rule clear enough so that you can easily understand it? Does it avoid unnecessarily obscure terminology? Does the explanation provide clear examples? If you're investigating something complex like the comma, is the explanation presented incrementally? That is, is each major rule followed by practice sentences (or are you expected to remember three pages of rules before you tackle any practice sentences)? And does the explanation start with the simpler rules (e.g., commas in a series before commas with restrictive and nonrestrictive clauses) so that the student can build a sense of mastery?

Exercises. Do the exercises provide enough practice? Try the exercises yourself and assume that the student will have more trouble than you do. If you just about feel comfortable with the rule after trying three practice sentences, the student will probably need more than three. You might also check whether the exercise has five to ten straightforward applications of a rule before any tricky ones or exceptions. (I once found myself trying to teach the punctuation of restrictive and nonrestrictive clauses from a handbook whose first practice sentences were like the following: "The Jean Smith who attended my high school is now working in a gas station." That's a difficult first sentence for a rule that many students find confusing to begin with.) You may well find that most handbooks don't offer enough practice exercises: they try to save space by skimping here. So you might then turn to workbooks like Eugene Ehrlich's *Punctuation, Capitalization, and Spelling* (1977), which provides lots of practice for a small range of problems.

Answers. Unless you're very confident, you probably want to be able to check your answers against those of another authority. Are answers provided in the back of the handbook or in a separate instructor's manual? And do the answers make sense to you? Answer books are not always correct—in fact, I often think of options other than what the answer book implies is the only correct one. If you have trouble understanding one of the given answers, or perhaps disagree with it, by all means consult another tutor or teacher. And if you have trouble understanding a lot of the answers, you may want to find a better exercise.

Relevance. No matter how good an exercise is in itself, it's useless to a student unless it's relevant to his needs. Completing lots of exercises on using commas with words in a series and with introductory phrases won't be particularly useful if his main problem is with restrictive and nonrestrictive clauses.

A note of caution about usage and mechanics generally: the rules are slowly but constantly changing. Acceptable punctuation in eighteenth-century essays, for instance, would not always be considered acceptable in twentieth-century essays. And different handbooks may espouse different rules. If you find puzzling discrepancies among handbooks, talk about them with another tutor or teacher.

Computer Exercises

Another source of drills and exercises is the computer. Many students—and instructors—find it fun to do computer exercises—especially compared to doing yet another workbook exercise.

> I think the whole idea of having grammar lessons and exercises on the computer is wonderful. I really had a lot of fun using the computer even though none of the exercises I did were very difficult. I think it's a great way for anyone to practice up on grammar skills. Even though rules and grammar can be explained, often they don't sink in until you actually try to put them to use. Another good thing about the computer is that you get an immediate response. It's better than doing exercises on paper, having them corrected, and then finding out what you did wrong. A lot of times by the time you find out what you did wrong you've forgotten about the exercises anyway. With the computer, when you make a mistake you find out instantly, can correct it, and practice the correct way right away to reinforce it. You also get instant gratification when you answer correctly! (Ellen McVeigh)

M. F. Withum explains why she found computer lessons helpful.

> Even though I knew most of the answers and answered the questions
> correctly, doing the exercises helped clarify many things in my mind.
> I think that this is primarily because . . . writing and grammar books
> absolutely bore me. Also, listening to English teachers talk about
> writing puts me to sleep. (No insult intended!) Yet, by doing these
> often amusing exercises, at my own pace, I learn a lot more. I find that
> the constant interaction with the machine keeps my attention span
> much longer than just reading a book. Further, the machine, to me, is
> much like a toy. Even though I hate video games—which I consider
> an insult to my intelligence in most respects—this is more than that.
> It's a gadget, and I love gadgets, as well as a challenge—which is
> something I'll never say no to. I think that I also like it because I'm
> like most humans in that I hate to think that a machine can outwit
> me. Even though it's not the machine at all, it feels like it really is the
> machine you are competing with. And I, like others, refuse to capitu-
> late to it. Instead, I find myself totally absorbed with it for a full hour
> or so—learning little things the whole way. Rarely can I honestly
> admit to having been totally absorbed in an English grammar class
> for an hour.

Another advantage of computers is that they have infinite patience:
a well-written lesson will give a student as much time and practice
as she needs and won't make snide remarks.

But try the lessons first before you ask a student to take them.
Are the explanations clear? Do they avoid unnecessary terminology—and explain any unavoidable terms? Do the examples build
from easy to difficult? Are there enough examples of each type? Is
the tone neither abrasive nor condescending?

Diane Ciarletta has mulled over the merits of computers.

> If a tutee comes to me and wants me to explain about a grammatical
> point, is it copping out to refer her to the computer, rather than trying
> to meet the challenge of explaining it in person? I often wonder if the
> student may somehow feel cheated, or may feel that the tutor doesn't
> know what she is talking about and has to rely on a machine. (Even
> though a tutor is considered a resource for information, I still feel
> there is an expectation that the tutor should know everything.)
>
> Getting back to the computer issue, I'm wondering how effective an
> interaction with a machine is as opposed to the personal interaction of
> a tutoring session. When we tried out the computer lessons in tutoring
> class, I thought they were really neat and fun, but I didn't use them
> long enough to assess if they were effective teaching tools.

My psychology class last year discussed the issue of computers replacing personal teachers in the future, and present research shows
that computers are often more effective in teaching children as mea-
sured by improved grades and higher standardized test scores. However, even though this method produces better external performance,
I still feel that a student loses something internally when he learns
solely on a mechanical basis. There is no room for emotional expression, a very essential part of learning.

Thus, although the computers are an effective teaching vehicle, I
am still left with a question as to whether the gains outweigh the
losses. For my own use, I think a combination of both would be the
best solution.

Computer-assisted instruction is at present most common in
working with problems in grammar, mechanics, and usage. (It's
hard to imagine how a computer could ever respond fully to a piece
of writing that a student has composed, though recent programs
will, for instance, show a writer where she has used a passive construction or unusual spelling.) But it's just a supplement to the tutor
or teacher, who needs to supervise the student's progress. The same
is true for other self-paced materials: workbooks with answers,
tapes, cassettes, filmstrips. All of these can provide a change of pace
and many students enjoy working with them, but you need to supervise and be available. For one thing, you often need to make explanations.

Beyond Fill-in-the-Blank and Sentence Exercises

You can then move the student from computer and workbook exercises that foster passive knowledge to exercises that encourage students to use their knowledge actively. Being able to fill in blanks
correctly does not guarantee that the student actively uses that
knowledge in his writing.

Thus, instead of turning immediately to handbook rules it may
be useful to dig for general principles with the student. Such an
inductive working out of rules can help a student to understand and
absorb them. Suppose, for instance, that you are working with a
Japanese student who has trouble using articles, especially, you
decide, with countable and uncountable nouns. You might start by
asking what general principle the following use of articles suggests:

       a dog
       a table
       a piece
       sugar
       information
       justice

Why don't the last three items take "a"? The answer is that they are not countable nouns: you can count dogs and tables but not usually sugars (only grains of sugar) nor informations (only pieces of information).

Often, too, students prefer your off-the-cuff explanation to poring over the dense print of a handbook. And your explanation can be tailored to a student's needs. Jen Ciaburri, for example, was working with a student who hadn't realized that there are distinct rules for using commas—who had thought that separating words in a series meant throwing in a comma after every sixth or seventh word. So Jen needed to demonstrate that commas have important functions. She began thus:

> I suggested that instead of doing numerous dull grammar exercises I would explain the various uses of commas, which she could write down and we could discuss. I began by explaining what "words in a series" meant. I said it was three or more items . . . in a listing. . . . Next to this, we wrote some example sentences like "He was running, talking, aching, and gasping for breath." "Mother wants eggs, milk, bread, and butter at the market." "Mary is pretty, shy, and thoughtful."
>
> To show her further why it makes sense to do this I read the sentences without commas. Mother then wants "bread and butter" (in the sense of a piece of buttered bread instead of two separate items). Mary, without a comma, would be taken as pretty shy and thoughtful instead of pretty (in the sense of beauty), shy, and thoughtful.

Once the student understood some of the functions of commas, she was motivated to start learning what otherwise seemed like arbitrary rules.

After doing some handbook exercises, you could also move a student from sentence to paragraph exercises: instead of just supplying punctuation or correct spellings for isolated sentences, the student can supply them for a whole paragraph. Or he could correct any fragments and run-ons that appear in a paragraph. Or he could correct any inappropriate prepositions. Such exercises give a student practice in correcting errors in a slightly more realistic context than sentence exercises do.

Another bridge between passive and active knowledge is controlled writing, which is closer to composing than filling in the blanks is. Sometimes the writing may be tightly controlled, with only one correct answer: a student may be asked to change a passage from the present tense to the past, or from the singular to the plural. (For more of these autotutorial exercises, especially valuable with basic writers, see *The COMP-LAB Exercises* (1980), by Mary Epes and others.) Sometimes exercises are less tightly controlled: you could remove transitions from a published paragraph and ask the student to supply plausible ones.

You could also prepare an exercise that uses sentences the student has written. You could, for instance, take a six-sentence paragraph and ask him to combine sentences so that he'll have three, or dismantle sentences so that he'll have nine. Or you could ask him to rewrite a passage in a different tense or in indirect discourse, or to rewrite it so that he uses three semicolons correctly or so that it needs no apostrophes. Be sure the student knows that the goal is not necessarily to improve the passage (the past tense may or may not be more suitable than the present), but to give him practice in manipulating forms.

Frequently it's difficult to find appropriate bridging exercises in handbooks. You and the student may therefore create your own, like the paragraph-transforming exercises I have just described. But creating good exercises is harder than it looks. Be sure to try taking the exercise yourself, and then perhaps ask a friend to take it, before you give it to a tutee. It's easy to make an exercise too difficult. You may find, for instance, that when you try dismantling the student's six sentences you can't get more than eight, so asking him to produce nine would be unduly frustrating. And beware of getting locked into a single correct answer: the student may come up with a viable response that you hadn't anticipated.

In addition, the sentence-combining, imitation, and sentence-generating exercises described in the next section can help to bridge fill-in-the-blank exercises and the student's own writing.

Style

Style is a matter of judgment rather than outright error. And you should usually tackle style only after eliminating most errors. Style can be improved by eliminating awkwardness and impenetrability and by seeking vividness and grace.

In reading a paper in which style could be improved you might ask the following questions:

- Have you expressed your meaning as concisely as possible?
- What details and images could you add? How can you make the reader see, hear, taste, smell, feel what you're saying?
- Would a comparison or analogy communicate your point more effectively?
- Do you emphasize the points you want to emphasize? Have you made use of emphatic positions at the beginnings and ends of paragraphs and sentences? Are subordinate ideas syntactically subordinate? Could greater sentence variety provide greater emphasis and interest?
- How does the prose sound when you read it aloud?

If wordiness and impenetrability are a problem, try the following techniques. Often a student talks more effectively than she writes: if she can, without looking at a passage, tell you its ideas more clearly than she has explained them on paper, perhaps she should read her writing out loud, to find passages she has trouble speaking. Or she could underline her verbs to see whether she is relying on colorless verbs (like "is") and needs to convert abstract nouns to verbs (e.g., "elimination" to "eliminate"), to make her writing more direct. Or she could underline all appearances of "-tion," usually a sign of an abstract noun derived from a verb, and try to convert these nouns to verbs. Or she could circle prepositional phrases, and revise to eliminate as many as possible, especially when they appear in long strings. Or she could write down the four or five key words in a sentence and build on these words to rewrite the sentence.

> The fastest most painless way to express my idea in a shortened form is to pick "key thought" words out of the sentence. From these I know the point that I want to make and the style that I want to make it in because I took it right from the original sentence. To me, this is much easier than trying to just rewrite the sentence to make it shorter. . . .

> Once I have my thought words I "relink" them into a more concise sentence. (Jen Ciaburri)

Suppose that you want a student to revise the following sentence: "The attempt by the president to impose a uniform standard of excellence in academic grading by the elimination of idiosyncratic standards of individual professors was a failure." The student might decide that the key words are "president," "impose," "grading," "professors," and "failure." She might also realize that she could replace the verb "was" with the verb lurking in the abstract noun "failure." Her sentence might then become "The president failed to impose a uniform grading standard on the professors."

M. F. Withum found that she could communicate how colorless a student's writing was simply by asking the student to count appearances of the verb "to be."

> I read one brief, eight-sentence paragraph to her and asked her to count the number of times she used "is" or "are." Needless to say, she was astonished and pleading with me to stop when we got to fourteen. It was then that I suggested that she use more varied verbs. I told her that different, creatively used verbs in clear, concise sentences would eliminate the "simplistic" tone . . . which she feared.

A number of exercises can help a student improve her style. Sentence combining is one: it entails combining short sentences into longer, more complex ones. The point is not that longer sentences are necessarily better, but that a student can increase her flexibility, her choice of options, by practicing sentence combining (and also sentence dismantling). Take, for example, the following short sentences.

> LaVonne leaped at the masked intruder. The intruder had managed to elude the guard dogs. LaVonne wrestled the intruder to the floor.

They don't flow smoothly, but they can be combined. Sometimes you can ask a student to follow a specific pattern when combining sentences, such as being sure to include a "who"-clause. Sometimes you can ask her to combine in any way she likes. Or to come up with, say, four different versions and to decide which ones work best in different contexts. Here are several options for the above set of sentences.

1. LaVonne leaped at the masked intruder, who had managed to elude the guard dogs, and wrestled him to the floor.
2. Managing to elude the guard dogs, the masked intruder was leapt at by LaVonne, who wrestled him to the floor.
3. Leaping at the masked intruder, LaVonne wrestled him to the floor. He had managed to elude the guard dogs.
4. The masked intruder had managed to elude the guard dogs, but LaVonne leaped at him, wrestling him to the floor.

There are many more options. But even these four can provide a basis for discussing choices. Which are generally more effective? Which would be most effective in a paragraph whose primary subject was the intruder, not LaVonne? (I'd be inclined to say that 1, 3, and 4 are generally more effective, and that 4 would probably be effective in a context focusing on the intruder.) For lots of sentence-combining exercises, some controlled and some free, see *The Writer's Options* (1982), by Donald A. Daiker and others.

Another useful exercise entails imitating passages from an anthology like *The Norton Reader*. You can ask the student to imitate a sentence or paragraph by following a pattern.

Pace, timing, economy—all are essential for an effective joke.
_____, _____, _____—all are essential for an effective interview.
_____, _____, _____—all are _____ for a(n) _____
_____.

Or you can ask her to imitate the style in an extended passage while writing on a different topic.

Still another exercise derives from Francis Christensen's generative rhetoric, described in "A Generative Rhetoric of the Sentence" (1978), among other places. Starting with a base clause like "Jenny grimaced," a student can practice adding phrases and clauses, at varying levels of generality. She might, for instance, come up with a sentence like the following: "Without rising from her precarious perch, Jenny grimaced, her body coiled so tightly that she seemed not to breathe." The levels of generality could be diagrammed thus:

2 Without rising from her precarious perch,
1 Jenny grimaced,

    2 her body coiled so tightly
      3 that she seemed not to breathe.

The base clause is level 1, additions modifying it are level 2, additions modifying level-2 elements are level 3, and so on. (A similar approach works with paragraphs: the thesis statement is level 1, and the other sentences are assigned to levels according to whether they are coordinate with or subordinate to the thesis statement and each other.)

Over the long run, regular freewriting can help—it helps not only in generating ideas but in generating force and flow in writing. Celeste Cobb discovered that such practice gave her style greater force and personality.

> When I was younger I used to love to write letters. I would write to the person as though I was talking to them face to face at that particular moment. They were literally a written form of my thoughts. They usually proved to be quite earthy, fun to read.
>
> But as I have gotten older, my letters have become much more difficult to write. I don't like to write letters any more. And thinking about it lately I have discovered why letters have become such a task for me. I am structuring my letters; I am not always writing what I am feeling, but what I feel this person will be interested in. I write a letter that I feel could never incriminate me, reveal poor grammar, poor word choice, etc. But the other day, while sitting in the tutoring room with nothing to do, I dragged out my mail. I was suddenly inspired to answer one of my letters. I ripped out a piece of notebook paper, grabbed a pencil, and wrote and wrote. I had a great time writing the letter. When I got back to my dorm I seriously considered not mailing the letter, but instead revising it. But I didn't. I mailed the letter and got the most overwhelming response. This person who received my letter had frequently pointed out that my letters were "less than enthusiastic" but that this one was superb! The point is that what I did was essentially what I am doing in my journal entries.

One of the dangers of working on style, though, is that you may be tempted to impose your own on the student. It's important, here as elsewhere, to ask questions, to encourage the student to try out alternatives, to let her make the final decision. Diane Ciarletta explores some of these issues in a discussion of a tutoring session.

> One of my good friends came to me the other day wanting me to proofread a resumé cover letter. Since I am no expert myself at judg-

ing what a good cover letter includes contentwise, I could only really comment on her grammatical and structural errors. She had only a few punctuation errors here and there—a missing comma, a run-on and a few unnecessary phrases to be scratched out. However, after I read her letter over, I felt uneasy about telling her it was okay. There was nothing really radically wrong with her presentation, yet I felt overall that it could have been improved. Her style is very unlike mine, so maybe I was trying to judge it according to that—and not allowing for a difference in her manner of expression. I had to stop myself from trying to compare her work with my own standards and style. It caused me these disconcerting feelings; however, I just couldn't let her send it in without saying something. I felt that overall the letter could be presented more eloquently—but how do you say that, much less try to impose a style on someone who either doesn't want to use it, or doesn't know how? I wrestled with my uneasy feelings and finally decided (when she asked for an overall impression) to tell her what I thought. I said if she was shooting for a clear, to-the-point letter it was okay. But I said that maybe if she spent some time polishing and using some creativity the letter could become much more dynamic and outstanding. The purpose of these letters is to impress and stand out as unique. After all, employers read tons of letters every day—if yours is just ordinary how is it going to catch their eye? She got the idea—and we talked about some points she could have included. All in all, it was a good, *creative* session!

Diane's approach is sound: whether you're working on style or syntax or spelling, you want the student to be active and to share in the work. The final decisions are hers. More than when working on generating ideas and organizing them, it's easy to tutor grammar, mechanics, usage, and style by taking over and becoming directive. You may indeed need to play a major role in diagnosing the problem (even so, listen to what the student wants to work on). But be sure the student shares in deciding on priorities and approaches. True, she may feel that drills and rules and fill-in-the-blank exercises are what she needs, because they are all that she is familiar with. You may need to explain the value of controlled writing and sentence-manipulation exercises. But if she neither sees their value nor agrees to do them—if she feels that controlled writing is only a punishment imposed by you—she will resist and the exercises won't be very effective.

5 Special Writing Problems

Sometimes a student will ask you for advice on a writing project that you've never tried yourself—a book review, perhaps, or a lab report, or an explication of a poem, or a resumé. In part you can rely on common sense: if in a lab report you can follow the steps a student outlines for titration, even though you've never heard of titration before, she must be doing a pretty good job. Or if a book review for a history course simply recapitulates what the author said, you know there's something missing, even if you can't immediately verbalize what it is.

You should not just rely on your instincts, though. Ask first whether the instructor has provided instructions. Then you can turn to resource books. I'll outline approaches to a few common tasks, but you'll want to check other books too. An excellent resource for college writing assignments throughout the curriculum is *Writing in the Arts and Sciences* (1981), by Elaine Maimon and others. An excellent resource for writing in the real world, for resumés and business letters and memos, is *Writing That Works: How to Write Effectively on the Job* (1984), by Walter Oliu and others.

Plagiarism

You should be especially alert to the dangers of plagiarism. For one thing, as I noted in the Introduction, you don't want to be plagiarized—you don't want to give a student ideas or phrasing that he then adopts as his own. It's dishonest. And it's not fair to you, or the student, or the teacher. Your job is to guide a student, not to take over.

Similarly, a student needs to avoid being unduly influenced by any written sources he consults. One difficulty is that he may not understand when and how to acknowledge sources. He needs to learn when to include a footnote (or otherwise document his source). He probably knows that a quotation requires documentation. But so do facts and statistics not generally known (how does he know that 53 percent of the American public approves of flapdoodle?) and opinions and ideas (if three or more sources state an idea, it's probably sufficiently common not to need a footnote).

Some students commit plagiarism because they don't understand paraphrasing. Not only quotations but also paraphrases require documentation. And while quotations must agree word for word with the source, paraphrasing should be in the student's own words. Unfortunately, some students think they can change a couple of words in each sentence and then consider the wording their own. They're wrong. The wording and structure of the paraphrase need to be substantially different.

One way the student can be sure he's paraphrasing is to turn the source print-side down, so that he doesn't steal glances at it, and then to write his own account of what the source says. Another strategy is to tell himself that as soon as he has strung together three words that are the same as three adjacent words in the source, he's no longer paraphrasing.

Both strategies can help a student when writing a paper and, even earlier, when taking notes. For one cause of plagiarism is careless note taking: the student doesn't know whether his notes are the author's words or his own. He should be careful to use quotation marks in his notes when he's quoting directly, and be careful to use his own wording when he's paraphrasing.

Research Papers

The principles for writing library research papers are like those for writing other papers. But juggling a lot of research can make writing more difficult. Thus a student needs to have some system for coping with the research. Elaine Maimon and her coauthors in *Writing in the Arts and Sciences* (1981) give good advice on writing research papers, and Ellen Strenski and Madge Manfred's *The Research Paper Workbook* (1981) is an excellent tool for leading the student through the process of writing about research.

I'd encourage a student to start, before doing any research, by writing an instant version of the paper—in *Writing with Power* (1981) Peter Elbow calls it writing first thoughts. The student will probably be surprised by how much she already knows and feels about her subject, and in writing an instant version she can start organizing her thoughts and finding a focus, perhaps also a tentative thesis and organizational scheme. She shouldn't feel locked into a position by this early version, though—she'll probably change her mind about some things as she does her research. But after writing an instant version she'll know exactly what to research: she can take notes only on material relevant to her focus or thesis, not on everything that looks remotely interesting. And the instant version can provide the student with a framework for her final draft, so that she'll be less tempted to rely on the organizational structures and approaches of her sources.

As for the research itself, a student can approach each book or article with a technique called SQ3R, described by, for instance, Lynn Quitman Troyka in *Structured Reading* (1978). First, the student can *survey* the material—get an overview by examining the title, any headings, and the first and last chapters or paragraphs. (And if the survey suggests that the work is not relevant to her research, the student need not pursue the work further.) Then she should ask *questions* about the work, preferably questions related to her focus or thesis. And she goes on to *read,* to *recite* the main points at the end of each short section, and finally to *review*—summarize or outline the material and answer her original questions.

While questioning, reading, and reviewing, the student can take notes. The traditional advice is to use note cards.

> When taking notes, one has to be really careful to put what is written in one's own words and not plagiarize. Also, for me note cards are essential. Most of my friends just go from book to book and write down whatever information they need on a piece of paper. I've used this approach before and I've found it's horrible for organization, as everything invariably gets mixed up or lost.
>
> But note cards should correspond to some mental or actually written down outline. For example, if I'm writing about . . . the good and bad aspects to the Industrial Revolution, I'd probably have one section of notecards on the good aspects, one on the bad and another with general background on the Industrial Revolution. Any quotes can be copied down and only one idea per card. Also you can keep track of

your sources on a bibliography card, and sources for footnotes and page numbers can be written down next to the information to be footnoted. (Karen Curry)

Like the instant version, note cards can help a student to avoid one of the special dangers in writing research papers: the danger that she will rely on the organizational scheme of her sources, rather than develop her own organization, based on her own thesis. (One sign of this problem is many consecutive footnotes from the same source.) But since note cards can be readily shuffled, they make it easier to develop one's own organization and then to slip in information from sources only where relevant.

Another danger is that a research paper will be just a series of quotations, loosely strung together. Such a paper should paraphrase more; the student should also incorporate her own analysis. In general, a student should have a good reason for quoting a passage— not just because doing so is less work than making a comparable point herself. For instance, maybe she's going to analyze the wording in detail. Maybe the passage contains an unusual or characteristic turn of phrase. Maybe the author is a well-known authority whose exact words need to be reckoned with. Or maybe, especially in literary criticism, the passage illustrates the point the student has just made about the author's style. Quotations should never speak for the student: she should make the point herself and use the quotation to support it. And usually short quotations are preferable to long ones.

Essay Exams

Many students may not understand what's expected of them in essay exams. Some think that an essay question should simply trigger an outpouring of all the facts they crammed the night before. They don't realize the key importance of their interpretation and analysis.

> To study for an essay exam, I would think a student should study facts, but at the same time keep in mind overall concepts that have been taught in the class. An essay exam is not an opportunity for a student to spew forth everything a teacher has taught, but an oppor-

tunity to show the significance of what has been taught, as well as do some analyzing. If a professor wants memorization, he/she can give a multiple choice or fill-in-the-blank exam.

To tutor a student needing help in studying for an exam, I think the tutor needs to find out what class the exam is for, as well as the tutee's views on essay exams, and the process she usually follows in studying. Also, some discussion of what has been taught might help the student to get her thoughts in order and decide what is important. If the tutee has ideas as to what the main concepts are, she might want to make an outline for a possible essay, listing the main concepts and filling in the facts to go with those concepts; however, I think it is a waste of time trying to psych out the professor and practice writing essays, usually. (Penny Penn)

Outlining possible essay answers is probably more useful than writing out full answers, but it depends on the student. More generally, it is valuable to make connections and see relationships, to organize the course material in one's own mind. It's important to study both facts and concepts. Some students do so by outlining notes on the class and the reading.

When I prepare for an essay exam, my usual approach is to read class notes, make a list of most important facts (from *memory* first and then from reading notes); from these I make up or rather highlight comparisons we've made in class. One experience last year made me realize that there are even better ways to study for essay exams and that is with a group of people. We got together and talked about most important things, interpretations, class notes, and made some guesstimates about questions. (Liz Como)

Barbara Emerson describes tutoring a student in preparation for an essay exam.

Our session mainly consisted of trying to get her to start thinking about what the question would be. Her teacher had given out a three-page paper on "IQ: Are the Japanese Smarter?" That is what they'll have to write on. Sally and I generated different ideas on what could be asked.
Examples:
• cause and effect
• compare and contrast Lynn study and Stevenson study
• discuss influence of their backgrounds (Lynn's British and Stevenson's American)

- prejudice of writer of article—he is Japanese
- how other writers might interpret
- your agreement with one or the other

Another hurdle in preparing for an exam is anxiety. Sue Haberberger has found a way to control anxiety and to organize her thoughts.

> Last week I had four midterms and by the time my fourth one rolled around I felt very exhausted. As a result of my exhaustion, I became very panicky and felt that I didn't know anything about the material that I would be tested on the following morning. In order to relax myself and see what I knew I freewrote. I don't know how long I wrote (it certainly was longer than ten minutes), but I was satisfied with the results. I relieved the stress I was feeling and I was amazed at how much I actually knew. Afterwards when I studied, I had basic building blocks in writing to work from to get a complete picture of how everything is interrelated.

Even if anxiety strikes during an exam, freewriting can help.

> The other day (while in the midst of an English exam!) I had a terrible case of writer's block. The professor had given us the questions in advance and told us we could bring both our books and outlines to the exam. I had studied quite hard for the test and was keyed up when I started to write.
>
> I soon realized that I hadn't written half of the first essay in thirty minutes. Since the class was an hour and fifty minutes long and there were seven topics to write on, I was understandably nervous. My palms were sweating and my ears were filled with the sounds of busily scratching pens.
>
> Fortunately for me while I was in this state of panic I remembered some tutoring wisdom. Instead of being concerned over every line I just looked at my outline and freewrote. Before I knew it I was whipping through the essays. I don't know if my grammar was the best or if the punctuation was all there, but I did get my thoughts on the paper. (Sarah Hutcheon)

When beginning an exam, the student should make sure she understands the question.

> First, I told her to read the question through entirely, very slowly. Second, go back over the question, making sure to read *every* word, and identify the *key* instruction words. Then, thirdly, underline or

circle the key words, so that if she found herself wandering off on a tangent half way through the question, she could look back to the key words to re-direct her focus. I also advised her to paraphrase the question in her answer, so as to help her concentrate on the question before jumping into the answer. (Susan Rich)

After carefully reading the question, the student should concentrate on figuring out connections and organizing, perhaps sketching an outline or jotting down notes. One tutor tells how she learned to do so the hard way.

My first attempts at essay exams were disastrous. I was so worried about remembering all the facts and figures that I often began without any organizing idea whatsoever. As a result, my exams were full of facts, yet the facts weren't properly organized. In addition, I'd spend so much nervous effort frantically racing the clock that I'd often find myself writing about everything in a course, while totally ignoring the actual question being asked. Since that time, however, I have discovered that pausing for five minutes or so before I begin answering the question is immensely helpful for collecting my thoughts. Not only does this brief pause allow me to analyze the actual essay question, but it also allows me opportunity to write a brief outline for what I plan to write. In this way, I can concentrate on my prose and presentation, rather than on just the facts. This also frees my mind of clutter, which often leads to writer's block. Also, as I write an essay exam, I only write on the right side of the exam book and leave the left side blank. This way, any time a stray fact, which I may have overlooked, pops into my head, I can add it to the existing paragraph without having to write in the margins. (M. F. Withum)

And it's more important to attend to ideas than to grammatical and mechanical perfection. Although it might be worthwhile to learn to spell key concepts and names, most instructors are tolerant of occasional lapses in correctness on an essay exam. One student, after taking a psychology exam, told a tutor

that essay exams were always hard for her because she becomes very involved in making a grammatically perfect essay rather than a complete one which contains all of the relevant information. She said that she spent about twenty-five minutes on each of the first two essays and by the time she got to the last two essays, she only could spend five minutes on each. . . .

I told her that the first thing she should do is figure out exactly how much time she can spend on each essay in the next exam. In this exam, she should have allowed herself no more than fifteen minutes per question. . . . Also, I told her that time should be allowed at the end of the exam so that it can be proofread.

I then explained to my tutee that professors don't expect perfectly written essays on exams. They realize that you don't have the time to write a nicely polished essay in an exam situation. What they do look for is content, however. My tutee said that her content lacked due to the time she spent working on grammar. (Sandra Prouty)

In general, a student doesn't need to write a full-blown introduction when answering an essay question, but she should at least start with a statement of her thesis: to guide the teacher in reading the essay and to guide herself in writing it. (She might, for instance, rephrase the question she is answering.) Then she needs to develop the essay around concepts, supported by relevant details. She should not jot down unsupported concepts nor chaotically unstructured details nor a scattering of concepts and details, but achieve a working marriage of abstract concepts and specific details.

Book Reviews

The most common weakness of book reviews is that a student simply recapitulates the contents of the book. He needs to be reminded to comment on the book—on how well the author has fulfilled her purpose, how cogent the argument is, how clear the organization and style are. And ultimately the student should indicate whether or not he recommends the book—although not with an "I recommend this book to all my friends." Instead, he could discuss whether it would be a useful introduction to someone who knows nothing about the topic, whether it's too complex for an introduction but offers insights that will generate heated discussion among experts, whether it's an excellent book for primary-school children despite occasional sex-role stereotyping.

Anne Rice describes what a book review can include, admitting that

sometimes I will get off track and start writing too much plot/summary in a review. . . . In a book review, you . . . write about your opinions of the book, about what you think the author was trying to do, whether you think the author did a good job, and whether or not you like the book . . . and why. You can also comment about the style of writing, whether it was consistent or not, whether you liked it or not, etc.

In tutoring a student working on a book review, you might start by asking him whether he liked the book and why—as a way of getting him to think about strengths and weaknesses, though he should be wary of too much "I liked" and "I didn't like" in the review itself. Book reviews comment not only on the content of the book but also on the kinds of things you look for in student writing: focus, organization, logic, convincing specificity, clarity, conciseness, accuracy, even proofreading. For example, does the author overwhelm the reader with details, without providing enough guidance and explanation? Is the style unnecessarily turgid? Or perhaps its complexity appropriately reflects the complexity of the ideas?

If a student has already written a draft, you might start by examining its structure. If the organization of the review closely follows that of the book—first the author said this, then that, then this—the student is simply recapitulating what the book said. It's better to organize the review in terms of strengths and weaknesses: if, for instance, the student is basically favorable about the book, he might start by admitting, say, that the author is wrong about a few details and then go on to stress how persuasive the author's argument is nonetheless.

Sometimes, if a student has trouble deciding how to approach the review and what to focus on, you can help him by clarifying who his reader is. He should assume that his reader hasn't read the book and wants to know whether she should.

Lab Reports

One visible difference between writing in the humanities and writing in the sciences is the method of guiding the reader through the paper. Scientists tend to use headings, unmistakable guideposts that allow the reader to thumb through quickly and find the section he wants to read. Since readers may not read an entire report but only particular sections, a scientific writer may repeat in each section some material from other sections. Humanists are likely to consider such repetitions inappropriate and headings a sign of weakness. They prefer a smooth-flowing paper, one with well-crafted transitions that move the reader from paragraph to paragraph. And scientists are likely to consider such carefully constructed transitions unnecessary verbiage.

The point is that lab reports and other scientific writing rely on headings—such as "Materials," "Methods," "Results," "Discussion"—and favor directness. But they still require careful organization and attention to clarity. One tutor describes their requirements.

> All of the lab reports I have done have usually been predetermined by my instructor as far as format was concerned. Each section was titled, the first being, say, method, then equipment, followed by results and conclusions. I have always felt that the main purpose was to basically get down in writing what you had done and what you had gotten out of it. . . .
>
> If someone came to me with questions concerning how to write a lab report I think I would first ask her for the format already given to her. I would advise her to follow the outline, and answer the questions in complete sentences. If she had no format I guess I would first look over the lab and then have her evaluate the experiment. I would then probably give her a general outline of what the professor may be looking for, and let her incorporate her results into the outline. The outline would be similar to what I gave above. (Celeste Cobb)

The most common problem with lab reports is that students don't appropriately separate their methods from their results or their results from their conclusions. The methods section should describe how the experimenter proceeded—so clearly that another experimenter could exactly replicate the process. The results section details the results that the student actually came up with in following the methods. These results should be factual: the measurements, not their meaning. Their meaning and significance should be explained in the discussion or conclusions section.

6   Evaluating Writing

A good tutor or teacher not only knows something about the writing process and about kinds of writing but also knows how to evaluate writing: she can gauge a paper's strengths and weaknesses and can advise the writer on how to improve. This chapter provides practice in evaluating writing. Ideally, you would discuss your evaluations with colleagues and share ideas on how to tutor the student writers. But in case that isn't feasible, I share some tutors' comments on essays, both here and in Appendix C.

First, try a ranking exercise—you could ask a tutee to try it too, especially one who needs to work on organizing paragraphs. Read the following four paragraphs (two written by the same student) and rank them from best to worst. There's no correct ranking—just be prepared to defend your choices.

A

As the American economy continues its downward trend, economists continue to emphasize the urgent need of an energy program. Some economists have investigated solar energy and feel it is the best choice. They contend that it will be inexpensive once instituted, and that it will not harm the environment. Furthermore they state that such an energy program will illiminate the United States fatal dependence on OPEC. In short, they state that the United States dependence on foriegn sourses has driven the econﬁomy into a recession and that such a program will reinvigorate the economy.

B

The use of fuel was never a problem for our grandparents but now the problem of fuel has become our concern. One problem is to find a way to produce solar power at a prices people can pay. But in order to do that we must become less dependent on foreign sources for our fuel. This would give the fuel producers an incentive to produce more fuel. The increase in production would bring down prices. When we become less dependent on them the production of fuel in our own country will increase. The key to energy is the increase of production in the U.S. and then the prices may go down.

C

We are aware of the high cost of oil from foreign countries for energy in this country. If we were to develop more and more solar power, we would have a much better environment. Granted, the initial cost of such a system would be high. We would also be a nation independent from foreign sources to meet the needs of energy.

In the long run the system would be cheaper and give us the benefits of clean fuels and independence from foreign sources.

D

There is a great need to develop more solar power to help alleviate the energy crisis. Granted, there are some disadvantages and one of them is the high initial cost of installing such a system. However, we would have a much better environment because we would have cleaner air. We would, also, be a nation independent from foreign sources to meet the needs of energy. In the long run the system would be cheaper and give us the benefits of clean fuels and independence from foreign sources.

(The paragraphs were written in response to a supplemental assignment for *Functional Writing,* by A. D. Van Nostrand and others, now revised and called *The Process of Writing* [1982].)

Which paragraph do you consider best? second best? third best? worst?

Chances are, you ranked A and D ahead of B and C. But there is no immutable order: people need to understand why they rank the paragraphs as they do—what their priorities are—and they should become aware of how their priorities differ from those of others.

People who prefer A to D tend to favor stylistic flow and scholarly context (and are not put off by spelling errors). Those who prefer D favor directness. And those who prefer B to C tend to prefer a smooth flow from sentence to sentence, whatever the underlying logic: the writer knows how to use sentence connectives. For example, the third sentence begins with "But" and includes a demonstrative pronoun ("that") referring to the preceding sentence—but what does "that" refer to? And does the writer really want to say that becoming less dependent on foreign sources will enable us to produce solar power that we can afford? Which is cause and which is effect? Those who prefer C, on the other hand, can manage to ignore the focus implied in the first sentence.

C and D are actually "before" and "after" paragraphs. What was C's problem? The writer might have known how to organize a paragraph but have forgotten to do so here—she might have discovered what to say while writing, might have done some exploratory freewriting and then forgotten to rework it. In that case all that would be necessary would be a nudge—perhaps simply asking how she could revise the paragraph to make it easier for a reader to follow. In fact, however, she seemed still at sea when asked probing questions, and the tutor became more directive, suggesting that she start with a thesis statement, discuss disadvantages and advantages, and conclude with a general statement.

Now let's turn to some longer writing samples—what are their strengths and weaknesses?

ESSAY QUESTION:
WOULD YOU RATHER BE A MALE?
WHY OR WHY NOT?

I was once told of a Scorpio's hidden desire to be a man but being born under that sign I can't see what they mean. Personally I get offended if a member of the opposite sex puts me down, however subtley, for being a woman and I get the uncontrollable urge to show him I'm not the typical weak female. Nothing is more annoying than to have "the dumb blonde" stamp taped across you. Men are never accused of being "flighty" or an "airhead" instead they are referred to as aloof. Another fact in point is when a woman dresses carefully she is called a *flashy* dresser, but if a man takes the same amount of time and care he is known as a *smart* dresser. I think what is really being discussed here is the sexual prejudice seen throughout society today. If men have "created" this culture, as I'm sure some will claim, then they must be doing *something* wrong. Women should be given the chance to see what they can do maybe to re-create our society. As I see it women have always had the advantage of intelligence over men but now importantly they have been endowed with female determination. Female determination is an attribute that men, obviously, lack.

Actually I see almost no advantages to being a man except that it may be more socially acceptable. Everytime a war crops up *men* are drafted into the army, navy and air force, and one of them is bound to get you. Men have always had the honor of doing all the heavy work around the home.

I suppose the main reason I'm glad I'm not a man is because, as they say in the movies, they're so dumb where women are concerned.

What would you say to the writer? What has she done well? What is her major problem? What should she work on first?

The student uses some striking details and has an effective conversational tone. She also has some idea how to use a punch line to achieve a sense of closure. But the paper lacks coherence. It's probably best to focus on coherence and organization before worrying about, say, spelling or run-ons. One tutor tells what she would say to the student:

You have some really good ideas here about why you are glad that you're female, but there are some problems with your essay, as well. I'd say that your main problem is a lack of organization, which stems, I think, from not really knowing what you want to say. It seems to me that you just sat down and started to write without really giving the subject much thought. That's a good way to generate ideas for an essay and it can even be considered a first draft of an essay, but it really needs to be revised. As I said before, you need to have better organization. What, exactly, is your organizing idea? What is the main point of your essay? What are you really trying to say? These are basic questions you can ask yourself in order to help you get a firm grasp on the direction in which your essay is going. Once you've established the organizing idea of your essay you might want to break down your other ideas into separate paragraphs and elaborate on each. It would be a good idea to give a brief idea of what these paragraphs will be about in your introduction. Then in your conclusion you can summarize what you've said just to make sure your reader has clearly gotten your point. (Ellen McVeigh)

In actually tutoring the student Ellen would probably have asked her about her writing process, before stating that she must not have spent much time on the paper (think how discouraged the student would be if she had indeed spent a lot of time). But I like Ellen's focus on stepping back and rethinking the essay as a whole, not just tinkering with words and sentences that might disappear in a later draft.

Another tutor basically agrees with Ellen but focuses more on the student's logic (and the comments are not directed toward the student).

> The paper's main problems are that it not only lacks organization but it has no central thesis. It also does not even address the assignment question. This type of assignment is typical of an argument paper, and the student would be better directed if she took some stand on the question. Thus, before she even begins to write she should first of all decide whether she would rather be male or female, and then list all the reasons and/or advantages she foresees for her particular decision. With this first step she should have a clearer objective and organization of the paragraphs. The indecision of her stance . . . is apparent in her paper. When she points out the sexual prejudices against women for being "dumb blondes" or "flighty" it sounds as if she is using these negative stereotypes of women as advantages for being male. However, her next statement is contradictory. She writes, "I see almost no advantage to being a man except that it may be more socially acceptable." Her arguments lack logic and development. For instance, she writes, "Female determination is an attribute that men, obviously, lack." Of course men don't have *female* determination! But what does that have to do with the price of rice? The student should concentrate on clarifying her ideas; this could be done by making an outline of her reasons for her argument. Then she should write a few sentences on each argument and then develop them into separate paragraphs. Since an argument paper is one where you can express personal opinions, I would encourage the tutee to talk aloud her feelings and get some sense as to what it's like to "argue in a paper." (Diane Ciarletta)

Diane's comments are good. I particularly like the advice to get the student to argue out loud, in preparation for arguing on paper.

Here's another student paper to evaluate:

WOMAN'S ROLE

It is definitely an understatement to suggest that women have come a long way in our society. The position that we have worked for, for such a long period of time, is no longer fairy tale, but a true story. Unfortunately, it is also true that we still must conquer a lot of red tape.

To women of today, family life is still an important factor, although not as much emphasis is placed on it anymore. We are no longer contented with playing the stereotypic role of the happy housewife, who sits at home all day awaiting the arrival of her favorite soap opera! We want the very best education we can possibly get, and work hard for our degrees. In essence, we are striving for careers, the working woman! This is so unlike the days of our past, where all we could handle—according to most of the male population—was a high school education and instantaneous marriage. It is attitudes such as these that have made our quest so discouraging.

Any woman in business automatically contradicts one of the general assumptions about women. It is difficult for a male to understand that in some ways, we are just as equal as they are. I think that they have been the stronger sex for just a little bit too long. Women overcome many bigoted attitudes. It is true that generally women have the same managerial qualities as do men. We have received the same basic educational qualities, so it should only follow that we may be equally as talented. Some women have even begun to take over in higher, executive positions which should prove that we can, and will provide.

The federal equal employment legislation has really helped women to overcome the fear of progression. It has helped to build our confidence in conquering an unnecessary barrier. It has also helped to reshape the public opinion of women's position in business. The position that we have strived for, is finally coming to life. We have broken through a lot of red tape, and we will break through more. It is an understatement to say that we have come a long way—because we have finally made it.

How could this essay be improved? What can the student build on?

Most tutors that I know recognize a problem with organization and clarity. One tutor sees these problems and pretends she is talking to the student.

There are some very good points in this paper. You mention some important aspects of the stereotypical woman and you seem to have a generally good understanding of society's attitude toward women. There are some problems, however. I would say your main problem has to do with organization. You try to say too many things all at once and you don't really seem to have a clear notion of exactly what direction you are going in or exactly what you are trying to say. You need to establish a main organizing idea and work from there. Another strategy is to list all of the points you've made and organize them into a coherent train of thought.

You also seem to be having some problems with word choice. I think this is partly because you aren't too sure what you're trying to say. It might help to really think about the words you're using to make sure they make sense. You could also read the paper out loud to yourself to make sure the words sound right. (Ellen McVeigh)

Another tutor recognizes problems with organization and tone and goes on to discuss vagueness (related to Ellen's discussion of word choice).

A tutor would have to find out exactly what this student means by many of the vague terms and general statements that she makes in her writing. Examples of this vagueness include (in the fourth paragraph) "legislation . . . helped women to overcome the fear of progression," (in the third paragraph) "one of the general assumptions about women," and (in the fourth paragraph) "It is an understatement to say that we have come a long way—because we have finally made it." I really think that the student would be able to include more specific—and less vague—information in her paper, if she could be made to explain what she means by these general statements (for a beginning) and write these ideas down. I would probably ask this student to explain what she feels are the "general assumptions about women" in our society, and what kind of "red tape" she feels women have had to "break through" to attain their goals. I think it would be helpful for this student to design an outline—expanding or rather supporting her general ideas by more specific ones. Then, with a clearer idea of how her pieces of information relate to one another and an idea of a possible sequence for this information, I think she could develop an organizing idea for her old and new pieces of information and a way of tying this information together. . . . (Cathy Coffin)

I would agree that the student needs to talk out her ideas, to clarify and specify her meanings. She needs to decide, for instance, whether women have finally made it or still need to cut through red tape. She does seem to have some sense of organization: introduction, paragraph on women leaving the home, paragraph on women in business, conclusion. Yet it's difficult for the reader to determine what each paragraph is about. The student could probably use practice in developing one-sentence theses—for paragraphs and entire papers. A tutor could help her to build an issue tree and to compose thesis statements.

As you evaluate more essays you will become more skilled. Don't be alarmed if you don't see all the possible improvements right away.

> During tutoring class my responses to essays and readings are different from the other students'. I wonder why I overlook certain aspects of a paper that they see. Actually, we do have some similar responses, which makes me feel a bit better. I suppose that I concentrate more on subject matter and organization rather than grammatical errors. I do not pick up tense changes as quickly as the other tutors. When reading an essay in class I first read for understanding and then for technical errors. When comments are given the other tutors point out grammatical errors that I have overlooked. Usually I pick them up after a rereading. At first I was concerned about my abilities because my responses are different, but now I realize that we are concentrating on varying aspects of an essay. I am now trying to read essays while looking for technical aspects as well as for organization. It is difficult to catch all the mistakes in one reading. That is why it is good to have all the tutors reacting and sharing thoughts. Each of us points out mistakes that the others overlook. This has been extremely helpful because I am beginning to view essays from different perspectives. I have found that reading the essays for class and then responding to them has improved my concentration and reading ability. (Barb Rose)

The following are more student essays for you to practice evaluating. Chances are, you aren't familiar with the material on which some of the essays are based. But, assuming that the writers haven't written anything factually wrong, you can still evaluate the effectiveness of the essays, analyzing their strengths and weaknesses. And you can consider tutoring approaches. For comments on the essays see Appendix C.

1. Aliosha and Miranda

> In both stories, "A Trifle From Real Life," by Anton Chekhov, and "The Fig Tree" by Katherine Anne Porter, the portrayal of the treatment of children is similar. The reasons why they treat them this way differ.

The Chekhov story is one about the betrayal of a child. Nikolai Ilitch Belayeff was a young man from St. Petersburg who was having an affair with Olga Ivanova. He was "dragging through a long and tedious love affair."[1] He paid a visit to Olga's house, only to find she wasn't home. He was seated on the couch prepared to await her return. It was then that Aliosha, Olga's eight-year-old son, entered the room.

During all his aquaintance with Olga, he had never really paid attention to, or noticed, Aliosha. Yet, now, he felt himself watching the boy. It was taken, while they were playing together, that Aliosha felt very confident with Nikolai.

Aliosha was rambling on about something that he wanted. He wanted a watch just like his father's. Nikolai questioned Aliosha as to whether or not he has seen his father. Aliosha begged Nikolai not to tell "mama" because it was a secret. Nikolai took Aliosha into the most strictest confidence, in order to find out the truth. Aliosha felt confident so he told his little story.

Pelagia, the nurse, takes Aliosha and his sister Sonia to see their father every Thursday and Friday. Before dinner Pelagia takes them to Angel's confectionary. It is here where the children see their father, and have all kinds of treats. Aliosha got very excited when talking about the pasties that "Papa" buys them.

Aliosha is a young boy who knows very little of the world around him. He lives in a fantasy world in which there are only happy thoughts. He receives pasties and sweet pears and is absolutely thrilled and satisfied.

Nikolai interupted the boy's story and asked if his papa ever said anything about him. Aliosha admitted that papa is very angry with Nikolai. Papa claims that it is Nikolai's fault that mama is unhappy and that Nikolai has ruined mama. At this Nikolai was extremely angered. When Olga returned home, Nikolai told her all that her son had told him. Nikolai stated "it appears that I am a wicked scoundrel and that I have ruined you and your children."[2] Aliosha's face became distorted with fear. He was shocked at Nikolai because he gave his word of honor.

Nikolai brushed him aside impatiently as he started to pace the floor. His mind contained the thoughts of the wrong that had been done him. And, as before, he was unconscious of Aliosha's prescence.

It was at this point that Aliosha felt pain. He was terribly hurt by an unfeeling and selfish adult. He had come face to face with deceit. Never had he imagined, until now, that there were things in this world besides watches, pasties, and sweet pears, "things for which no name could be found in the vocabulary of a child."[3]

Nikolai was a man who lacked an understanding of children. He didn't care how Aliosha felt about the pasties and sweet pears. Nikolai didn't realize, nor did he care, that these things are important in the eyes of a child.

The story of "The Fig Tree" is about the treatment of a young girl named Miranda. She is facinated by death and always takes care of dead things. She is always being told by her Grandmother to act like a young lady.

Miranda's mother died when Miranda was quite young and no one really explained what death meant and why people die. She only knew that "dead meant gone away forever."[4] She only knew the ritual of what happens when someone dies. When someone died, there was a long row of carriages going at a slow walk over the hill towards the river while the bell tolled and tolled, and that person was never seen again by anybody. Miranda realized that farm animals like chickens and little turkeys died more often.

Many times Miranda discovered creatures that she had found to be no longer living. She always burried it in a little grave with flowers on top and she put a smooth stone at the head. Everything that was dead had to be treated in the same way. "This way and no other,"[5] said her Grandmother.

There was an incident in the story including Miranda and a dead chicken that she had found. She had tried to give the chicken a proper burrial. When the job was done she heard a "weeping" sound. She was terrified that she had burried the chicken alive. Her Grandmother had called her so she had to leave the gravesite. Miranda was afraid to tell her Grandmother about the chicken for fear that her Grandmother would tell her that she did something wrong.

Miranda and her family were now on their way to their relatives house in Halifax. By this time she was extremely upset that the chicken was burried alive. She had to think of a way to make her family bring her back. All of a sudden, she started crying for her doll. She hated dolls because her Grandmother made her act like a doll.

Miranda secretly told her Great-Aunt Eliza about the "weeping" sound. She said that they are only tree frogs and that sound means that it is going to rain. Miranda was so very happy to now know that she had not burried the chicken alive.

Grandmother didn't understand children, especially Miranda.

She didn't give Miranda any responsibility, yet Grandmother really does care about Miranda.

She wants Miranda to act like a doll, still and not free. She wanted her to do the right thing and to stay put when told. Grandmother didn't want Miranda to run around like all the other children. She wanted Miranda to be a young lady. She was doing all of this for Miranda's benefit.

Both of the stories don't have the same subject matter yet they have similar types of characters. Each story has the young child who is treated badly by the adult. The children aren't treated fairly. Both of the children, Aliosha and Miranda, aren't treated like real people. In one story the child is betrayed. He has been scarred, if not for life, then for a long time, because of an inconsiderate adult. Someone who didn't care about his feelings. While in the other story, a young girl is always being put down and made fun of by her grandmother. Miranda is made to feel very selfconscious and insecure because her grandmother says that she asks too many questions.

Notes

1. Anton Chekhov, "A Trifle from Real Life," in *Story to Anti-Story,* edited by Mary Rohrberger (Boston: Houghton Mifflin, 1979), p. 263.

2. Ibid., p. 266.

3. Ibid., p. 267.

4. Katherine Anne Porter, "The Fig Tree," in *Story to Anti-Story,* p. 391.

5. Ibid.

2. Take-Home Exam

Question: What do you feel is the single gravest problem facing America's cities today? Why do you pick this particular problem rather than others? Suppose you headed a Presidential Task Force dealing with this problem. How might you proceed to deal with it? (An outline of steps would be appropriate here.)

Cities have long been known as the cultural, economic, governmental, population and communication centers of the world. Usually they are places where most people can find a job and earn a living and where some people can accumulate moderate or great wealth. In cities, people can also choose from a variety of cultural and recreational activities that add to the enjoyment of life. Nevertheless, cities have many physical, social and economic problems, not to mention governmental problems also.

One of the biggest problems that face cities today is economics. It is difficult however to single out economics as a main cause, because it encompasses so many of the other crisis the city faces today.

When one thinks of poverty, it brings to mind hunger and suffering. These are just mere symptoms. The cause is much deeper. Poverty might cause a person's unwillingness or inability to work. But where there is widespread poverty, such as inner cities, it is usually the result of such economic conditions as business and industrial depressions, financial crisis or industrial changes. So perhaps the cities biggest problem is unemployment.

It has often been stated that money is the root of all evil. So if money is a large factor in the city, it stands to reason, that evil must be close behind. Indeed evil lurks in the cities.

This paper will attempt to touch on some of the other problems of the city, but looking closely at these you can see that the main problem relates to economics.

Physical problems of cities include substandard housing and pollution. Poorly constructed, run-down, unsanitary or overcrowded dwellings consist of a city's housing. Governments have set up various programs to get rid of substandard housing. But population growth, lack of funds, the high cost of construction add to the problem.

Automobiles, factories, powerplants and other sources pollute city air. But the same things that cause pollution also aid a city's economy and give its people conveniences.

Social problems in todays cities include friction between people of different backgrounds, crime, juvenile delinquency, alcoholism and drug addiction. Such antisocial behavior arises in part from poverty and from the inability of some people to adjust to urban living. Sociologists point to urban society's impersonal relationship toward individuals as a cause of these inabilities.

Most people in cities enjoy a high standard of living. But even in the best of times, a city has many poor people. Poverty has always existed, but the wealth of today's cities highlights the problem. The poor see other people enjoying comfortable lives, and their resent-ment toward their condition grows. The anger felt by the poor toward society may lead to crime and violence. Government and social organizations try to improve educational and job opportunities for the poor and provide the poor with financial aid.

Complex economic and social factors sometimes lead to business slumps. During a slump, many workers lose their jobs and the number of needy people in the city increases. The workers collect unemployment and some recieve welfare.

Cities have made some effort to solve their problems, but much remains to be done. More money than is now available could partially solve these problems, but most of the funds would come from taxes. Some people favor extensive use of tax money but others oppose it.

Goverment regulation could also help, as with air pollution.

All city problems could not be solved completely even if everyone favored wide use of tax money and governmental regulation. The goverment may not be able to get enough money to releive such problems as poverty and substandard housing. Also money can not change the attitude of one group of people toward another.

3. In-Class Paragraph

Students were asked to write a paragraph on Jane Austen's *Sense and Sensibility* and to touch on the following concepts: drawing and music, courtship, divorce, inheritance. (The exercise was testing both knowledge of the book and ability to write a coherent paragraph, but you should focus on analyzing the latter.)

> The Society in which Elinor and Marianne lived in, consisted of many social rules. Each young lady and gentlemen was expected to do certain things and follow certain social rules. For instance, a young lady before she is married, spends most of her time in drawing and playing music. Dating was sort of a ritial, the couple must have the parent's permission and they must never be alone. Marriage was thought of as bringing together two houses. An ideal marriage was when a girl marries a rich husband. Divorce was consisdered a big scandal and only on the grounds of adultery. Inheritance was always a big issue. The oldest boy of each family usually receives the inheritance. Being wealthy was having a high social standing.

4. *Discussion of the* Crito

Assignment: Two to three pages. Briefly summarize, analyze, and discuss Plato's *Crito*. Are the arguments valid and convincing? Are they applicable to present-day situations?

This dialogue begins with a friend of Socrates, Crito, coming to see Socrates on the day before he is to die. He came with the purpose of talking Socrates into escaping Athens and in order to avoid his death sentence. Crito claims that enough money to do so has been set aside by Socrates wealthy friends. Crito's justification of the escape, stated simply, is that Athens was wrong in convicting Socrates for he had committed no crime. Therefore, he is right in escaping.

Socrates refutation of this claim is complex. He first states that one must never do something that is evil. He also claims that it is possible for a person to distinguish good from evil. Everyone has an idea (form) of what is good. Socrates then asks if it is right to *counter* an evil with an evil. No, says Crito. But, Socrates then asks, isn't that exactly what he would be doing if he escaped his sentence?

And why would this be evil? Socrates says that by living in a town you automatically make a silent agreement that you will abide by the laws of the town. One really has the right to live where ever one wants. Though he feels that he has been wronged by the men of Athens, he must abide by the compact and his sentence. To break it would be wrong, and consequently, evil, and everyone knows, one must never do evil.

Thus are the main arguments of the *Crito*. They seem to be quite sound. But, are they valid in today's society? I think so. His concepts seem to jibe with the general beliefs of today. Laws are inacted to protect society. Those living in a democracy, as we do, have usually agreed upon these laws and are expected to abide by them. However, here is an interesting question to pose: What would Socrates have said about draft evasion, or any type of civil disobedience, for that matter? He states quite clearly in the beginning of the *Crito*, "But, why, my dear Crito, should we care of the opinions of the many?" He felt that one should do what one feels is right. But, as you know, he also claims that one must abide by the laws of Athens if one is to live there. So, what is one to do: follow your conscience or the laws, if you feel, as is the case with draft evasion, that killing and war are wrong. Socrates seemed to have influenced several of his young disciples to abstain from fighting in the war against Sparta, so it might be assumed that his sympathies would be with the draft dodgers. But one can almost imagine him saying, "One must still adhere to the state. One must be willing to stand up for what he feels is right, and go to jail if the state says one must. Either that or leave the state altogether." One, of course, will never know what he actually would have said.

Socrates did justify his case to Crito, and Crito could say nothing to argue it. The last line in the *Crito* seems to summarize Socrates feelings about his death: ". . . let me follow the intimations of the will of God"

5. In-Class Essay

Question: Everyone has different ideas about the word *American* and what it means. Write about something that you feel is typically American so that somebody who did not live in this country would know all about it. (One hour)

American youth is remarkably different from the rest of the world. Teenagers particularily represent the new American culture. Most people from other countries don't understand why the American teen is different. Whereas the generation above us has many parellels to people in other countries, teenagers do not. For starters, teen's are very freer in the U.S. Many teens have their own cars or have accessability to their parents'. The diversement and quantity of clothes is another difference. This is due to money. Our economy may not be in that great of shape, however most teens have money to go socialize. Teenagers spend millions at movies, fast food restaurants, on records and many other things. Over the past decades all this freedom has not proved to better the U.S. teens. In fact there has been a rapid increase of drugs and drinking. These two catagories may be one of the biggest differences between American teens and teens from other countries. Some people think this drug and alcohol abuse has led to the high crime rate. In any event, the teenage crime rate has rose sky high in recent years. Of course all this is not a total reflection of teens. American teenagers come from broken homes which is also another difference. Teens from other countries typically do not come from broken homes. This portrayal of an American teenager is one of the best examples that sets Americans different in comparison to most other countries. The future values and goals of American teens are apt to also be different, making America increasingly different from other countries.

6. Cheryl and I

Cheryl Tiegs came into my life about two years ago, when I saw her on a commercial for Cover Girl Cosmetics. Now, when I say, "came into my life," doesn't mean that she "stopped by" soliciting my opinion of her new Cover Girl image. I mean that I finally associated a famous face with an unfamiliar name. In several ways, she helped me to set goals for improving myself, or at least cleaning up the rough edges in the cut of my jib, a sailing term. Some of these goals, her weight for example, I don't feel would be healthy, torturous, in fact, for me to try to attain. It is the *notion* of keeping the figures on the scale in mind, as you're biting into your fourth piece of Super Deluxe pizza, that is important, though.

My awareness of Ms. Tiegs, we're not on a first name basis yet, intensified when I discovered that she was five-feet, ten-inches tall, a half inch shorter than myself. My mother, by the way, will declare to her dying breath that I'm five-feet, nine-inches tall, attributing the discrepency to either a short-sighted nurse, or my tendency to stand on tip-toe. Cheryl Tiegs has shown my generation how attractive and graceful a tall women can be. Each generation has a woman to remind the general public of this fact. Katherine Hepburn, for example, symbolized this svelteness in the 1930's and 1940's, as well as "Grinning Willow" of the 30's and 20's B.C. Ms. Tiegs has simply added a few inches to the old standard of five-feet eight-inches. She exudes that *type* of confidence in herself that could be helpful to *anyone* in many aspects of life. Nothing looks more awkward than a tall woman standing stoop-shouldered. This only serves to tell people implicitly how conscious she is of her height.

My interest in Ms. Tiegs became keen when I read in *Time* magazine that she only weighs (gulp!) one-hundred and *twenty* pounds. Since my weight is constantly fluxuating, I feel it would be difficult to accurately disclose it at this time. In other words, either her bones are hollow or I'm "with child" and "expecting" around Labor Day. I have always known of women, who were exceedly thin as adolescents. Yet, by the time they were in college, they had either discovered Saga food or were auditioning for the part of the lamppost in the class play. I knew that I could never be in Tiegs' weight bracket. Still it was a *rude* awakening to discover that a women of my age should be a lot thinner. Dieting over the summer taught me better eating habits, a fairly good program for shedding undesired poundage, how to stand on my home scale on one foot, that the doctor's scale was probably "rigged" by Twiggy and the *ex-*

hilarating joy when someone asks if you've lost weight. Yeeeees, Maaam!!

Cheryl Tiegs also discussed in the *Time* article, the period in her life when she "zoomed" up to 155 pounds. Oh, if she only knew what it was like to *really* zoom! Her confession was helpful because it showed that she had to *struggle* to get her weight down and keep it there. Besides making a model's life more realistic for me, it fortified my spirits during those desperate times when I would have voted Republican for just *one* Twinkie!

Cheryl Tiegs has done a lot to raise my consciousness of how I look and how satisfied I am with it. By having a famous model approximately the same height as myself it has made my life a little bit easier. I just tell people that we're really twin sisters; she changed her last name to make things easier for the folks at home. She has helped me set goals for myself. Though I know that I will never attain them and some of them I wouldn't want to, still most of the fun and satisfaction comes from just trying and sometimes stepping *closer* to them.

7. Application for a Legal Internship

Purpose in Applying

My future career goal is to become a lawyer, and this internship would give me experience in the field that will be beneficial in the future. An internship like this is a rare opportunity for an under-graduate, and it will give me the opportunity to observe one legal specialty. The training and exposure to the law are two things undergraduates rarely have the chance to experience, which is why I am very interested in this internship.

Academic Studies

Several of my philosophy and government courses are preparing me for law school, and they would also be useful for the internship. Family law and torts, two of my government courses, were taught like law school classes. For these courses it was necessary to read and brief cases, and be prepared to discuss them in class. For my philosophy courses, we had to understand the legal principles of the cases we read in order to discuss the ethics involved in the decision. Morality and the Law focused on the right to privacy and how much power lawmakers should have in regulating private acts, such as sex. Philosophy of Law focused on questions such as what law is, what good law is, and why we should obey the law.

Practical Experience

My work in the Family Law Unit of Legal Services covered many of the administrative areas of a law office, including filing, sending out letters, and being the receptionist. To help the lawyers I even "gophered" when I did not have anything more important to do. My duties as receptionist included personal contact with clients and other lawyers over the phone and in person.

I also work at the Wheaton Library. When people submit requisition cards for books, I search the cards for two things: first, I make sure the library does not already own the book or have it on order, then I verify the information on the card and determine if the book is in print. The accuracy demanded in this job is as important as the accuracy demanded of any type of research.

Qualities and Skills

My work and school experiences have helped me to develop my organizational and communication skills. I have had to write papers or give oral presentations in most of my classes. I also realize the importance of dependability, especially when there is a deadline to be met. If you promise to finish a job at a certain time, you better have it done.

Summary

This internship is the type of employment I have been looking for and unable to find. I have skills that are necessary to a legal intern, and my motivation and diligence in working are useful in any job.

(Note: Pretend that you are the lawyer to whom this essay is sent. How well are your needs addressed?)

Part 2
How to Tutor

Part 1 focused on the content of tutoring: on the writing process—on strategies for thinking, writing, revising—and on practice in evaluating writing. Part 2 focuses on tutoring itself. In particular, it addresses what your basic stance should be, how to start a conference, how to cope with the middle and end, how to cope with limited time and grading, how to cope with other problems, and how to evaluate your effectiveness as a tutor or teacher.

7   Coach or Dictator?

Suppose that Ronnie brought the following paragraph to a tutoring conference with Maria:

> The use of fuel was never a problem for our grandparents but now the problem of fuel has become our concern. One problem is to find a way to produce solar power at a prices people can pay. But in order to do that we must become less dependent on foreign sources for our fuel. This would give the fuel producers an incentive to produce more fuel. The increase in production would bring down prices. When we become less dependent on them the production of fuel in our own country will increase. The key to energy is the increase of production in the U.S. and then the prices may go down.

Maria reads the paragraph and reaches the same conclusion that we did in chapter 6, "Evaluating Writing": it's hard to discern the underlying logic of Ronnie's ideas. Then the session goes like this:

MARIA: Well, yes, it's kind of illogical, isn't it? You probably just dashed it off at the last minute, right? I mean, you don't mean that in order to produce affordable solar power we first have to become less dependent on foreign sources. That's kinda backwards. Because we have to produce more fuel first in order to become less dependent, right? That's—

RONNIE: Umm, yeah, but—

MARIA: That's kinda the cart before the horse. Because only after we become less dependent on foreign sources can we take the time to work on solar technology. Uhh, what were you going to say?

RONNIE: It's just—it's just that if we produce more ourselves then prices will go down.

MARIA: Oh. I guess. But the logic isn't clear. That's what you really need to work on—logic. You've gotta make sure each sentence follows from the preceding one, okay?

RONNIE (tentatively): Uhh, yeah.

MARIA: What you really need to do is make an outline and then it'll all be clear. And you gotta be sure to start with your topic sentence.

> So if you just do these things and clean up the logic it'll be fine, okay?

Or maybe the session goes like this:

> MARIA: What do you think are your strengths and weaknesses here?
> RONNIE: Well, I have trouble finding the right words. They don't always sound right, so I usually spend a lot of time trying to find the right one. And I didn't have the time to spend on this paragraph so it just—it's lousy.
> MARIA: I see. But it isn't lousy. And it's an interesting idea—here in the last sentence you're saying that if we increase production the prices will go down. That's the thesis of the paragraph?
> RONNIE: Yeah.
> MARIA: Let's see. (Reads) "One problem is to find a way to produce solar power at prices people can pay. But in order to do that we must become less dependent on foreign sources for our fuel." You're saying that in order to produce solar power we have to become less dependent?
> RONNIE: Yes. Well, sorta. Solar power at prices people can pay.
> MARIA: Oh. But why solar power?
> RONNIE: Well, any kind of power—that's just an example.
> MARIA: Ohhh. You mean that to produce *affordable* power we need to become less dependent. I see. But isn't there still a step missing?
> RONNIE: What do you mean?
> MARIA: I mean, maybe if we bought lots of cheap foreign fuel we could provide affordable power.
> RONNIE: Oh. But what I mean is if we produce more fuel, and one way is to harness solar energy, we wouldn't have to depend so much on foreign sources.
> MARIA: Ohhh. That's a good sentence, what you just said—that explains the connections I didn't catch at first. Here, can you write that down so we can remember it. . . .
> (Discussion of later sentences continues.)

Which version of the tutoring conference is better? On the basis of the information given here (we can only imagine facial expressions, gestures, intonations)—the second. Why? Because Maria takes less control and is more responsive to Ronnie. It's still not a perfect interaction. As in all tutoring conferences there are false starts, but Maria listens to Ronnie and eventually they make genuine progress.

Let's examine the two sessions a little more closely. Even a quick glance at the first transcript shows how much Maria dominates, how much she talks. She even interrupts Ronnie when he tries to say something. She does go back and ask him what he was going to say, but then she doesn't really listen to him—doesn't really hear his point—and she goes on to make her own point about logic. Look too at how she starts: she makes a negative pronouncement on the paragraph's illogicality. And then she states that Ronnie must not have spent much time on the paragraph. She probably said that to help him save face, but how's he going to feel if he did spend a lot of time? Notice too how her apparent questions—her "isn't it?" and "right?"—don't really require answers. She may have heard that it's a good idea to ask questions, but they should be real questions that require answers. Still, though, she does focus on concrete aspects of the paragraph—at least she does early in the conference. Later she talks more abstractly about logic, and it's not clear that Ronnie knows how to apply the abstraction to his writing. Then she trots out typical panaceas—using an outline and starting with a topic sentence—without clarifying their relevance to the paragraph, again assuming that Ronnie will know how to apply the ideas. And finally she seems to rush him out the door. She never gives him a chance to state his concerns.

The second version is not perfect either. Maria lets Ronnie get away with discussing only weaknesses, not strengths: she could be more convincing in finding strengths in the paragraph. And it would have been better to discuss energy generally, including the problems of trying to increase production, so that Ronnie could rethink the complexity of the issues and not leap so quickly to a somewhat simplistic conclusion. But Maria does listen. Reading a couple of sentences aloud, as she does, is a useful technique. And she asks questions that get Ronnie to fill in gaps in his logic himself—and then asks him to write down the connection.

Such a comparison of transcripts should suggest that at least as important as knowledge about writing are interpersonal skills. In both cases Maria understood the paragraph's problems. But only in the second did she help Ronnie to understand them.

It's important for a tutor or teacher to be friendly, relaxed, interested—and to listen. One tutor gained a deeper understanding of the tutor's role by herself being tutored on an intentionally weak paragraph.

> I found it extremely helpful to experience what it feels like to be the student requiring help. While I realize that our paragraphs were sup-

posed to be poor, I discovered how easily a student could become defensive about a piece of writing she has created and initially felt proud to turn in. I have come to realize the importance of an understanding and encouraging tutor. It is difficult enough to receive a poor grade on something someone has written, and a tutor should do something other than just criticize it further. . . . An impatient, condescending, and rude tutor could conceivably cause a student to feel so incompetent that she would lose self-confidence and perhaps even give up writing. Originally, I thought a thorough command of grammar and the other mechanics involved in writing were the most essential aspects of tutoring. However, now I feel that knowing how to deal with people seeking help is far more important. . . . A tutor's goal is essentially helping a student learn to help herself, not just to demonstrate whether a semicolon or colon is called for in a particular instance! (Sydney Herman)

Perhaps the hardest thing for a tutor or teacher to learn is that he is a guide or coach or counselor, not a dictator. The tutor or teacher thus needs to learn restraint. He should not make corrections but help the tutee to correct and improve herself.

8 Getting Started

You've been sitting around for hours, it seems, waiting for a student to show up. At last she appears in the doorway. This is it, you say to yourself, and you take a deep breath. You smile. You introduce yourself. And then, after a pause, you panic. She's silent, staring at the wall. What do you do now?

Assessing Feelings, Attitudes, Context

First, you need to get to know the student. Even with one-shot drop-in tutoring, it's important to spend some time this way. You could ask the student about herself, her attitude to writing, her previous experiences with writing, how she sets about writing, her course, her assignment, her strengths and weaknesses. One tutor describes her first meeting with a student.

> Last Friday's session lasted forty-five minutes and we spent about fifteen minutes just getting acquainted. My feeling about the session was extremely positive—I felt the rapport between us was very good and that the tutee really wants to work on improvement.
>
> The tutee was a bit uncertain about how the tutoring process was going to work. . . . We talked and laughed about how we were both new to the tutoring process, etc. And I asked her about her classes, how she was doing, etc.
>
> And then the tutee began talking about the papers she had written, the assignments she had weekly in English 101 and Basic Writing, and she expressed her concern about a critical analysis of a book she had to write for Religion—due November 10. She wasn't sure what I could help her with during the sessions. And we talked about how I was there for whatever she wanted help on, and to just talk about how she was feeling about her writing or her courses if she needed sometimes. (Terry Wood)

Such preliminary talk serves several functions. One is that the student will relax and feel comfortable and start trusting you. She'll also have a chance to express any anger or frustration or resent-ment—to get them out of the way. Only after expressing such feel-ings will she be able to concentrate on her writing. And if she's angry about an instructor's negative comments, for instance, you may be able to use her anger as a springboard for action: how can she improve so that the instructor will be less negative?

Observe as well what the student communicates indirectly. Does she give short, gruff answers? Does she avoid eye contact? Does she cross her arms and glare at you? Then it's especially important to draw her out and find out what's bothering her. Maybe she broke up with her boyfriend. Maybe she's furious with an instructor. May-be she's in despair, convinced that she can't write, that she never could and never will. (Then you might discuss your own problems with writing and whether it's possible to improve.) Or maybe the student is embarrassed about needing to see a tutor, as one tutor admits she was when, during her freshman year,

> I had received a poor grade on my paper and was advised by my professor to see a tutor. Believe me, I did not want to go. . . . I felt extremely embarrassed. I felt like an absolute moron. How could any-one be as stupid and poor a writer as me? The moment I walked in the door I was so nervous I thought I was going to die. My legs and arms started to shake. I couldn't stop them. I got so hot and nervous that my glasses steamed up. (By the time the session was over I thought I had best go back to my room and change my wet clothes.) When the tutor read my paper I felt sure she was going to think I was the most stupid person in the world. I thought she would laugh at me. (Ann Kohler)

In such a case you might admit how much you yourself benefit from being tutored, how much tutoring can help anyone. In general, you should be sympathetic and understanding—but avoid agreeing that it's impossible to learn how to write, that an instructor is stupid, or that the student is.

You'll benefit from preliminary talk too: for one thing, it may help you to relax. And if you're relaxed and caring—if you make eye contact, smile, nod in agreement—the student will feel even more comfortable and also motivated. She's also likely to feel comfortable if you make a point of sitting beside her rather than the other side of a table, if you quickly shove aside other work, if you uncross your arms and legs, if you avoid toying with your pencil or drumming on the table, if you lean forward in interest, if you speak clearly and straightforwardly.

In addition, preliminary talk gives you a chance to explain a little about what you can and cannot do, what the student should and should not expect. Does she expect a quick fix or a lecture? Now's your chance to explain that you'll provide some guidance but she has to help herself.

Preliminary talk will likewise give you an idea of what the student's problems are and how to solve them. Maybe if she tells you how she writes you'll know why she has difficulties. If she says she must write a perfect introduction before writing the rest of her paper, you'll know why she has such a writing block—and if she learns that she needn't write the introduction first, many of her other problems may disappear. If she says she simply throws in a period whenever she feels she's running out of breath, you'll know why she has so many fragments and short sentences. One tutor had trouble understanding a Korean student's word choices until

> Finally, I did what I should have done first; I asked her some questions about her writing problems, courses, how she viewed the work, the difficulty of language (ours—spoken or written), and whatever else she could add. Then, all sorts of things started to come out that I had not known and which helped me a lot. The most important thing of all is to follow her way of thinking. A tutor should pay great attention to process rather than a finished product. . . .
>
> She turned out to have her good vocabulary because she translated her Korean words through a dictionary and then found what she hoped was a pretty accurate equivalent. So, most of her good vocabulary came down to a matter of luck. This explained why she couldn't tell me the reasoning behind a particular choice of words or the meaning she intended. (Karen Kielar)

Maybe too, if you're tutoring a student who's writing for someone else, you're familiar with the instructor and her expectations— or with expectations common in that discipline. It's helpful to know what different instructors value: originality? correctness? organization? logic? You may realize that creative writing teachers are likely to value originality, that philosophy teachers are likely to value logic. You can also examine the instructor's assignment or comments on a paper—and even, with the student's permission, talk to the instructor. Then, if you know the teacher's priorities, you'll know where to start with the student, so that you and the teacher will be working together, not at cross-purposes.

Another kind of problem is that in some courses a student may learn a radically new approach to writing. As she tries to use the approach her writing may first get much worse than it was before. And she may become depressed. But if she realizes that she's going through a phase that many students go through, she may gain the courage to keep trying. One tutor describes her own experience in such a course.

> I know that when I was taking it I hit a real bad point where I just couldn't write. I was aware of the . . . concepts and wanted to use them but couldn't make it work. I think that is where you make the transition from your old writing to your new. I can still remember the paper. (Gayle Tangney)

Learning that others have had similar experiences, have gotten worse before getting better, can help a student survive a low point. The process is a little like getting instruction in tennis or golf or violin after you've been playing awhile. At first you play worse, because you're unaccustomed to the new technique. But once you learn the new technique you should play better than ever.

Preliminary talk may not only help you assess a student's feelings, attitudes, and problems; it may also help you to avoid embarrassment.

> Before a tutor begins a session, she should question the student about the type of work she is reviewing. For example, one tutor found out in the middle of a session that she was helping a student with a take-home essay exam. (Melinda Wadman)

It's not clear whether a student is entitled to tutoring on a take-home exam. Certainly not on an in-class exam. But some instructors treat a take-home like an exam while others treat it like a paper: you should check with the instructor to find out whether tutoring is permissible.

Be alert too for problems that may require specialized assistance that you're not trained to give. Perhaps the student has a sight or hearing problem—and needs glasses or a hearing aid. Perhaps she has trouble understanding what she reads—and could work with a reading tutor (if available) as well as a writing tutor. Perhaps she has a learning disability, such as dyslexia (does she transpose letters and words?), and getting it professionally diagnosed might alleviate some of her frustration and enable her to seek specialized help. Perhaps she is severely depressed and needs to talk with a professional therapist.

Preliminary talk can thus generate trust, defuse anger, relieve embarrassment, clarify goals, provide insight into a student's problems. Sometimes, though, a student wants to bypass mere chatting and get down to business. You shouldn't force her to talk about herself; you should respect her privacy. But it may be that if you explain some of the benefits of preliminary talk—explain that it's not mere chatting, for it can help you to understand her writing process—she'll agree.

Gaining Time to Read the Paper

Once you've gauged the student's feelings and context, you may be able to settle down to work on his writing. If, furthermore, you have a file of his work, and you looked through it before the session, you have some idea of what to work on. But if the student has brought a paper with him you'll want to spend some time reading it and thinking about it. It's important to give yourself time here, but sometimes difficult, since the student is waiting with bated breath for you to divulge the sacred mysteries of writing. And maybe the paper is due within the hour. So what do you do?

Maybe you or the student could read the paper aloud. Or, if you would like to spend time reading the paper by yourself, maybe you can ask him what his problems are and give him a relevant diagnostic test or section of a book to read or exercise to complete, while you read his paper. Maybe you can ask him to write down what he thinks he has done well and what he feels he should work on. Maybe you can ask him to come back in half an hour. Maybe you can encourage him, next time, to see you several days or a week before the paper is due and to give you the paper the day before you work with him. Here is what one tutor did:

> Carol . . . had received back a paper from a professor with a comment about going to see a writing tutor. She was not pleased with the grade on the paper and wanted me to read it and see if I felt that maybe she could use the help of a writing tutor. Well, I wasn't going to spend much time helping her, but finally decided that I would, and am glad now that I did. I think that the one and a half hours that I spent with Carol were just about the most rewarding time I've spent with a tutee

yet. Before working with her, or speaking to her about the paper, I read it through, and on another piece of paper wrote down specific and general comments about the good and bad points I thought the paper contained. Then I went over these comments with Carol and we discussed the six-page paper in great detail. We came to a conclusion that what her paper needed most was a new organizing idea and a better way of developing this idea. We found that she had the perfect means of starting her paper over again (if she had to) in her concluding paragraph. This paragraph contained all of the "meat" of the paper and was almost a perfect introductory paragraph in itself. What made the time spent with Carol so rewarding for me is that I felt I gave her some workable ideas, and she understood these ideas and saw how she could use them. I felt that we had really communicated. When I think back on this, what really helped me (to help her) was the time spent reading and reflecting on the completed paper before I sat down with the tutee directly. (Cathy Coffin)

Notice how Cathy did this preliminary reading. She didn't mark the paper up; she didn't "correct" it. Instead, she made notes, so that she could discuss the most important points with the student.

Starting with Strengths

When you turn to discussing a student's writing, it's a good idea to start with her strengths. The same holds when discussing exercises as well. For one thing, she may be demoralized and need the encouragement: writing requires self-confidence. For another thing, she may not know what her strengths are. As Mary Alice Taylor notes,

> It's just as scary not to understand what you're doing right as not to understand what you're doing wrong.

Mary Alice had been receiving high grades on papers that struck her as pedestrian, and it took her awhile to realize that a "pedestrian" paper that fully develops a thesis may be preferable to a stylistically exuberant paper that is full of sound and fury but proves nothing.

So it's a good idea to start by praising a student for what she's done well and to continue to interject praise while you're tutoring. Praise her for her one correct use of the apostrophe, for her one successful transition, for having a clear focus, for having interesting ideas. But beware of overpraising.

A tutor should be careful when praising a paper because the tutee can inflate what the tutor says. For example, if a tutor says the paper is satisfactory, the tutee may be expecting an A or a B. If the tutee then receives a C, she may become disappointed in the tutor and discouraged in seeking further help. (Melinda Wadman)

Still, praise is important in motivating a student—just be sure it's realistic praise. Not "This is a super paper. I'd be surprised if your professor didn't think so too." But "I like the conclusion—I like the way it brings everything together. I can now understand how all the parts of your argument fit together. But I wonder if you could make some of these connections earlier, to make it easier for the reader to follow. . . ."

Sometimes you may feel that you can't find anything to praise in a paper. You probably can if you try. But if you're really hard pressed, at least show an interest in the student's topic, or agree that it's difficult to sort out ideas when discussing such a complex issue. You can also admit how badly you did on your first college paper or how hard you too find it to come up with enough details to develop your points.

In addition to praising the student's strengths, you can ask her to tell you what she considers her strengths and weaknesses. Make sure she discusses strengths, though, and doesn't just get caught up in the litany of her weaknesses.

Acknowledging the Student's Agenda

When a student does tell you her weaknesses, she's telling you what she wants to work on. It's important to know her agenda, for if yours differs you may have trouble getting anywhere, as one tutor discovered when she was being tutored.

I do not think I have had a more valuable experience than the one in which I played Tom Tutee. I really wanted Paula to take over and guide me through the paper. Instead, she questioned me slowly to try to clarify my organizing idea and was more interested in the structural format of the paper.

There was a real conflict in our tutoring session and I now understand how frustrating it is to be a tutee. A tutee comes in with an idea of what she would like done and tries to direct the tutor. . . . The tutor knows what she wants to do and the conflict arises. I feel it might be a good idea to ask the tutee what she would like to do with her paper and also tell her what I (as tutor) would like to do. (Ann Schipani)

Try to put yourself in the student's position and understand her point of view. Explain your own position. But remember that she'll be more motivated to work on what she herself thinks is important, so be willing to compromise.

Setting Goals

Then you and the student can set some realistic goals. You and he might decide to work on run-ons: first you'll go over some handbook rules and exercises; then he'll try some computer lessons or a self-instructional text; then next week he'll bring in a paper he's been working on and you'll go over it together. Or your goal might be to rework a paper to make the introduction preview what will follow, so that a reader will find it easy to follow the paper. In fact, the reason for providing such a preview in a paper is similar to the reason for setting goals when tutoring: so that the audience can see where everything's going. A preview of tutoring goals also provides a manageable focus—so that the student doesn't feel overwhelmed by the need to fix *everything*.

To summarize, when first working with a student, or when beginning a session with a returning student, you might keep the following principles in mind:

- Find out where the student is coming from: his course, his assignment, his mental state, his feelings.
- If he has brought a sample of writing, give yourself time to read it.
- If you're working on a piece of writing or an exercise, try to start by praising him for something done well.
- Get him involved by asking him to tell you his own strengths and weaknesses and by finding out what he wants to work on.
- Set realistic goals, and make them explicit.

9 Down to Business

What do you do once you've become acquainted with a student, discovered the purpose of her paper, and agreed what her strengths and weaknesses are? Here's a transcript of a successful tutoring session (ellipses here indicate pauses):

> The first problem that I had to handle was to make Karen feel relaxed because she was really upset and nervous about the paper and everything else that she had to do by Friday. Just the fact that the session was being held in my dorm room was a big help in making her feel comfortable.
>
> The session went something like this:
>
> KAREN: My teacher handed me back my first paper and said that it was unacceptable and that I had to rewrite it. She also suggested that I go and see a writing tutor (nervous giggle) so that's why I'm here.
> ROBIN: Okay. First let me ask you who your teacher is, and what the assignment is.
> KAREN: Oh—Mrs. Clark. And we were supposed to write a comparison between these two books [stories]—two books that we read. I already started to rewrite the paper and I tried to stay with the point more because she told me that I kept getting off the track.
> ROBIN: Okay—well, why don't I read the first paper and then the rewrite. Then we'll see what we can do.
>
> . . .
>
> All right—you've covered a lot of good points in the first paper but you do tend to get off the track, but I think we'll be able to fix that. Now—I don't want to discourage you but in the rewrite—you cut out one of the characters—you only talked about one of the books— why did you do that?
> KAREN: Well—I wanted to make sure that I stuck to one point. . . .
> ROBIN: Okay—but by doing that—are you really doing what the assignment called for?
> KAREN: Well—no, I guess not.

ROBIN: All right. Let's take a look at the original paper and the rewrite, 'cause you have a lot of good points, but I think that the most important thing right now is to get that other character back in there. What do you think?

KAREN: Yeah—but I don't know how to do that.

ROBIN: Okay—I want you to try something. Take a pencil and paper and right now—write down all of the similarities and differences that you can think of between these two characters—make two columns.

. . .

KAREN: Okay. I did that.

ROBIN: All right—let's take a look. From this list you can figure out what you want to write about. Can you see that?

KAREN: Oh yeah! You're right—that makes sense . . . but I have a lot of these things in the first paper.

ROBIN: That's right, you do, but—you can't find them. Look at this paragraph—the idea's in here but you have to really look for it. Do you see how, maybe, you're telling too much of the story here? And not enough of your own ideas, your interpretation?

KAREN: Okay—I see what you mean—but I have to tell what's going on in the story!

ROBIN: To a certain extent—I agree—but you don't have to totally relay the whole story—because your teacher, your reader, has also read the story and knows what's going on. So all you really have to do is say enough to let her know what you're talking about and you don't have to give that many details.

KAREN: Okay—all right—I get it.

ROBIN: Okay—do you know what you have to do next?

KAREN: No. Well, yeah—I can start writing the paper but . . . I don't know how to organize it.

ROBIN: All right—this is where you use your list that I just had you make up. Sort through your list and figure out where you want to start.

KAREN: Okay. (She goes through and writes down all her ideas in the order that she wants to cover them.) Okay—how's this?

ROBIN: All right—you have all your ideas down—that's good. Now, what is the purpose of an opening paragraph?

KAREN: To tell what you are going to talk about in the rest of the paper.

ROBIN: Exactly. So what you have to do is indicate the organizing ideas for each paragraph—in some sort of order, of course—that way the reader will know just by reading the first paragraph what your paper is about.

KAREN: All right. Let me do that then. . . . I'm not good at transition, though, so can you help me with that?

ROBIN: Sure—why don't we go through the first paragraph together.

First, why don't you go through your list of ideas and number them so you know what you want your order to be and that will be the order in which the paragraphs will come.

We went through that first paragraph and worked on organizing her ideas and also on working out transitions between the ideas. She was happy with her paragraph when we were done and she left with confidence that she could write the rest of her paper. I told her that I would read the rest of her paper when she finished, if she would come back, and she said that she would.

Karen came back the next day with her completed paper for me to read over, and it had improved 100 percent. There were only a few problems, that I could see, in transition between paragraphs.

I did a lot more of the talking in this tutoring session than I normally would have done but in my opinion this tutee needed me to show her how to organize her paper and to specifically point things out to her. (Robin McAlear)

Such a transcript omits gestures, intonation, facial expressions—all important in tutoring. So we have only an approximation of the session. But it was certainly an effective one. Robin broke the work down into concrete, manageable steps. Instead of just saying that the first paper had a lot of garbage that had nothing to do with its thesis, and expecting Karen to figure out how to apply such general advice, Robin discussed a specific paragraph. She also explained why Karen should, say, forecast her paper in the introduction—so that "the reader will know just by reading the first paragraph what your paper is about"—instead of simply telling Karen what to do. And Robin asked Karen to demonstrate her understanding of each step (and not just say she understood). My one quibble would be to be careful about advice not "to give that many details." Details are important. But they are important not in themselves nor as part of a plot summary: they are important as support for the writer's ideas. And Robin certainly communicated this notion to Karen, for the paper improved dramatically: the details were now supporting her arguments, not just retelling the plot.

Serving as a Sounding Board

Often a student doesn't need as much directed guidance as Karen did. She may simply need to talk through her ideas with a sympathetic audience; she needs a good listener. Does she not know where to begin on a particular assignment? What is the assignment? Has she read the work on which she is supposed to report?

> I found that, in telling me enough about the book for me to get a fairly good idea of how it should be judged according to the prescribed criteria, she got a better idea of how to rate it herself. For instance, one thing she was supposed to discuss was character development. I got her to tell me about the various characters, talked a little about flat and round characters in general myself, and asked her if she thought the main characters stayed the same, or if the readers saw different sides of them. A lot of the time I found if I merely recapped what she was telling me, she'd discover she'd known what she was trying to say all along. (Caroline Brown)

Or is the student supposed to write an analysis of experiences that she hasn't sorted through yet?

> Tonight I had a sophomore come to me because she was having some problems generating ideas for her government paper. The assignment was very open and the only requirement was that she write about what she learned from her experience working on Margaret Heckler's campaign. The primary problem . . . was that all she did for the campaign was telephone. She felt that it would be difficult to write five to seven pages on telephoning.
>
> We then began talking about Heckler's campaign itself, and the student began to realize that she could probably include some of her impressions of the campaign in the paper. She also mentioned that other people who worked in her office with her didn't seem to do anything. And, since the paper was to be an analysis, she decided that writing about her impressions of the people in the office would also be a good point to mention.
>
> Her ideas continued to flow as we continued talking. Although I added a few of my own thoughts, I soon realized that just my presence as a sounding board for her "thinking out loud" was really all she needed. . . .
>
> Before she left, I suggested that since she wasn't planning on starting the paper for a day or two, it would be helpful for her to write down the ideas we talked about. That way, she wouldn't forget them and also wouldn't be starting from the often excruciatingly frustrating point of a blank mind. (M. F. Withum)

Or perhaps the eleven-year-old brother of a friend refuses to talk about poor grades on his book reports?

> I was visiting Steve's house when I noticed that his normally energetic mischievous brother was unusually sedate. I mentioned it to

Steve, who said that Ken had been cut from intramurals at school because of two poor grades on book reports. He was also grounded at home. He wouldn't talk to anyone about it and he hated school now.

We both wanted to do something, but what? Ken is an avid reader. He is the type to ask for books for his birthday and Christmas. The problem obviously lay in the presentation of what he had read. It was difficult to approach him at this point about his problem but something had to be done. . . . Luckily one of the reports was done on *Tom Sawyer,* a book which I had at home.

I returned that evening with the book to "study." Ken was still dejected as I sat down and pulled out the book to read. I read for about an hour and then closed the book and sighed hopelessly. Steve then asked what was the matter and I said that I was supposed to have the book read by Monday so I could summarize it for my class, but I had an exam and I would never have time to read the whole thing. Steve looked at the book and said there was no problem. Ken had read the book and he could tell me about it. Ken was reluctant at first but he eventually consented. He gave a great oral summary to me. He loves telling stories to people and I made sure I was extra attentive and asked questions to get him to go into even further detail. When he had finished I thanked him and told him it was great. Then I said I wished I had some kind of written summary to refer back to. Ken was silent until Steve gave him the "if you don't say something about having a paper I will" kind of stare. Finally he said that he had a paper but it wasn't good and he had to rewrite it so I couldn't use it. I told him I would help him with his paper if I could borrow it. He consented.

As we read his paper, Ken admitted that he knew it wasn't very good. He knew what he wanted to say but he couldn't write it the way he had said it to me. I suggested that he "talk" his paper to someone first. Then make an outline of what happened when in the book to help him stay on the right track. A good way to do this is to list all the chapter titles. Next to this he could elaborate on the important points that he wanted to write about. . . .

He rewrote his paper that afternoon. . . . (Jen Ciaburri)

Your job is to listen, to encourage the student to talk. Sometimes all she needs is someone to listen and encourage.

I had a very interesting tutoring session last night. The girl next door came in with a paper she was writing for an English class. It was a poetry analysis, and the assignment's length was 500 words. I think it was this fact that scared her and caused her to have a mental block. She kept thinking that there was no way she could write that much on such a short poem. When she came in my room she had already written the introductory paragraph and was organizing her main points for the body. The thing that was so interesting about the session was that I didn't have to offer her any help. She didn't need it. All she did was talk about how she was nervous about getting it done. She read me what she had written and I thought it was very good, and I told her so. She then breathed a sigh of relief and said, "Oh, you've helped me so much!" Honestly, all I did was listen to her and give her a few words of encouragement!

Thinking about the session afterwards, I realized that what Marie needed help on was not her paper but her confidence in writing. (Diane Ciarletta)

Being Silent

A surprisingly effective technique—a way of making oneself be a sounding board—is silence. You might, for instance, try counting slowly and silently to ten before answering your own question. For if you don't speak, chances are that the student will fill up the silence. Then he can do some thinking out loud and work his own way to an answer. Even if he doesn't speak, he has time to think.

> I think an important part of a tutoring session is the tutee coming up with her own answer to questions and errors in her writing. The tutor *has* to learn to let the tutee figure things out for herself—everyone learns better that way. The statistic saying that the average teacher in a classroom waits two seconds for a student to answer is an important thing for a tutor to remember and avoid doing. If the tutor blurts out the answers without letting the tutee respond she is doing the tutee a disservice. This is bound to discourage the tutee because people feel better when they come up with solutions to their own questions and problems. There is nothing more frustrating than speaking with someone who finishes one's sentences. It is even worse when the tutor blurts out the answer before the tutee has a chance to think about the question. . . . Even if a question remains unanswered in a session—it is something for the tutee to ponder for awhile, and she might even find a better answer than the tutor could give. This would give a tutee further confidence in herself and her writing ability. (Barbara Shea)

Mirroring

Another technique for encouraging the student to speak is to mirror what she says, to summarize what you hear her saying: "You don't agree with this critic?" "In other words, the economic problems were the most important ones?" "You mean you think Mao was effective?" Such mirroring not only reassures the student that she has a sympathetic listener and draws her out, but it reassures you that you understand the student's problems and ideas.

Confirming

You can also encourage the student to speak by confirming any problems he senses.

> Last night I had a short tutoring session with . . . Kim. She was working on her English paper and started off just asking me if one of her sentences was a run-on. It was and I told her so and asked her if she knew how to correct it. She told me that there should be a semi-colon in place of her comma and I explained that if she had kept the comma there it would have been a comma splice. She went on to point out another sentence that she thought was a run-on. This sentence used a conjunctive adverb, and again she had left out the semicolon, but after identifying that it was a run-on, she knew how to correct it. This went on for a while, but with each of the problems she pointed out to me, she knew how to correct it. I continued to read through her paper, and basically there were some sentences that sounded awkward because of a left-out word or phrase or faulty punctuation. If she didn't catch these sentences herself, I would ask her if a specific sentence sounded awkward to her and she usually had no problem correcting it.
>
> I think this tutee basically knew where she had problems in her paper but just wanted me to confirm that there were problems. After she pointed out these problems, she usually knew how to correct them. I don't know if she was careless in writing her first draft or what. I suppose she was just confused about certain points in her writing and wanted my approval after she had corrected them. (Anne Rice)

Recording

Occasionally you can even help the student by recording what she says.

> I remember helping a friend who had mono. She had to write a story and all she wanted to do was sleep. I got a piece of paper and got her to come to a lounge with me (to get her away from her room—and her bed). We worked it out together. She thought it out, and I wrote it down in outline form so it would be organized. In no way did I do work for her. She told me what came next. For my own personal touch, I illustrated the outline as she thought. I tried to keep her enthusi-

astic. . . . Now I'm not suggesting that everyone do this but it's an idea. . . . Sometimes a mediator between a struggling writer and paper is great! (Beth Brown)

Recording can thus free a student's creativity. But it does have some drawbacks. For one thing, a student may feel less ownership in what she's written—she may feel that it's your paper, since the notes are in your handwriting. You'd also need to take special care not to fill in gaps or to make decisions for the student: you might be tempted, for instance, to decide on the structure of an outline for her, whether something is a subtopic or new topic. And you'd also need to be careful of taking outright dictation, of recording a draft as the student composes aloud, since you'd probably supply too much editing help with punctuation and spelling.

Asking Questions

If a student is reluctant to talk—if he needs prodding in thinking and writing and revising—you can ask questions. Asking questions can encourage him to think and also to be less defensive, as Mary Alice Taylor noticed in a writing class.

> Yesterday's Poetry Writing class ended up being a great lesson to help in tutoring. It was very interesting to see the various methods used to criticize constructively. I find the question to be the best method. If you ask someone why she used a particular phrase, word, etc.—by making her answer she may see the problem herself. If not, you can continue asking questions, each time maybe getting a little more specific. I noticed people's reactions to the methods others used to criticize their poem. One girl said, "I don't like the second stanza at all. You should eliminate it. . . ." The poet immediately jumped on the defensive and closed her mind to the rest of the suggestions. This is why I think it is so important . . . to use the utmost care in phrasing suggestions because a tutee will close her mind to all said after something is phrased wrong.

Open-ended questions are generally better than leading ones, and definitely better than ones requiring only yes or no answers. "What do you want to work on first?" Not "You should work on sequencing first, shouldn't you?" Or "How can you revise this sentence to make it easier to read? . . . Can you condense it, maybe eliminate some words?" Not "Shouldn't you eliminate these words here?" If a student has trouble with open-ended questions, you can become more specific. But it's best to start with broader questions, if only to gauge the student's thinking and his approach to writing.

Finding ways of asking probing questions that will challenge a student to think can, however, take practice and ingenuity. Terry Wood shows such ingenuity after looking through a student's notes for an analysis of the poem "Auto Wreck."

> These ideas were, I thought, not the major ones expressed by the poem, and so I asked her what she thought the whole poem was getting at. She said she didn't know. I asked her what she thought the poet was getting at at the end when he talked about the way the spectators at the scene of this automobile accident felt. She said she didn't really know.
>
> At this point, I was feeling somewhat frustrated. I had particular ideas about what the poem was saying but I knew I could not communicate them to her. And I was at a loss as to how to start the tutee putting together her own ideas about the poem's meaning.
>
> I thought to move the poem out of its particular setting and to ask the tutee to apply it to herself—how she would feel if she were witnessing an accident. We talked awhile about this and then tried to apply the poet's lines to the tutee's thoughts. This worked somewhat better—the tutee could see that some of her ideas about the questioning of why people die so suddenly, and how we never think it will happen to us, may also be some of the same things the poet was trying to say.
>
> This discussion fit in with some of the tutee's earlier ideas about certain symbols in the poem; and inversions, such as the idea that the spectators felt pain and constraint similar to the injured party, might now be worked in with the idea of the spectators' reaction to death.

Terry's questioning was pretty open-ended, offering a new perspective that led the student to discover new meaning. Sometimes, though, your questions may be more directed or Socratic—you may have a fairly good idea of possible answers and you ask relatively specific questions. If, for example, "How can you make the paper less choppy?" and "How can you improve transitions?" don't work—if a student knows that he has a problem with transitions but doesn't know how to improve them—you may need to become more directive.

> We looked at two paragraphs in particular, and I asked her what exactly was the connection between the two. She was able to *tell* me

rather clearly so I asked her to look at the two paragraphs and come up with one sentence to say what she had just told me—to use as a transition sentence between those two paragraphs. She was able to do so easily. (Robin McAlear)

Modeling

One kind of modeling is to share how you would approach a student's difficulties if you were the student. Paradoxically, one way of being sensitive to a student's needs is to use the pronoun "I" instead of "you": to say "I would" instead of "You should." Rather than insist that the student do as you do, you can simply share an approach that has worked for you, thus serving as a role model.

Or you can model the reactions of a reader by responding as an interested reader—or better yet, a naive reader—not by pronouncing absolute judgments but by sharing your responses and perceptions. Consider the difference in impact between these two statements: "This sentence is wrong" and "I have trouble following you here." Which statement is less offensive? Which statement is likely to encourage the student to drop her defenses and learn from the discussion that follows?

The student is in fact likely to bristle with disagreement if you insist, "You simply have to use better transitions." More tactful guidance can take the form of "I found it a little hard to follow the paper as I read it. Now I can step back and see where the argument's going, but then I couldn't. When I'm working on a paper I always have to go back and figure out transitions. That's what I think you could work on. I'd try to get other paragraphs to follow as smoothly as this one does here. . . ."

Another approach to modeling is to share one's own writing with the student. I once worked with a student who was deeply upset by a professor's criticism of a paper. After she had vented some of her feelings, I showed her one of my manuscripts, which this same professor had similarly covered with red marks. She wasn't the only one to "suffer," I suggested, and, further, I noted how helpful he was being when he covered a page with red, sharing his keen insights into language.

Terry Wood has also shared her own writing with a student:

After I finished reading, I suggested my idea of moving her intention, her main point, to the proposal beginning. And she agreed somewhat, so we tried some rearranging. But I could tell she wasn't quite sure if this was the best idea or if she understood what I meant. I went to my room (the session was held in my dorm) and got my [successful] Scholar proposal so she could read it, and then she understood what I had been talking about, and decided that it might be the best thing to do in her case as well.

Sharing your writing can also demystify the process of writing.

We were struggling with how to organize a compare/contrast paper and she said something about "Oh, this is so easy for you—do you just come up with a thesis right away?" I laughed and told her that the only reason it seemed to her that writing was easier for me was because I had had more practice than she. I then did something which we mentioned in class—showed her two rough drafts I had done for two different classes. Both were scrawled, scratched, red-inked, and arrowed—showing her that even for a writer with experience the first draft is tough. I also told her that I don't hesitate to change the thesis to match a paper in which the original emphasis has shifted. She seemed much more comfortable after that. (Deborah Williams)

You can even physically model the process of writing, as Muriel Harris suggests in "Modeling: A Process Method of Teaching" (1983). You can, right in front of the student, draft a paragraph and talk about what you're thinking as you write. Perhaps as you are capturing your ideas you can't immediately think of the right word in a sentence, so you leave a blank, to be filled in later. Thus you dramatically demonstrate to the student that she doesn't need to write a word-perfect first draft. Like you, she can revise later.

Reading Aloud

Another technique is to read a paper aloud. The student could read it to you, or you could read it to him.

One of the best techniques I've found in tutoring is having the tutee read out loud. This has many benefits. It often helps if the tutee's problem is run-on sentences or punctuation. I also had one student with problems in paragraph organization read a problem paragraph out loud. After she did so, she had less trouble in reworking the paragraph to make more sense. I think having a student read out loud is also beneficial because it's a way of giving the tutee a more active part in the tutoring session. Some tutees have problems discussing a paper, and I've found that this is a good way to get them started. If you ask someone to read out loud, they can't just shrug and say, "I don't know." (Tina Cunningham)

Reading aloud not only encourages the student to be more active but gives him a new perspective on what he has written—he hears as well as sees the paper.

Agreeing on an Assignment

You can similarly efface yourself—prevent yourself from dominating the conference too much—by giving the student a chance to work alone. You and he can agree on a task, such as listing ideas or rewriting a paragraph or working through an exercise, and then he can go off to complete it. Such a strategy can give him confidence and independence. It can relieve a self-conscious student of the anxiety of performing—of talking and answering questions—extemporaneously, and he can spend as long as he needs to, without worrying about taking up your time. It can also free you to read the student's paper or to work with another student if you're barraged with tutees.

Deferring to the Student

And throughout a tutoring session—not just at the beginning, when you acknowledge the student's agenda—you should defer to the student. Try to imagine her point of view. And remember that tutoring is a partnership. Remember that the writing is ultimately hers. Remember that she'll learn more if, instead of slavishly following your directions, she uses your advice to reach her own conclusions. And often you are more effective if you remind the student that she will make the final choices.

I made a point to caution her that it was her proposal and that she should only accept the advice which seemed most appropriate. I found that, in saying this, we were better able to work together, both tossing out ideas. Also, . . . the tutee made any marks or corrections on the paper herself with her own pen. I don't feel it's my prerogative to change and rearrange sentences and paragraphs; my interest is to stimulate conversation and offer advice. (Terry Wood)

In another session, the first of a series, Terry again defers to the student, asking what the student wants to work on.

She decided she'd like to go over one of the papers she had already passed in for English 101 and which she had to revise. The tutee chose the paper and, in fact, made the decision to work on a paper this first session. The tutee really ran the session and decided what she wanted to cover . . . , which I found quite positive. I think we saw ourselves as equals during the session, and at no time did I feel I was doing more than making suggestions to a fellow student.

This paper was an examination of what the tutee believed a character in a story—Katherine Mansfield's "Garden Party"—would do in her future life, in her life outside and beyond the context of the story, based on what the tutee inferred about the character's personality from reading the story.

The paper had good ideas but had little focus or organization and looked more like a piece of freewriting. After reading the paper, I talked with the tutee about her ideas and how she arrived at them. This led the tutee to discuss how she writes and I asked her if she liked to write. She said, "No," and she explained that she usually sits down the night before the paper is due and forces herself to write and . . . to get every word on paper correctly the first time—she has never thought to freewrite before or to write a workable first draft. I explained both techniques to her.

And I worked with her at applying the freewriting, note-taking idea in revising this paper. We had a long discussion of why she thought the heroine of "The Garden Party" would be different in her future life, and how she would be different specifically. I thought that some of the paper ideas were ambiguous and not clearly supported.

And as she spoke about her ideas she jotted them down, and then we talked about specific examples in the story which supported her theory. She wrote down these also. Then we talked about setting up paragraphs. We discussed how my tutee's main idea should be stated. And then we broke down the particular instances which supported this main idea into paragraphs. The tutee separated these ideas so she would later know how to arrange them when she sat down to write the revision.

Consciously deferring to the student can also help you to restrain yourself from taking over.

I have to really rein in on myself and ask the tutee to explain herself—telling her that I do not understand the subject at all. For instance, a tutee came to me with a paper she had to write for an economics class. I've never taken an economics class. I told her this and then asked her to start with the basic premise of the economic principle she was to explain and asked her questions when I felt confused or tried to sum up what she said in fewer words. We then made an outline of what she had told me. I think it helped—both the "freetalking" and the fact that I admitted I knew nothing about the subject—thus destroying the myth of the omniscient tutor. (Deborah Williams)

Sometimes you may even have a student who seems to take complete charge of a session.

I had an unexpected tutee burst into Meneely last Monday, clutching a paper and talking about: "I hate to write these history papers—I'm never taking history again, but I'm almost finished and Mr. Calitri has looked it over—can you help me?"

I could tell she was a seasoned tutee when she filled out the information in the tutoring log book. I asked, "Have you been tutored before?" "Oh yes, it was a big help," she answered.

Control of the situation was in her hands—I felt like a backseat driver, clutching the seat while she just bombed through her paper.

The paper was amazing—it had been reworked to the point that I couldn't read it. But she could, so she read, I listened. She commented on her problems (I *like* long complex sentences . . .) and kept asking continually for my reassurance that she could finish the paper in two hours. I would just smile, and she would continue.

I did point out a place where she might rearrange her sentences to lead into one another and how to regroup paragraphs. She would ask me for word choice selections, but reject them in favor of her own. That was fine.

Finally, she stopped and said, "Well, your hour is up. You've been a tremendous help. Thanks so much!"

"Thank you," I said, "and good luck."

She left and I just sat there, amazed at the whole experience—so this is tutoring! (Dianne Holcomb)

It may feel odd when a student takes that much control, but such a conference is nonetheless effective.

Using Appropriate Body Language

You can reinforce other techniques by using appropriate body language. Chances are, if you are genuinely interested in the student and in helping him to help himself, your gestures and expressions will be appropriate. You'll smile. You'll make eye contact. You'll quickly put aside any other work. You'll uncross your arms. You'll lean forward in interest. You'll sit beside the student to look at his paper with him. You'll avoid doodling and drumming on the table. Such subtle cues can make a big difference to a student, as one tutor acknowledges.

> The other day I was at Springfield College visiting a friend. While there I mentioned to this guy Steve that I had a paper to write this week. We began talking about it and, as it turned out, he was taking a course very similar to the one I had to write this paper for. Steve asked me if I wanted to speak to his professor to get his views on the ideas I was playing with. . . . At first I was reluctant to do so but Steve insisted, highly praising this professor.
>
> The next day I walked into this professor's office nervous as anything. I felt, "Who was I to take up his time when I didn't even attend his college?" Well, to cut this story short, this professor, through nothing more than his body language, immediately put me at ease. He greeted me by standing up, shaking my hand, flashing a smile and looking me directly in the eye while introductions were made. When he sat down at his desk (I was sitting in front of and across from him), he always leaned forward as if to bring us closer. His hand gestures brought me into the conversation as if he was almost reaching out to pull ideas out of me. An occasional reassuring smile told me I was on the right track and when he did lean back in his chair it was merely to think deeply about what I had said.
>
> Anyway . . . at the end of only twenty minutes I felt very comfortable with this professor and he even asked me to show him the final paper if I was ever up again. I only hope that, merely through body language, I can make my tutees feel as at ease as this man made me feel. (Sue Moore)

For the most part, you won't need consciously to monitor body language. But I've discovered at least one situation when self-consciousness helps. Sometimes by late afternoon, after four or five conferences with students, I'm emotionally exhausted and not as interested as I should be. It doesn't seem to help if I give myself a mental pep talk, admonishing myself to be interested. But if instead I recognize that I'm slouching back in my chair and distancing myself from the student, and then tell myself to lean forward as if I were interested, to fool the student, I fool myself as well. I magically become interested in the student's work. Assuming the right posture helps me assume the right attitude.

You should also be alert to the possibility that a student may use different body language and have different customs if he comes from another culture. His preference for sitting four feet instead of two feet away may not be due to aversion but to a different sense of personal space. His refusal to make eye contact may not be due to boredom but to his culture's norms regarding deference to authority. His lateness may not be due to disinterest but to a different sense of time and punctuality.

Let me suggest another way in which consciousness of body language can help you. One of the goals while tutoring is to share responsibility with the student, to get him to contribute as much as or more than you do, to encourage his active participation, to give him more control. One way to monitor active participation is to note how much the student talks, and you can consciously increase his share of talking, as noted before, by asking questions and delaying your own comments, perhaps by counting to ten. You can also encourage the sharing of responsibility through seating arrangement and through what I'll call sharing the symbols of power. You and the student should usually, when talking about a draft, sit side by side, so that both can look at the paper. And so that both can have control of the paper. If the paper is in front of you, then you are in control. If the paper is between you and the student—or, better still, in front of him—then he has more control. And you can encourage the sharing of control by placing the paper appropriately.

Another symbol of power is the pen or pencil. If there's only one pen, who holds it? I remember watching a videotape of two students tutoring each other, first one, then the other. As they switched roles, the first tutor handed the pen to the second one. Although their tutoring was actually quite good, I asked about the implications of the pen switch. Is the one with the pen the one with authority? Could they perhaps increase the tutee's share of authority by letting her hold the pen?

Marking Progress

It's important not only at the beginning of a session but throughout to praise a student for what she's done well—for every step of progress. Now that she's done such a splendid job of listing ideas or of completing the handbook exercise on colons, she can go on to sorting her ideas or writing a paragraph that uses three colons. The sense of accomplishment will give her confidence to continue. And, of course, in order to give her frequent praise you'll need to break a task down into manageable steps.

Gauging progress also requires getting frequent feedback from the student. Don't assume that she understands an explanation, even when she politely agrees that she does—get her to demonstrate her understanding. Get her to tell you what the correct word endings are or where she should use apostrophes, not just to nod in agreement that the sentence could be improved. Get her to tell you how she'll revise her introduction or how she'll guide the reader through her paper, not just to say that she'll do it.

Ending

A final note: on ending. If you're working within a time limit—perhaps the student is assigned to work with you for an hour, or perhaps your tutoring hours end in half an hour—try to end on time. If you don't you may find it difficult ever to break off work with some students—they'll start to think you have endless time to give them. Students may also start thinking they can afford to be late, since you'll stay late. And, of course, if another student is waiting, you're being unfair to him. In any case, be sure that your tutee is aware of any time constraints from the beginning, and try to remind him ten or fifteen minutes before you stop.

Finally, try saving a few minutes at the end to summarize—or better still to let the student summarize—what you've done. Be honest in appraising his progress. And discuss any plans for the next meeting: what your goals are, when and where you will meet, what you and he will do before the meeting.

In general, the student should do as much of the work as possible. You can listen, ask questions, avoid interrupting him. You can ask him a wide variety of questions, including what he considers his strengths and weaknesses, whether he feels comfortable with a particular sentence, what his central idea is, what broader context it fits into, what the main categories of his argument are. By helping students to help themselves you show them that they do know how to write, that they can revise. They learn skills that they can use in the future; they learn to become independent.

10 Constraints on Conferences

In some circumstances you may have to cope with external constraints on conferences. One constraint is limited time; another, the need to grade the student. Both constraints may tempt you to become more directive in conference, more authoritarian. But while there may be value in having you take more control, in having you guide the student quickly and efficiently, I'd encourage resisting the temptation as much as possible.

Time

A student may come for help fifteen minutes before you're scheduled to leave. Or you may schedule regular fifteen-minute conferences for each student in your class. Is fifteen minutes long enough to do anything?

Sure it is. In fact, the pressure of working within a time limit can force you to concentrate on the most important points in a paper. Commenting on everything that could be improved will overwhelm a student: he can do better if he works on overcoming two or three weaknesses at a time. Tutors or teachers who feel that Big Brother is watching and will punish them if they don't mention everything that's wrong can wean themselves from their compulsion by having timed conferences. It's worked for me.

Still, time limits have a disadvantage. They may encourage you to take too much control—in order to cover enough during the limited time. That's something I need to work on: encouraging the student to take more initiative, allowing room for the student to voice his concerns, even in a fifteen-minute conference.

But if you do conduct any conferences with time limits, you should make sure the student understands the time constraints right at the beginning, so that he won't feel he's being kicked out because you hate him or you're bored or he's done something wrong.

Grading

Another kind of constraint is having to play an additional role in conference: not just coach but also umpire. If you're not only helping the student to write better but also judging her writing—perhaps grading it or reporting on it to another instructor—the second role can interfere with the first.

This dual role is like the dual roles that writers must play: they must both generate writing and criticize it. Just as an effective way for writers to juggle such conflicting roles is to separate the two—first generating, then criticizing, so that the criticizing doesn't interfere with the generating—so too might tutors and teachers separate their conflicting roles, as Peter Elbow suggests in "Embracing Contraries in the Teaching Process" (1983).

Thus if you need to evaluate students, in addition to tutoring them, you might clearly separate the two processes. One approach is to give the student a grade and then have her come to conference. But I find it more helpful to go over a paper in conference and then to change roles at the end and state a grade. For one thing, the second approach encourages the student to come to conference less defensive and therefore more willing to listen and to share. (Students also give me less grief about their grades when we confer first; perhaps they listen better and can see the rationale more clearly.)

Another approach is not to discuss grades at all during conferences, or at least early conferences, but to do the grading later in the semester. Perhaps at the end of the semester each student can submit a portfolio of her best work for a grade.

Still another approach is to involve the student in the grading. Just as tutoring can be a joint effort, so can grading. A student can suggest a grade and a rationale for it. Then you can discuss the paper and the grade with her—though here, unlike most tutoring, you have the final word. One advantage of such an approach is that it may make the grading process less threatening to the student (though it might reinforce a student's intransigence). Another advantage is that you can clarify your standards: if the student feels she deserves a particular grade because she spent so much time on her paper, as my students sometimes do, you can suggest that time spent is not a valid criterion.

Finally, I find it valuable, as do some of my colleagues, to do some "pure" tutoring in addition to tutoring students who are in my courses. I find that my approach to students who just drop in—who are not writing a paper for one of my courses—is less directive. And that reminds me how to be less directive with the students I am grading.

11 Problems with Attitudes and Feelings

Each student you tutor is different, and so is each writing task; what works with one may well not work with another. So you need to fish strategies out of your repertoire, perhaps trying several different ones to find one that works. In addition, though, you may come across students that you have particular trouble working with. For ease of discussion I've grouped the problems that follow into those that derive primarily from the student's attitudes and feelings and those that derive primarily from your own. But that's an oversimplification. Usually a problem derives from the interaction of your own and the student's feelings and attitudes. Your own lack of confidence and defensiveness, for instance, may fuel a student's hostility.

The Student's Attitudes and Feelings

Procrastination

Many students know that they're supposed to start writing a paper long before it's due, but they keep procrastinating anyway. They dash it off at the last minute. Then they expect you to tutor them at the last second. Maybe they don't understand what tutoring is. Maybe they think that tutors and teachers should simply proofread and correct mistakes instead of questioning and guiding a writer through the full process of writing. These students may even insist that you correct their papers instead of tutoring them.

> They are firm in wanting the answers to very specific questions. As we've discussed in tutoring classes, specific answers are supposed to be avoided. But this type of student is so persistent that it's very

aggravating to deal with her. Just as you think you've convinced her that she can solve the problem herself and she begins to do so, up pops another question and you find yourself ready to give the answer. I'm not exactly sure how to deal with this problem, but I think there may be some promise in deciding to talk a great deal less than I'm apt to with other students. It seems that once you've made your general point . . . , you simply have to let her fumble around and more or less talk to herself. Once she sees there is no response from you, she is much more inclined to start thinking of her own solutions. This might be especially effective when the student is in a great hurry to get the paper over with. She'll know that she can't just sit there and do nothing because if she does, so will you. (Karen Kielar)

You can also tell the student that she should come earlier and that, even though she has brought what she'd hoped was the final draft, you won't limit yourself to superficial comments.

The other day Beth came to me with a finished, typed draft of a history paper. She told me that the paper was due the next day, and couldn't understand why I raised my eyebrows at that. I explained to her that I didn't like to tutor papers that were due the following day because it limited both my tutoring advice and her ability to change the paper. I asked her what she would do if I had some real serious criticisms— would she change her already typed draft or would she keep the paper as is? We talked about this, and she realized that any problems or questions that needed to be ironed out should be done before the paper is ready to be passed in. Even though she only wanted me to proofread her paper and give her an opinion, I told her that I wouldn't hold back on any criticisms or problems, and it would be on her hands to choose to retype or leave it if I found anything really wrong. I proceeded to read the paper and found that it was a well-organized, well-written, logical essay. I told her and she seemed very relieved. Still, I see this last-minute reading as a problem because I feel that I am inhibited in my advice. If I say that major changes need to be made the student is up the creek, but if I don't mention the problems I see then she is up the creek too. I am making it a policy from now on to explain to my tutees who want me to "proofread" that it's on their consciences and in their hands to listen to comments on the night before the due date of a paper. If they don't mind the pressure . . . then I shouldn't either. (Diane Ciarletta)

Diane's approach is sound. The issue of proofreading, though, deserves further comment. Although you may decide that you cannot proofread a paper, be careful about immediately turning away students who ask for proofreading. Some students will ask for proofreading because that's a socially acceptable way of asking for help with writing (it's "only" proofreading). Yet these students may well have other problems, and you would do well to warn them, as Diane does, that once they ask you to look at a paper you won't limit your comments to minor details.

Such a warning may be especially important with the student who habitually comes at the last minute, the student who

> always wants me to tutor her paper fifteen minutes before it's due. In this case, she wanted me to read over her education paper, which she said was awful but which I knew she didn't want any negative comments on. Whenever I tutor her, if you can call it that, she refutes everything I say and will not bend. Well, she did the same thing this time but I refused to hold back. I told her I could give it no more than ten minutes because I had an appointment to go to and that I was going to tell her everything that was wrong with it. She didn't like it, and I was probably being somewhat insensitive because she's very insecure, but I felt she had to learn and that it's not my place to shelter her or just give her empty encouragement. . . . I was tactful, I think, about my criticism but it was honest as well. (Terry Wood)

Like Terry, sometimes you need to be less supportive and sympathetic—you need to become firm, even stern, perhaps giving an ultimatum. Mary Alice Taylor was working with a bright student who was writing everything at the last minute, coming in for quick tutoring checkups before passing the papers in, and usually receiving B+'s. Mary Alice sensed the student's potential, sensed that she could do even better if she only pushed herself more, by writing drafts early and allowing them to sit for awhile before revising. So Mary Alice gave an ultimatum: the student had to get a draft of her Friday paper to Mary Alice by Wednesday, or else Mary Alice would refuse to tutor her any more. When Wednesday came, the student strolled in but hadn't written her draft. Mary Alice scolded. Then, right afterward, the student drafted the paper, and she revised it the next night. When she received an A, she started writing early drafts regularly.

Anxiety

Students who lack confidence in their writing may have poor self-images and may be depressed and anxious. And they may well be anxious about more than just writing. They may be depressed about school in general or about their lives. New students may be anxious about whether they will measure up academically and will find new friends. Students from overseas or from some American subcultures have the added burdens of trying to survive in an alien culture, in American academia, perhaps speaking an alien language. These burdens can be exhausting: during my first month or two in Fiji, where I worked for two years, I slept about twelve hours a day. And the students may even be fearful of losing skills in their native language or dialect.

You need to try to counteract these feelings, or they'll interfere with anything else you try to do. The first step is to listen to the student, allowing her to get it off her chest, to clear the air. Listening to her will also give you a better idea of her concerns and thus how to address them. Occasionally, though, a student may have such severe problems—may be constantly calling you to talk about them, for instance—that you should direct her to a professional counselor. You're not trained to counsel such a student, and you could cause more harm than good.

After hearing the student out, you can bolster her confidence, pointing out strengths. And show interest in her ideas—show her that she has something to say that's worth writing about. If you can interest her in communicating, you'll motivate her to work on her writing. Ask her questions about what she has written. She mentions liking sports? Which ones? When did she play? Is she on a team? How is the team doing?

It's also helpful to assure the student that everyone has to struggle to overcome writing difficulties, including you.

> She was really depressed. I tried to reassure her but there was not much to compliment her about. I told her she had some good ideas and I asked her about the subject. I told her that on my first paper, I had gotten a C too.
>
> After talking with her for awhile I realized that she had been panicked by her first paper. She was also confused about the material so that led to a confused paper. She was also offended by all the markings (corrections) on the paper so I showed her a good paper of mine. It had at least three to four markings per page.
>
> We began by working on an organizing idea and finding things which would go in an introduction. I felt that she needed the structure of an introduction to organize her thoughts. I told her to follow in sequence from her introduction. . . .

I was working on my own paper and I showed her my introduction so she could see the structure. I feel that that might have been a mistake. She commented on how good it was but I don't think she realized how many hours I spent doing it. It might have intimidated her because of her C−; I don't know.

. . . She had other problems but I did not mention them because I will see the rewrite. If they reappear, I will deal with them there.

Upon leaving, she was still negative so I tried to reassure her that organizational problems are usually easy to overcome and that her rewrite would be much better. (Pauline Meehan)

In addition to encouraging the student and breaking the work down into manageable steps, Pauline admits her own weaknesses—an excellent idea. It shows that tutors are human and that the student is not alone in having to struggle with writing.

Thus it's important to sympathize and encourage, but then there's the danger that an anxious student will become too dependent on you. It's gratifying to know that a student needs you, but she may need you too much. Perhaps you're happy to tutor her outside your regular hours, but then

When I went home last weekend she had the nerve to be upset with me because I wasn't there to tutor her two English papers. (Eileen Salathé)

You may need to get tough, to remind a student that writing a paper is her responsibility, not yours; that she's mature enough to stand on her own two feet; that if she continues to depend on you so much, you may have to insist that she go to another tutor.

Hostility

On the other hand, students may be hostile and angry. And some of that hostility may be directed at you. They may criticize you directly, or their tone of voice or facial expressions may imply that you don't know what you're talking about. Or they may blame you if their grades don't soar.

Today was my first unpleasant tutoring experience. A girl I had worked with on a rewrite came back and complained that her paper had only gone from a B− to a B. I explained to her, as I had done the day she showed me the paper, that we could have done a lot more if she had come in earlier. . . . When she first came to me she had said she wanted to work on her grammar and punctuation. I had asked her if she wanted to change any of the organization and explained that there were some structural problems. But she told me the teacher had specifically complained about the other difficulties. Thus when she got the paper back she saw that the teacher had written, "Good work with the mechanics, yet disorganization is still a problem." She clearly believed it was my fault, even when she left, yet I really feel that when she wrote the second paper she didn't put as much thought into it as she should have. But I still felt as if I let her down. (Sydney Herman)

It's hard not to feel responsible, yet you shouldn't. Try to be objective with yourself: the paper is ultimately the student's responsibility, and improvement in writing isn't always reflected in improved grades. And think about what the student's blame is communicating. Is he feeling frustrated? Then you might concentrate on tangible, achievable goals and praise him for each step of progress.

Terry Wood reflects on the hostility she encountered when she agreed to glance over a student's introductory paragraph.

The tutee's attitude during the fifteen-minute session was a difficult one—she seemed very suspicious of my abilities, and I sensed that she really didn't want to be tutored by another student. And this was a bit hard for me to deal with. I found myself tensing up and being less giving than I would normally be. The tutee did not seem to want to accept my advice and I felt uncomfortable and somewhat annoyed. It seemed to me if this girl wants tutoring help she has a certain responsibility for how well the session goes. I realize it's difficult for a lot of people to go to a tutor . . . , but I think that in the same way that a tutor should be open and warm, a tutee should also give something in return.

I don't know if this extreme defensiveness is encountered often and I really had not anticipated it. But I am thankful, in a sense, that I came to realize I might encounter such an attitude. I'm afraid I wasn't as patient as I should have been in this instance—I spent fifteen minutes with the tutee and completely went over the introductory paragraph with her, yet I ended the session there—but hopefully next time I'll learn to handle it better. Maybe in the future I should go back and talk to the tutee some more about her writing in general so we can establish a bit more rapport.

It's hard not to become defensive. But if a student criticizes your hair, your suggestions, your approach to tutoring—step back and think why he's doing it. Probably out of insecurity and frustration. And if you can manage not to take the criticism personally, if you can focus instead on overcoming the insecurity and frustration, the criticism is likely to disappear.

Aloofness

Maybe the student says she couldn't care less about her writing. Or maybe she's shy, keeping her eyes lowered and responding to your questions with monosyllables. Or maybe she's so polite that she doesn't want to bother you. In all of these cases the student seems to distance herself and remain aloof. You should of course respect her privacy, but you could probably work with her more effectively if you overcame some of the distance.

The first kind of aloofness, the seeming indifference, may mask anxiety. So you can talk about how difficult you find writing, how hard you've struggled, but how you have in fact improved. Or the student may not be aware of the value of writing. So you can discuss its value, how it not only helps one to communicate but also to think, how most careers, including the one she is aiming for—systems analysis or electrical engineering or whatever it is—require a good deal of writing.

With a shy or overly polite student, you can work especially hard at gaining trust and encouraging assertiveness. Keep asking her questions and show interest in what she says. Possibly too her politeness is a way to avoid facing up to difficulty.

> Carrie stopped by and wanted to cancel the tutoring session for tonight, because of my cold. She thought I should sleep! I think I managed to convince her that I would be healthy enough to do it. She also said she didn't want to infringe on my time.
> I think perhaps she doesn't want to deal with these English papers. She's trying to shelve them and think about economics only. I honestly feel that if she devotes some time to each she'll feel much better, and be able to concentrate better. (Janine Clarke)

Like Janine, you can try to assure such a student that she's not imposing. And you can ask her whether she's actually trying to avoid facing difficulties.

Prejudice

Sometimes a student may not take you seriously because of your sex, your race, your class, your age. The student may feel that someone with your accent or sex appeal or skin color couldn't possibly be a good tutor. Or he may be embarrassed about being tutored by someone younger than he is. Or he may feel that a white couldn't possibly be sensitive to the needs of a black, or vice versa.

In any of these cases, it's valuable to confront the issue head on. If the football jock looks up and down the hallway before sidling through the door, and looks startled when he sees you, muttering something under his breath about chicks, you can ask if he's embarrassed about being tutored by a woman. You can explain how everyone can benefit from being tutored—even a tutor. You can tell him you won't broadcast the fact that he's being tutored—that is, you'll respect his privacy, treat his tutoring confidentially. And finally you can offer to bow out if he still feels he would work more effectively with a male tutor. Similarly if a white looks at you with surprise upon learning that you're a tutor, and in the course of a conference denigrates all your advice, you can ask if she was surprised to see a black tutor and why.

Another way in which prejudice manifests itself may not at first seem to be a problem: a woman student may be too eager to agree with you, especially if you're a male. Or a minority student may find it easier to deal with whites by seeming to conform to stereotypes, by seeming to be eager to please, and he may not admit that he doesn't understand something. Tutors who notice such a problem should work especially hard at sharing responsibility—at encouraging the student to talk, to start out by stating what he wants to work on.

In general, it's valuable to discuss possible prejudices, to ascertain what the student is thinking and feeling. You can also work especially hard at being tactful and at sharing responsibility.

The Tutor's or Teacher's Attitudes and Feelings

Tutors and teachers too can by guilty of the sins of anxiety, hostility, aloofness, prejudice. You may be anxious about your tutoring ability and be so apologetic that the student loses confidence in you. You may be angry because someone else has made a snide remark about your work, and you express your hostility by being too critical of the tutee. Or you may have unconscious prejudices, and your expectations of a student will in fact affect his performance in covert ways. Sometimes, if you realize that your feelings or attitudes are affecting your behavior, you can clear the air by admitting as much to the student: "I just got a C on a paper too, so I know how you feel. I think that's making me more critical now than I should be."

Sometimes a student will anger you, and here too you can acknowledge your feelings. He may anger you by being critical, by being late, by being sarcastic, by expecting you to stay up till 3 A.M. to read his paper, by generally expecting you, it seems, to be his slave. Erupting in a fury of passion is not helpful, but you can let the student know how you feel. "I understand how worried you are about your paper," you may say, "but I generally go to bed about eleven. And it makes me angry when a student expects me to drop everything else to help him. Next time, if you start your paper early, I'd be happy to help during my regularly scheduled hours."

Terry Wood explores her feelings regarding

the nonchalance two tutees displayed about my having time for them. They seemed to feel that since I was a tutor I, of course, had extra time to look over their papers. And what bothered me most about these sessions was not that they asked for help—I advertise myself as a tutor and could easily have said no if I hadn't wanted to tutor them— but that they left the paper with me, or had me sit in their rooms while they went off and ran errands, etc., and I read their paper. They didn't seem to want to "waste" time going over their papers with me but they expected me to spend a good deal of time with them. . . .

One of my friends asked me to look over her eight-page research paper for her eighteenth-century literature course. And it was an extremely boring topic to me but I got through it and then I began to go over page by page what I had problems with. I had initially told her I would give her one hour and only one hour because I had a lot of work to do and she agreed. But then after we had spent nearly an hour together—and her laundry was done—she asked if she could go down to put her clothes in the dryer right away because she had to get dressed to go out. I said no because I think it was her responsibility to leave that hour completely open. And she ended up keeping me one and a half hours, which was all right, I guess, because I think we worked well together and that she changed her paper a lot for the better. But I'm still angry about her attitude and am even more angry about the fact that she had written the paper a few days before . . . and had not even taken the time to reread it before the session. Her having done so would have allowed things to move more quickly and more effectively. I think a tutee has to realize she has *at least* half the responsibility to any tutoring session.

The other tutee I had this week asked me to read a ten-page book review of hers for a government course. She had me read it twice and she did listen to my comments. But the second time I read it over she asked me to make extensive comments in the margin while she went off to work on her other assignments. This struck me as unfair and not as what a normal tutoring session should be. I told her I wouldn't make the extensive written comments but would only go through a paper that closely if the tutee were there and we were both discussing it. She did understand and asked if I would read it over then just for basic clarity and organization. And I did and we discussed the paper.

But I do feel that sometimes tutees have unfair expectations of tutors—that they'll always be there, that they can leave all the work up to the tutors, and that a tutor can turn a mediocre paper into one deserving an A. These are things I am not willing to do, nor do I have the time or energy for it. But I do know that ultimately it is up to me to define a tutor's role for my tutees. I think I have to work more on telling tutees with unfair expectations that they are asking for too much.

A similar approach—honestly admitting your feelings—also works if you find you are disconcerted by how good a tutee's writing is, possibly even better than your own. You may feel envious, possibly defensive. Jacqui Belleville honestly recounts her feelings when working with such a paper and tutee.

Well, as much as I hated to admit it, his paper was *excellent*! I've never read anything so well-written by a peer in my entire life. The paper was supposed to be on the meaning of war. He struggled with his feelings on the topic and that's why he was nervous enough to ask my opinion. (Normally, he's pig-headed about admitting dependence on others.) He didn't write it like a normal essay; it was in story form. In fact, his characterization and imagery were so vivid and intense that I suggested that he submit it to a magazine. It had everything a short story needed, including the discreet clues that led the reader to understand the character's motives.

I had to put aside my initial feelings about his paper, though, in order to give him some constructive criticism. After telling him I thought it was excellent, I pointed out that he tends to be inconsistent. By that I mean that he'll use colloquialisms throughout an entire paragraph, and then switch to very specialized language. He was aware of this and seemed pleased that I'd noticed. He complained that his teacher hadn't noticed it yet. He seemed to really want to improve that discrepancy in his writing. In all truth, I admitted to him that many writers do this for the sake of style, and that as long as he knew what he was doing, the inconsistencies added to the paper. It wasn't a case of false agreement, or tense; I believe it was an endearing aspect of his style. Had he been unaware of it, then maybe I'd be more worried about it.

I didn't like this session at all. The reason is that I became jealous of his talent with every word I read! I shocked myself with these feelings. But I was really bowled over by the power of his writing, a power that I know is in me too, but that I can't seem to bring out. I can't bring myself to pass in an innovative type of essay for a class. I'm too afraid of being shot down for not adhering to the assignment. Denny's the opposite; he's a real nonconformist. He possesses a freedom in his writing that I can't seem to bring out. I know it's there, but I'm afraid it might not be any good!

I told him that reading his paper made me jealous. He didn't react the way I thought he would. I thought he'd get cocky and brag about his talent. Instead we talked about ways of freeing myself into a kind of looser writing. Not loose, but less structured. Structured writing is great, but I think I've lost some of my desire to be creative with assignments. After all, when a class only has two papers due all semester, who wants to risk an F just to be creative! I'm so obsessed with writing a clear, concise, point-by-point essay that I don't take the time to experiment with creativity.

Jacqui's honesty with the student enabled her to collaborate with him effectively—to share ideas in both directions. In general, honesty with a student about whatever is on your mind can help to clear the air; it also helps the student to see you as a real human being, neither a convenience to be taken for granted nor a god to cringe before.

Honesty is thus one tool for improving your tutoring; self-reflection is another. When a student is not fully responsive, try to figure out how you might have contributed to the problem. One tutor probes such responsibility when she explores what went wrong with a visit by an international student.

Back in high school my family had a French student, Monique, come to stay with us for a month. She knew a little English—about as much as an English-speaking student would know of French in Elementary

French. If we talked to her very slowly, with gestures, she usually figured out what we meant. Poor Monique! She got frustrated a few days after her arrival, and absolutely gave up on her English, speaking only in her rural French accent. This was fine for the next couple of days. Since I had been to her section of France before, and had learned many of the slang expressions they use there, we survived pretty well. But one of Monique's main reasons for coming to America had been to learn "American" as well as she could. We tried everything to make the transition to English easier for her, from talking in "Franglais," to talking slowly and simply, to translating what other people said to her. Nothing seemed to work—she always clicked "American" off, and grew amiable when we reverted to our (very) imperfect French. . . .

Monique . . . was a great lesson to me and my family. We may have doused her with *too* much "American" English upon her first arrival—but I think that catering to her encouraged her to get lazy—and to rely on us. I know that many students here, too, rely too heavily on the tutors. . . . Maybe, sometimes, we encourage them to be lazy? (Dawn Carroll)

Certainly the problems were largely Monique's fault, but Dawn thoughtfully explores how she and her family—as, in effect, tutors—might have reinforced Monique's stance.

Thus, to help you gain perspective and keep growing as a tutor or teacher, it's a good idea to reflect on your experiences—perhaps by writing in a journal, as Dawn does. What went well in a conference? What could you have done better? What could you have done differently, and what might have been the result?

Were you tactful? Were you understanding? Did you share authority with the student? Who held the paper?

Were you condescending? One clue is how you now feel about the student: are you appalled by his weaknesses, so appalled that you wonder how he ever passed the eighth grade? Chances are, he glimpsed your feelings.

Were you too authoritarian? One clue is to gauge how much you talked: more than half the time? more than two-thirds of the time?

Were you too harsh? One clue is the student's response: did he become defensive?

Were you too encouraging, too nice? Does he feel he's done better on a paper than he actually has? Or is the student starting to take advantage of you? Perhaps he keeps dropping by at 1 A.M.?

Were you surprised that a black (or a woman or whatever) could write so well? What does that say about your unconscious prejudices?

Do you feel that any problems with the conference were the tutee's fault? Is there anything you could have done differently?

All of us experience some failures, some incomplete successes. And it's important to try to learn from them.

> I experienced a difficult follow-up on a tutoring experience today. . . . The tutee came to me upset over the grade she had received on the paper we had previously discussed. The paper was based on a poem and we had discussed the ideas she wanted to introduce and how she wanted to organize them. And I had told her that her ideas were excellent, as I had thought they were, and I had felt her paper was going to turn out well. But she came back to me with the paper in hand, and she had received a "D" on it.
>
> Fortunately, the tutee did not blame me in any way, but she was visibly quite upset and I initially felt some responsibility for having encouraged her so much. Then I read the paper and discovered that the problem was not with her ideas but with her sentence structure, paragraphing, word use, transition, grammar, etc. The writing was very poor. . . .
>
> We talked, the tutee and I, for some time about the paper. What the talk amounted to, in essence, was a "pep talk." The tutee was extremely discouraged by the grade and . . . it was my responsibility to give her a sense of perspective about it. And it was a hard thing to do—I could imagine how badly I too would feel if I had received a D. But I told her that it is not uncommon for a student in 101 to do poorly on her first paper, and I assured her that the content of the paper was good and that it was the form that needed work. I advised her to see her professor as soon as possible, and I strongly urged her to set herself up with a tutor whose hours fit well into her schedule—mine do not.
>
> She listened and did see her professor, who also suggested tutoring. And I have been talking with her about her progress often.
>
> This experience was a good one for me. I'm certain that problems like this will crop up from time to time and I think it's very important to cultivate the counseling and listening skills so necessary to encourage a student who feels powerless and without ability to write. And it's important to know how to handle a situation where my tutoring help may not have yielded good sound writing even though I've done the best I felt I could. (Terry Wood)

Staying in Touch with the Student's Perspective

It's important to understand the student's perspective, to imagine how he feels. You can stay in touch with the student's feelings by writing and by being tutored. Terry Wood recognizes the value of struggling with writing herself when she tries to review a book of poetry.

> I can't write my poetry review; my rough draft is a mess and I lost my pen. I can't write it; my roommate has the radio on a top-forty station and I'm about to tear up the book of poems. I can't write the paper; my preceptees [advisees] keep coming in. I can't write it; it's late and I'm tired. I can't write it; there's noise in the hall. I can't write it; I have Art reading to do. I can't write it; I have to check when my next English paper is due. I can't write it; I just remembered my Art paper is due in a month. I can't write it; the book of poems is awful. I can't write it; I'm hungry and need to go to the candy machine. I can't write it—how will I organize it? I can't write it—I know what I want to say but can't find poem excerpts which point out what I mean. I can't write it—it's due on Thursday!
>
> I can't write it—I have to stop this! Relax . . . Freewrite—I did— fourteen pages full. And I feel a little better. But I want it to be finished. I can't wait to type. Right now I think my favorite thing to be doing would be typing the final page of this poetry review. Oh, if only I could be typing—and this is funny because I *hate* to type and can't except with one finger.
>
> I hate these feelings and I always get them when I'm beginning a paper. But I want to remember them. I want to remember how frustrating it is so I can relate when my tutees talk about it. I want to be able to sympathize and to tell them I feel that way too. I wonder if it ever goes away?

It's also valuable to be tutored—to stay in touch with what it feels like to be tutored by being tutored oneself. Some tutors and teachers stay in touch by practicing peer-group editing with colleagues. Others make a point of being tutored. One tutor, after receiving an unusually low grade, mentions how much she wishes she'd been tutored.

> I was very disappointed to get my history book review back and see that I got a C on it. I have never gotten a C on a paper before—I have also never written a book review essay before. I was really quite embarrassed to be an English tutor and get a C on a paper. The

professor did not like my transitions (he thought I was repeating myself too much). He thought a lot of what I had written was awkward. After reading over my paper quite a few times (after getting it back), I realized that many of the things he had criticized in my paper I would never have recognized on my own (I did proofread my paper). This proves to me the value of having an objective person look over the paper and give ideas. I think someone else can notice my writing problems better than I can myself. It is very difficult to separate oneself from one's work. I would have loved to go to a tutor and have her look at my paper. (Barbara Shea)

Another tutor, also dismayed by a low grade, did seek tutoring help.

I've come to the conclusion that being tutored is really a good experience. I took my latest paper for Mr. Donnelly's class to Mary Lu to be tutored for several reasons. (1) I can use all the help I can get with this class because I really don't know what to expect from the man. (2) I've always had problems in proofreading and writing my own papers. (3) It really is wonderful to get some positive feedback on my writing. (4) And lastly, since Mary Lu and I both have had few tutees, tutoring each other can give us the experience we need to become good tutors.

With both of us being tutors, our sessions (we had two) have been somewhat different from what I think my past tutoring sessions have been like. It's almost as though we've achieved the ideal tutoring session! We work together to point out the problems with the paper, and I had *plenty* of questions thought out before I saw Mary Lu. My questions about word choice and punctuation, combined with her questions about my sentence structure and the general flow of the paper, I think, made for a really well-rounded final draft. And when she pointed out specifics about sentence structure and clarity, more often than not I had questioned the very same thing.

The first session we had was pretty long. We went through the whole paper and decided that I had really chosen a topic that was too big to handle in two and a half pages. Although I first felt depressed at the prospect of beginning again, Mary Lu encouraged me so much that I really got into rewriting it. She has an interesting perspective on what I should watch for and has given me valuable pointers for avoiding the misuse of semicolons and dangling phrases. So as I was rewriting the paper, I focused on how Mary Lu would react to it, instead of becoming paranoid about how Mr. Donnelly will react to it. Consequently, I'm not as nervous about the paper as I was before.

The second session was a lot easier because we had spent so much time on content and structure in the first session. I'm pretty confident about my abilities now, and I owe a lot of that to the support that my tutor gave me. It really was a valuable experience being tutored. It helped her get more experience as a tutor and it helped me to see the tutee's point of view more clearly. I'll be able to understand the hostility that may arise when I suggest that major changes be made in the paper. I've felt the hostility, and I've seen how it can be broken down. Mary Lu was very good at this. She kept saying over and over how it really wouldn't require that much extra time and that I really had most of my ideas clear so that rewriting it became a painless prospect. She's going to let me tutor her some time in the future and I will definitely go back to her with my next paper. (Jacqui Belleville)

Finally, one way to gain understanding of a tutee's problems is to try to write like him, as Sydney Herman discovered when asked to bring an intentionally weak piece of writing to be tutored on.

I noticed, in writing my "bad" paragraph for videotaping, that it is now easier for me to create a poor piece of writing. I recall the difficulty I had in purposely writing a badly structured and punctuated paragraph in the beginning of the year. I attribute this change to my new understanding of what constitutes common errors, how to recognize them, and how to fix them. By working this process backwards, I found it much easier to write a typically bad paragraph. Perhaps, to the casual reader, the ability to write poorly may not sound extremely impressive. Yet I pride myself on it since I feel it demonstrates my newly developed understanding of the errors many students make.

In general, writing and being tutored can help you to be sensitive to a student's attitudes and feelings and to your own. Understanding what a tutee goes through can also give you a fuller appreciation of tutoring.

I have said many times in the past, "I can't write, I can't spell, and I want to go to sleep." Maybe that's why I enjoy tutoring; I've been there. (Beth Brown)

12   Evaluating Tutoring

It's gratifying when a student you have tutored rushes up to you delighted with the B− she has finally received on a paper, or when you can give her the B− that she has finally earned. You feel that you've made a difference. But grades are not the only way, or even the best way, to evaluate your tutoring effectiveness. Many factors affect a grade, and a student may well improve her writing without improving her grade. Furthermore, grades don't even attempt to measure some of the changes that tutoring may effect, such as greater self-confidence or a more positive attitude toward school. Instead, you need to get some distance and objectivity to help you gauge the strengths and weaknesses of your tutoring, both what you should continue doing and what you could improve.

The Student: Attitudes and Writing

Whether or not the student's grade improves you can still gauge your effectiveness by examining your impact on the student: the student's attitudes, writing process, and written product. Has he gained confidence? Does he write more fluently, with fewer stops and starts? Has he started writing multiple drafts? Is he no longer waiting till the last minute to start his papers?

You can also examine the papers a student writes—what a paper looked like before and after tutoring. How much change should you expect? That depends on the student and the circumstances. But here is an example of how much improvement you can hope for. Amy Sweetnam first wrote this draft:

> A year ago I broke my leg; this experience was something very special for me. Apart from what physically happened, I have seemed to gain a different outlook on many things. These new attitudes came from the stages that one goes through after breaking a leg.

The first part of the time I was idle. Here I learned to be patient and to accept the fact that I was going to be there for awhile. Then came crutches and movement. This was the way I spent most of my time. During this time I had to cope with my feelings of depression and inferiority. Also there was dealing with other people—the questions and stares one attracts when hopping on crutches with a cast. Finally, there is working back which gives one the largest sense of achievement imaginable. I gained a great deal of appreciation for my legs and being able to walk alone again.

This experience was definitely something important to me. I saw things I had done all my life in a different light. I feel as if I've grown more in the past year than in any other year. I am glad I had this experience, but I am also glad the end is near.

What Amy most needed to work on was developing her ideas, fleshing them out with more details. Her tutor asked her questions, got Amy to talk about her experience more: Why was the experience so special? How did she change? Why was it so difficult to be idle? After tutoring—and work in class—Amy wrote this version:

I had a broken leg for a year and a half, and I am just recovering now. This experience was something very special for me. I seem to have changed in so many ways. These were not physical ways, though; they were mental attitudes. My new outlook on things came from the stages one goes through after breaking a leg.

The first stage was confinement. This can also be broken down into two parts. One being a week in the hospital. I was so heavily sedated that the week passed quickly with little recollection. The next part of my idleness was at my house. Here I spent most of my time on my bed, adjusting pillows, using both hands to move my leg and dreading the next time I had to get up. My mother sat with me for many hours, and my closest friends were good for a visit a day. The hours in between, though, were filled with TV and smutty novels. I did not think much about things I could not do. My mind was filled with smaller problems like how to sleep on my stomach and how to move the pillows so I could see my TV.

The next big step was crutches and movement. This is how I spent most of my time. During this time I had to cope with my feelings of depression and inferiority. My largest depression came from watching others jump up and leave the room. This, which once came easily to me, now took five minutes of adjustments before movement could come. I felt awful for people with me because of how slow I walked. Also there was dealing with all of the out-and-

out stares complete strangers gave. Then having to answer the
same questions over and over; for example, "What happened to
you?" "Is it broken?" even "Did you sue the driver?"

Finally there is working back which consists of getting muscles
back into shape and trying to walk normally. Leaving your crutches
behind gives one the largest sense of achievement imaginable.

I gained a great deal of appreciation for my legs and being able
to walk alone. This experience was definitely something important
to me. I saw things I had done all my life in a different light. I feel as
if I've grown more in the last two years than in any other years. I am
glad I had this experience, but I am also glad that the end is near.

Amy's second draft is hardly perfect—it still needs work. In some
ways it has even more imperfections than the first draft: the first
has no sentence fragments yet the second does. But the second draft
shows significant improvement in its development of ideas and use
of detail. And that's the kind of change you can aim for in tutoring:
not perfection, not improvement in all areas, but significant improvement in one or two.

Checklists

Another way of gauging effectiveness is to examine the tutoring
process itself. You can, for example, complete a checklist like the
one given here.

Personal Checklist of Tutoring Skills

Listening	Infre- quently	Some- times	Most of the time

I try to be an *attentive listener* by practicing the following techniques:

1. I show that I am interested in what the student is saying by:			
a. Making regular eye contact.	1	2	3
b. Smiling, nodding, and making other gestures that signal my concentration and receptiveness.	1	2	3
c. Leaning forward in interest, undistracted by anything else.	1	2	3
d. Sitting beside the student, not hiding behind a desk or table.	1	2	3

	Infre-quently	Some-times	Most of the time
2. I avoid interrupting, even for the purposes of clarification, until a student has completed her message.	1	2	3
3. In order to indicate trust in the tutee's abilities to make thoughtful judgments, I allow a period of calm silence (wait time) after a student has apparently finished talking. In this way I can avoid cutting off a tutee's statements, and provide enough time for reflection and self-criticism.	1	2	3
4. I give my full attention to what the student is saying by:			
a. Taking notice of how he is delivering his message, including nonverbal cues.	1	2	3
b. Thinking chiefly about what he is saying, not reveling in my own thoughts on the topic or planning my next brilliant statement.	1	2	3
c. Framing my response in the context of the student's experience, whenever possible.	1	2	3
d. Yet sharing my own experiences with writing, to show the student that he is not alone.	1	2	3
5. I encourage a student to answer her own questions, or at least to try to answer them.	1	2	3
6. To check my understanding of what the student has said, I briefly paraphrase the tutee's idea(s) in my own words.	1	2	3
7. Using the following techniques, I ask questions in a manner that stimulates thinking and reveals a student's strengths and weaknesses:			
a. I avoid verbosity and make my questions brief but specific.	1	2	3
b. I don't overwhelm my student with too many questions.	1	2	3

	Infre-quently	Some-times	Most of the time
c. On the average, I wait more than five seconds between asking a question and saying something myself.	1	2	3
d. I avoid answering my own questions.	1	2	3
e. I try to ask open-ended questions, sometimes directive (Socratic) and sometimes nondirective (discovery)—not questions that require simple "yes" or "no" answers.	1	2	3
f. The intention of my questions is to enlighten, not to intimidate.	1	2	3

Explaining

I try to give *clear explanations* by practicing the following techniques:

	Infre-quently	Some-times	Most of the time
1. Since I don't want to do all the talking (or the work!), I give short explanations with appropriate examples or demonstrations.	1	2	3
2. I ask the student to perform a task that will help me measure his grasp of the concept or skill.	1	2	3
3. In addition to giving my own examples, I also ask students to provide examples after they have understood my explanation.	1	2	3
4. Although I sometimes share my experiences with the student, I am cautious about insisting on approaches based on my own experience because I am aware that the student's background may be different from mine.	1	2	3
5. I observe the student's learning habits and structure my teaching approach to her needs.	1	2	3
6. Whenever possible I model a useful behavior rather than give a long explanation.	1	2	3

	Infre-quently	Some-times	Most of the time
7. When it comes to learning/teaching, I am suspicious of all panaceas and flat "yes" or "no" answers.	1	2	3
8. Once I identify a tutee's typical learning style, I point out his strengths and weaknesses in the hope that the student will become more aware of how he learns best.	1	2	3
9. I delay my correction of a "wrong answer" so that I can first question my own preconceptions. (There may be another way that I've never considered to look at the issue, and it may be more important for me to understand *why* a student answered the way she did. Sometimes, with enough wait time, a student may self-correct.)	1	2	3

Summary

1. I try to make each tutoring session a joint effort with at least 50 percent of the work coming from the student.	1	2	3
2. I try to make sure the student has as much or even more access to the paper we are discussing and the pen or pencil.	1	2	3
3. I find out what the student already knows, I discover what she needs to know, and then I show her how to learn what she needs to know in a way that best suits her individual learning style.	1	2	3
4. I try to concentrate on real learning and self-improvement, not just on earning better grades. (I am aware that certain types of growth are not measured by grades.)	1	2	3

(Adapted from Thom Hawkins, University of California, Berkeley, © 1978.)

Here is an example of a tutor's self-evaluation:

> I found the personal checklist of tutoring skills to be a useful way to evaluate myself. . . .
> I feel that my use of nonverbal signals is frequent and I always show the student that I am interested in what she is saying.
> I find that only sometimes do I allow a period of calm silence after a student has spoken, and honestly I was not doing it to demonstrate trust in the student's ability to make thoughtful judgments. However, when it was pointed out I can see why that would be a good method to increase her confidence in her judgments, for by quietly reflecting about what she has said I am demonstrating that I find her comments worthy of thought and consideration. In addition, it allows her further analysis of what she has said.
> One of my main problems is listening with my *full attention* to what the student is saying, rather than formulating what my opinions on a subject are, and how to express those opinions. However, I notice that I listen a lot better now than when I first tutored. And I can see that . . . . I express myself in terms the student can relate to and understand, rather than be confused by. I usually encourage a student to answer her own questions, and she is usually surprised by how much she knows.
> In answering the summary questions I found that only sometimes are my tutoring sessions a fifty-fifty joint effort. Sometimes I find myself thinking (usually wrongly) that I have to *show* the student what she's doing wrong, what she should be doing, and how to do it. However, more and more, I've been pushing the student to analyze her own errors and make suggestions to correct them. I notice that when a student can explain what's wrong with something she wrote, she is much more eager to go on and identify and correct other problems. It tends to provide her with confidence, and this ability to detect and correct one's errors independently is the goal of every student.
> I found the question about whether I try to concentrate on real learning and self-improvement, not just on earning better grades, very interesting. For I notice that while my goal in tutoring is to help a student understand her errors and use this understanding to improve her writing, her goal, nine times out of ten, is to get an A, even if it means psyching the teacher out and writing exactly what she thinks the teacher wants. . . . When tutoring I try to stress that personal improvement and *real* learning are far more important than memorizing a particular format. However, I can understand why the ultimate compliment and ego booster comes in the form of an A! (Sydney Herman)

Sydney has also tried asking a tutee to complete the checklist, to see where their judgments differ.

I was a little nervous at first since I realized the truth could hurt, but I was extremely curious to see if my ideas about my skills (or lack thereof) were the same as hers. When she turned it in I was really glad I'd done it because it reassured me and also opened my eyes to a few things.

On the section about the nonverbal skills we were pretty much in agreement that I generally demonstrate the suggested techniques. However, I was surprised to find that she felt I left too long a period of silence after she said something and she even felt awkward sometimes. I, on the other hand, had been sure that I never left a long enough time. . . . I guess when you're a tutee you probably feel the tutor is sitting there . . . thinking about how wrong you are.

We also disagreed on another question, the one which asks, "The intention of my questions is to enlighten, not to intimidate." I had thought my questions were nonintimidating; however, she said she felt intimidated sometimes, since she couldn't always answer them. But then again if she could always answer them she wouldn't need me. So I guess the definition of intimidating must be taken into consideration here. Furthermore, I was glad to note that she found I did ask her to provide examples of what I had explained, for I felt I didn't do it very often.

For the summary question I had put down a 2 for the question which asks if I make each session a joint effort, with the student doing at least 50 percent of the work. However, the student gave me a 3 and said she had been surprised at how much she had had to participate, as she had expected the sessions to be more of a lecturing procedure. She also felt, as I did, that I try to help students concentrate on their overall learning ability, rather than just trying to get an A all the time. And she felt that had helped her in the long run since she learned skills that are applicable to all her writing needs, not just one isolated case.

Sydney did a good job of getting the student to offer criticism, for students are often reluctant to criticize. Sydney also did a good job of interpreting the comments. But I might add that the student's feeling that silences were too long might not have been altogether negative—it might be related to her expectation that a tutor would lecture. Sydney's silences probably helped the student to play a more active role.

Interviews

Other tutors have tried to evaluate their effectiveness by interviewing tutees.

I talked to Melanie about the tutoring program. She seems to really like it, although at first she said she felt she was forced to go. Now that she has gone, however, she really thinks it's a good program. She said that in the past she thought that people who went to tutors were really stupid (and this is the popular opinion of others, she said), but here at Wheaton everyone goes to tutors. She thought that was really good. She said she has talked to other people about it and she said a lot of people came to tutors before papers were due. (Nancy Cicco)

Diane Ciarletta reports the dialogue in her interview.

TUTOR: In general, how did you find the writing tutor to be?

ANNE: I found the tutor to be extremely helpful with my paper. She did not intimidate me in the least. I thought she might look down on me for coming to a tutor, seeing as I am a sophomore and took a freshman writing course last year, but she made me feel comfortable.

TUTOR: What kind of things did you work on?

ANNE: We worked on organization and clarifying my ideas. I had a problem with focusing on one topic, and I was so overwhelmed with the paper.

TUTOR: How did the tutor go about working on organization?

ANNE: She started on my introductory paragraph and we talked out loud about the points I wanted to bring across in the paper. This helped me to clarify my ideas in my head, and I had a better perspective on things. After we worked on the introduction we started on the body. The tutor explained to me that once I had my main points . . . , I should take a paragraph for each point and expand on it. We took the first point, and I had some ideas on it, so the tutor told me to freewrite a paragraph. I read it over and we worked out some of the kinks, like spelling and punctuation.

TUTOR: Did you work on anything else? Did the tutor have any other advice?

ANNE: She also told me that I had "thesauritis"—that is, I spend too much time looking up words in a thesaurus instead of using a more common word. I used one word that was way out of context, and the tutor suggested I only use a thesaurus if I was stuck. . . .

TUTOR: Would you go to a tutor again if you had to?

ANNE: I most definitely would. As a matter of fact, I have another paper due for English Friday and I plan on seeing a tutor to help me.

You may need to do a lot of probing to come up with constructive criticism, not just praise. You may need to stress that you sincerely want to improve. But if you persevere, you may come up with some useful and surprising insights. Dawn Carroll describes the different evaluations she received from her sister Merry, who found working on a high school paper "more of a game than real work," and from Kim, a college friend.

> Kim said that the questions I had asked got her thinking and made it easier to come up with her ideas. What I got from talking with *her*, though, is that I'm a little stand-offish. Tutoring her was not at all like *talking* to her. Usually, our conversations are easy, smooth—after all, friends normally talk that way with each other. But that time, she said, I was a lot different—more tentative, stiff.—Maybe I was scared of tutoring?? The difference between what Merry and Kim said is pretty big! I think that maybe dealing with my sister was much easier—first, because I've known her so long, and second, because it didn't seem like a "real" tutoring session. Kim, on the other hand, is only a friend—and sometimes we (I?) try to treat friends more gently/courteously than relatives (you can *always* make up with your sister, but sometimes you don't see a friend for *weeks*!) Perhaps I didn't feel as if I had the same freedom with Kim as I did with Merry?

Dawn sensitively explores Kim's criticism. It may be that some change in attitude, some aloofness, is appropriate when tutoring a friend—after all, instead of comfortably agreeing with a friend's complaints about the unfairness of the world, you should, as a tutor, help her to improve her writing. Kim may simply have been disconcerted by receiving constructive criticism from a friend who had previously been unconditionally supportive. On the other hand, if you find yourself becoming stiff and formal, you may want to work on relaxing: greater ease often comes with greater experience, but you can also try, say, spending a few minutes discussing a party last weekend or plans for Thanksgiving before turning to the student's writing.

Videotape

Still another way of gauging effectiveness, of giving yourself a chance to see how you perform, is through videotaping. (Or, if you do not have access to videotape equipment, you can listen to yourself on tape or cassette. In all cases you should have the permission of the tutee.) Videotaping may be frightening at first, but it's worth it. And try to be videotaped at least twice, perhaps once at the beginning and once at the end of a semester. The first time you're videotaped you're probably a little shocked, not just by how you perform but by how you look and sound: Is my voice really that nasal? Does my stomach really stick out that much when I sit down? Do my hands really fly about that much when I talk? The second videotaping is less of a shock, and you can focus more on your tutoring performance. But you can learn a great deal from both sessions.

> Videotaping forced me to see how others perceive me. I saw myself talking too much—I hardly let the student get a word in edgewise. It was shocking at first and then distressing, but after I thought about it, I was really happy I was videotaped. It certainly showed me that I shouldn't talk that much in a tutoring session and that I should let the student express how she feels about the paper. (Amy Halpern)

Videotaping shows how you can improve, but also what your strengths are, as another tutor recognizes in a balanced analysis of her performance.

> Although I was nervous at first, I really got a lot out of it. Besides having another chance to tutor (at least to practice)—it was good to be able to see myself in action. I realized a lot of the good things that I did, but I also got a chance to think about how I could have done things better. I was glad that I asked the student to talk about exactly what she had to do. But if I had a chance to do it over again, I think I would ask the student more questions. I also realized from last week's session that if you deal with a student's major problem first—a few of her other problems will also be discussed. Being on the tutee side of things let me see the situation from a different perspective. You really have to be careful about criticizing a student. I know that if someone told me, "Well, this is bad and this is stupid," then I would become defensive. Therefore, I was really glad that I remembered to point out my tutee's good points before diving into her major problems. The most important thing that I realized from this session on videotape was that the more relaxed a person is—the more she will accomplish. Being approachable is a basic characteristic which all tutors will need in order to be effective. (Jane O'Sullivan)

Videotaping is particularly good at letting you see what you're otherwise unaware of: how you physically respond to the student, what your body language is.

> It was the strangest thing to see myself tutoring on the videoscreen. I never realized how I appeared to the tutee. There were many things that I had not thought about before—body language, eye contact, interest in voice, to name a few. Body language is very important in a

tutoring session. The way the tutor crosses her legs [preferably top leg toward the tutee], for example, can signify whether she is genuinely interested in helping the tutee or if it is just another bother to her. Even if body language is not an obvious thing, a tutee will pick up at least on a subconscious level how interested a tutor is in helping with the paper. I noticed when I tutored Karen . . . that I was leaning towards her and looking at the paper at the same time. By looking at the tutee, maintaining eye contact, I showed Karen I was talking to her, involving her in the discussion about her paper. I looked up enough to let her add her own thoughts about her paper. . . . I made my voice sound interested and encouraging to prove to Karen that her paper was worth talking about. . . . As a tutor I put myself into a helping and encouraging state of mind—the correct body language, eye contact, and interest in voice followed naturally. (Barbara Shea)

In later videotaping sessions you can analyze your performance even more systematically. You could fill out a checklist after watching yourself. You might also watch a clock as you review your tape and note who was talking at every fifteen-second interval. Were you talking more than half of these times? You could likewise analyze what you said. What percentage of your sentences gave explanations, what percentage asked questions? Were your questions effective? Did they elicit more than "yes" or "no" responses? Did you allow enough silence? How long was the longest silence? Do you notice anything about the tutee's verbal or nonverbal behavior that you didn't notice while tutoring? For example, did you interrupt him? What does his behavior tell you about his thoughts or feelings? Why didn't you notice it before?

If you're videotaped when you first start tutoring, and again later on, you'll probably notice considerable improvement.

After being videotaped last week, I looked back at the journal entry I had written after the first taping. The first change I noticed about myself was the lack of nervousness. True, part of this ease was due to knowing everyone better; however, much of the lack of nervousness was due to more experience at tutoring and an increase in self-confidence. Most of the feelings, though, that I encountered the first time, I still have. After reading a paper, I still feel sheer panic that I won't be able to recognize what's wrong, or won't be able to explain or help the tutee; however, after the panic subsides, I feel I have more control now than I used to; I feel I'm more capable of handling different kinds of situations. I also wrote in my first videotaping entry that the person I tutored talked about as much as I did; she talked a lot. I felt this last time, also, that we both talked a lot; however, what we said was more productive, and I think this is a result of tutoring and what we've learned in class. My increased experience makes it easier for me to express myself to the tutee, and the more coherent the tutor is, the easier it is for the tutee to grasp the situation and help solve the problem. (Penny Penn)

Like Penny, you can learn a great deal about your tutoring by being videotaped. Interviewing a tutee or completing a checklist or examining a tutee's writing and attitudes can likewise give you the perspective you need to keep growing as a tutor or teacher.

Part 3
Beyond Tutoring

This part goes beyond tutoring in several respects. It addresses the value of keeping a journal, the unexpected consequences of tutoring, and ways of reaching a broader audience.

13 Journals

It's a good idea for tutors and teachers to practice whereof they preach—to be writers themselves. A particularly valuable kind of writing is a journal. You could freewrite for ten minutes, perhaps three times a week or daily, and respond to classes, to readings, to issues such as plagiarism. You can analyze sample student essays (see chap. 6, "Evaluating Writing") or your own tutoring conferences. Keeping a journal is a way of thinking about an issue, recording your thoughts, integrating theory and experience, reflecting on successes and failures—and, if you share your journal, communicating with colleagues or an instructor or supervisor. Most importantly, the journal is a way of exploring ideas. It can also be a place to try out stylistic effects. But the journal is primarily exploratory—don't worry about getting your words and punctuation just so.

Keeping a journal gives you perspective on your tutoring.

> Writing down my experiences has really helped me understand my accomplishments and difficulties. Besides explaining things to the tutees I had to recall my explanations for the journal. Thus I began to really understand and remember the sessions. They really helped when I had a tutee with similar needs to one already tutored. Having to explain things also improved my knowledge of technique and style. . . . (Sydney Herman)

The journal can also have a therapeutic value.

> When I write my doubts and anxieties down on paper it seems to lessen their importance. . . . It puts things into perspective and does not let them get blown out of proportion. (Barbara Shea)

In general, journals are for freewriting, for exploring ideas, for learning while writing.

> Often I find myself being surprised when I later read over what I've written. I may not even be aware that I hold a particular opinion until I've written a journal entry. (Tina Cunningham)

171

The excerpts quoted in this book suggest some of the topics you might explore in a journal. But if you still can't think of what to write about, try some of the ideas that follow.

The Writing Process

- How do you write? Describe in detail the process you went through for the last piece of writing you did. What are your ideal writing conditions? Do your experiences suggest possible advice for a tutee?
- How does a tutee write? Does he use strategies that others would find helpful?
- How valuable have you found a particular writing technique—e.g., drawing an issue tree, freewriting, making an outline? How valuable have tutees found it?
- What aspects of your own writing do you want to improve? How can you go about it?
- What aspects of your tutee's writing do you and she want to improve? How can she go about it?
- Is it possible to learn how to write, or must one simply wait for inspiration? What are your own experiences and those of your tutees?
- How would you help a student writing a letter of application for a summer job? Writing up a lab report? Studying for an essay exam? Writing a poem?
- How would you help a student with a problem in such areas as spelling, word choice, providing transitions, writing a conclusion?
- How would you explain plagiarism and documentation to a student writing a research paper?

The Tutoring Process

- Describe your most recent tutoring experience—in detail. Record as much of the dialogue and nonverbal communication as you can remember. What did you do well? What will you improve next time?
- What are the ideal conditions for tutoring? How was your last tutoring session less than ideal? How could you have brought it closer to the ideal?
- What kinds of comments are helpful to a tutee? What kinds are not?
- How do the dynamics of tutoring change if you're not just tutoring but also grading the student?
- What kinds of problems should tutors and teachers not attempt to tackle? When should you refer a student to someone else, such as a dean or psychiatrist?
- What should you do if you don't know the answer to a question?
- What should you do if you discover that you've given a wrong answer?
- Can you possibly be too encouraging? What are the dangers?

- Can you possibly be too helpful? How?
- If a student who has dropped in needs extensive help—if she needs to come regularly—how can you encourage her to keep coming?
- If a student who is supposed to meet with you regularly is resentful or reluctant, how can you motivate him to work on his writing?
- What are the functions of silence in a tutoring conference? How can you increase your tolerance of silence?
- Ask a fellow tutor or teacher to tutor you. What did you learn— about writing, about tutoring, about being tutored?

Tutoring Materials

- Discuss how well a particular exercise—published or unpublished— worked with a tutee. What parts of it worked well? What parts worked less well? How could you improve the exercise?
- What materials have you found helpful while tutoring? What materials do you still need? What can you do about it?
- Does computer-assisted instruction have a place in a writing program? Do audiovisual materials?
- Draft a letter to the author of a writing text that you have found helpful. Be specific about features that have been helpful (with whom? how were they helpful?) and features that could be improved.
- Draft a letter to me about how to improve this book. Feel free to enclose quotable journal entries.

The Tutor or Teacher

- How do you perceive your role? How do you want others to perceive you?
- What makes a good writing tutor? A good writing teacher? Are they different?
- What is it most important for a tutor or teacher to know?
- What are the advantages of being a writing tutor or teacher?
- What are the disadvantages?
- Has your own writing benefited or suffered? If it has suffered—if, say, you are now more critical of your writing and find yourself blocking—how can you overcome the difficulty?
- What were your fears when you started tutoring? Have you overcome them?
- Write a letter addressed to a new tutor or teacher, discussing what she most needs to know as she starts tutoring.

The Tutee

- How can you be sure that you understand a student's difficulties? Or be sure that you have communicated with the student?

- How can you be sure that you understand the student's point of view?
- What can you learn from your students?
- How can you recognize prejudice (against race, gender, class, age) in yourself? What can you do about it?
- Is tutoring ESL students (students for whom English is a second language) different from tutoring other students? Are attitudes different? Are assumptions? Are errors?
- How would you accommodate the needs of a student who is deaf? Or blind? Or in a wheelchair?
- Try writing a paragraph like one written by one of your students—not a parody but something that he might actually have written. What insight does it give you into his writing process?
- Try writing up a tutoring session from the student's point of view. How did she feel?
- Write what you know of a student's writing processes. What more do you want to know about his process?

Problem Cases

- How would you deal with a student who has received a D on a paper, has been referred to you, and refuses to make eye contact?
- What can you say if a student tells you that ever since she started coming for tutoring her grades have been getting lower?
- What do you say to a student who calls at 1 A.M., desperate for tutoring help?
- How should you respond to a student who asks, "Do I need a comma here?"
- How can you tactfully extricate yourself from a tutoring session that has lasted an hour or more and that you feel should end?
- How can you motivate a student who is overwhelmed by his utter inability to write? Or who is not convinced that writing well is a useful skill? Or who feels that he writes well enough and doesn't need tutoring?
- What can you do if three students come for help at the same time?

Ethics

- How much help can you give a student who brings in a draft of a paper? Where do you draw the line? Should you proofread? Write in corrections? Why or why not?
- What do you do if a student insists that you simply correct errors on her paper?
- What do you do if a student wants you to tell her what grade you'd give her paper—to assure her, in effect, that she'll receive a good grade—when you are a tutor and not a teacher?
- What do you do if a student wants you to disagree with a grade he

has received from someone else? What if you actually do disagree with his instructor's grade?

- What do you do if a student disagrees with a grade that you have given her?
- What do you do if a student complains about a teacher and wants you to agree? Or complains about a tutor?

Evaluation

- In the middle of the semester, if your tutoring is connected with a course: how is the course going so far? how would you improve it?
- At the end of the semester: evaluate the course. What worked well? What worked less well?
- Evaluate your tutoring. What are your strengths? Your weaknesses? What will you try to improve in your next session?
- If you were to be graded on your tutoring, what grade would you give yourself? Why?
- Interview a tutee, one of your own or someone else's (with the other person's permission). What did she learn from being tutored? What was especially valuable about the tutoring conference(s)? What was less valuable?
- Ask a student, right after a tutoring conference, what percentage of the time he felt he was talking. Do you agree? How do you account for any discrepancy? Should he have talked more? How could you have encouraged him to?
- Ask a fellow tutor or teacher to observe a tutoring conference (with the tutee's permission). What did you do well? What could you improve? How do you account for any discrepancy between her view and yours?
- Tape a tutoring conference (with the tutee's permission). What did you do well? What could you improve?
- Can tutoring effectiveness be evaluated? How would you evaluate it?

Publicity

- If you're attached to a writing center, how could it reach more students? How can the center become less intimidating? How can tutors become more approachable?
- How could you improve the publicity for a drop-in center?
- If you have a drop-in center, draft a letter to the school newspaper to explain the purpose of the tutoring program and how willing the staff is to help students.

Keeping a journal can thus help you to reflect on the tutoring and writing processes. And it helps you to stay in touch with the process of writing and the writer's perspective even more directly— because you're writing too.

14   *The Perils of Tutoring*

Tutoring can be exhilarating. But there are also personal perils. Your teachers may expect too much of you, or you may expect too much of yourself. You may have to cope with a plethora of students, or with a dearth of them.

Great Expectations

Occasionally, if you're a peer tutor, and a teacher knows you are, she may seem to expect too much of you. Or she may mortify you by asking how a writing tutor could still have problems with dangling modifiers. One tutor copes with some of her anger by writing about it.

> Even though I enjoy being a tutor immensely, there are some disadvantages. . . . The biggest disadvantage is that a lot more is expected of me (especially from a certain professor who shall remain nameless!). Here I am, a tutor, and all of a sudden, I'm supposed to know everything there is to know about everything! Get serious! I'm still an undergraduate, the same as everyone else! I'm in college to learn, not to teach! People don't seem to understand that in being a tutor, I'm learning a lot more than I could ever actually teach someone. I think being a tutor is a great learning experience. If I did know all the wonderful little points of grammar that I'm "supposed to know" because it's "expected of a tutor," I'd be teaching his class and not taking it. (Jacqui Belleville)

If you run into a similar problem, try writing about it. Try talking about it with someone sympathetic. Then, once your feelings are in control, talk with the teacher—explain your feelings calmly and ask how you can improve.

Tutor's Block

Great expectations can lead to tutor's block: you may start blocking when you try to write. Usually tutors and teachers learn to write better because of tutoring—there's nothing like teaching something to someone else to learn it yourself. You may also learn new writing strategies. But sometimes a tutor or teacher becomes so aware of what to look for in a piece of writing or of what is expected of her writing that she starts blocking—she can't get words down on the page.

> Since I have become a tutor I've found that I put more pressure on myself to write wonderful A+ papers. Now that I have this "tutor status" I feel that I should be "above mistakes." After all, how can I help others to write papers if mine aren't great themselves? I am presently working on a paper, and nothing I write can satisfy me. I keep thinking of all the ideas I learned from tutoring class to apply them to my own paper. It seems as though what I beforehand thought of as my "natural instincts of writing" now need to be pondered and thought through logically instead of just flowing. I am surprised at this reaction, since I would think that being a tutor would give me more self-confidence in my ability to write. Being able to critically analyze others' mistakes should help improve my awareness of my own mistakes. This has certainly happened, but now I feel I'm becoming too much of a perfectionist and too self-critical for my own good. I think I am producing better work as I am getting more practice writing, but it's taking way more time than usual. Because tutoring has made me more self-critical, I feel I am pushing myself harder and expect more from myself. (Diane Ciarletta)

The remedy for excessive self-criticism is to find ways to loosen up, so that you don't have to do *everything* on the first draft. Try freewriting. Try just to get ideas down without worrying yet about spelling or wording or whatever. Diane had been accustomed to planning her papers thoroughly ahead of time, then writing a near-perfect draft. When she became stuck on a paper two weeks after writing the above entry she remembered that other tutors had found it useful to write discovery drafts. So she tried freewriting and, as she notes in chapter 3, "Once I started I couldn't stop!"

Too Many Students

First Sandy drops in, while you're staffing a drop-in center, and he's struggling as usual to find a thesis for his English paper. Five minutes later Juan stops by to ask you to check his prepositions in an engineering report. Then Anita stalks in, barely controlling her anger over receiving a D on the book review for which she, unlike some people she could mention, had actually read the book. You're swamped. How can you tutor all three?

You could, of course, decide to work with Sandy first and set up appointments with the rest. Or you may be able to switch from one to another (though it takes tact and skill to juggle even two at a time). Sandy could list ideas on his topic and start drawing arrows connecting similar ideas while you turn to Juan, who starts underlining all his prepositions while you turn to Anita, . . . Or, if the students had similar problems, you could work with them as a group. They could work together on an exercise on punctuation or plagiarism or dangling participles. Or they could read one another's drafts and, after commenting on strengths and stating what they see as the author's central idea, point out where they have trouble following the author.

Or perhaps your problem is not that you're swamped with tutees while you work in a drop-in center, but that students keep bothering you when you're not supposed to be available for tutoring. They may call you at home. Or if you're a peer living in the dorm, they may come to your room. It may even seem as if they have a sixth sense that tells them when it's least convenient for you to help them.

> I think there is probably a formula somewhere: as your own workload becomes close to unmanageable the number of people seeking the light (or dim bulb) of your knowledge will increase proportionately. Thus $WL^2 = T^4$. (Deborah Williams)

You have other work to do—not to mention sleeping—but it can be difficult to say no. Still, for the sake of self-preservation, learn to give a gentle, tactful no. Explain when you and other tutors are available. Suggest the value of starting a paper early. Sympathize with the student's predicament. But remind him that you have your own coursework and sleeping to do.

Too Few Students

On the other hand, you may have too few students. Perhaps you make an appointment to meet a student—and maybe you even spend time preparing materials for her—but she doesn't show up. Don't take no-shows as a comment on your tutoring; they could result from any of a number of causes. And it's not your responsibility to ensure that the student comes—it's hers. But there are a few things you can do to encourage her to appear.

In the first place, when making the appointment you and the student could agree on a clear goal for the meeting, in addition to a specific time and place. It may be helpful to draw up a tutoring contract, perhaps an official duplicated form, specifying your names, goals, plan for next meeting(s), time, and place. Both you and the student should sign (she's made more of a commitment if she signs the contract). And, if possible, give the student a copy of the contract. In any case, if you're going to devote time to searching for or preparing materials, be sure she knows. And, finally, be alert to nonverbal signals (such as a refusal to look you in the eye or a nervous eagerness to agree with anything you say), in case she's agreeing to another meeting simply as a way of escaping right now. If you suspect that she may not keep the appointment, you could explain how it would inconvenience you if she doesn't, and you could stress that if something does come up she should be sure to let you know.

If you are also grading the student you can offer her other incentives to keep the appointment as well. One is to make it clear what the requirements are for passing the course. Does she need to confer with you at least once a week? Does the syllabus state that each student must have four conferences with you? Still another incentive is to reveal the grade on a paper only in conference.

What if, despite all your precautions, the student still doesn't show up? If tutoring is required for course credit, you can of course report her or lower her grade. If you see her again, try to find out tactfully why she didn't show. Did something urgent come up? Is she so spaced out that she has no sense of time? Is she feeling discouraged? Is she trying to avoid her writing problems by avoiding you? Absence (like lateness) is often a symptom of a larger problem that you might explore. In addition, be sure the student understands your point of view—be sure she knows how she has inconvenienced you. If she comes for tutoring later on, at an inconvenient time, you can tactfully refuse to tutor her right then.

Or perhaps your problem is not that you've been stood up by a particular student but that too few students drop by. It may not be your responsibility to drum up business for a drop-in program, but it's frustrating not to have anyone to tutor, and you may be able to help avoid the frustration. Methods for publicizing the program are discussed in the next chapter. In addition, if your school is residential you might try to reach out to more students by instituting night hours in the dorms.

> This is a dissertation on why I think dorm tutoring is beneficial to a tutee. The tutoring room can be kind of forbidding to an insecure tutee. A dorm room can be much more comfortable and puts a student at ease. I also feel that it is much easier for the tutor. I'm less stiff and feel less like I'm lecturing at the student and more like we're having a comfortable conversation. Besides, the chairs in my room are much more comfortable than the desks in the writing room! Seriously, though, there are so many advantages to tutoring in your own room— or even in the tutee's room. If she is tutored in her own room, I think she's put at ease because she's on "home ground." She also has all her old papers right there for reference. The hours are also more convenient—both for tutee and tutor. Day classes can interfere and a lot of times a student won't come see a tutor because she has no free time. Night tutoring helps this problem. Probably the only disadvantage I can see to tutoring in the dorm is that all the writing materials, books, guides, and exercises, etc., are in the tutoring room. (Julie Along)

True, you're likely to lack resources in the dorm—not just books and exercises but also furniture. Is there a second chair to draw up to the desk? Or if you sit on the bed, where can you put the paper you're working on? You may also be more susceptible to interruptions.

> Whenever people come to my room to be tutored, other dorm residents pop in and begin to talk. It is as though people do not take tutoring seriously. The same people who would leave right away as soon as they saw me doing homework come right in and sit down and start a conversation when I am tutoring. I have to tell them that they will have to leave. (Barbara Shea)

Evening hours in the dorms may also be inconvenient for day students. But you could have tutoring in the writing room during the day and in the dorms at night.

Of course, if you do try dorm tutoring, you may need to be especially strict about hours. We've found that dorm tutors are called upon for more tutoring than writing-room tutors are—but outside scheduled hours. If your hours are 7 to 9 P.M. and someone blithely trips in at 11:30, you should feel no hesitation about saying no. Be polite but firm, and explain when you're available and that you have your own work to do.

Night hours may attract night owls, but you still may be faced with a dearth of tutees. One way to alleviate some of your anxiety is to write about it.

> Let's see—what shall I write? I still have not had any tutees and I'm really feeling apprehensive, guilty, inadequate, etc., but I truly have tried dragging people into the tutoring room yet have had no success. So here I sit, not that the time is wasted, for it's not. This free time gives me a good opportunity to explore my feelings and ideas about tutoring—and about how wonderful I could be if a tutee dropped in. Oh, sure! Easy for me to think that because I have not been "put to the test" of tutoring. It sure isn't due to lack of enthusiasm or interest. Perhaps next semester Wheaton could offer a new course—for those who want to tutor but must not share in the tutoring experience. We could call it "The Tutor's Torture"—it would be an endurance test of sorts to see how long a tutor could maintain interest in an exercise she was forbidden to participate in. Sort of like waving candy in front of a child—we could entice tutors with the idea of tutoring, train them to tutor, but never allow them to experience it. The ultimate torture (the final exam) would be to tie them to their seats every Wednesday afternoon of the semester for an hour and a half and force them to listen to the exciting and fulfilling experiences of the other seasoned tutors. This is certainly a torture for teasing all trembling, terrified, torpid tutors! (Susan Rich)

Just hang on. Students will come, especially if you lure them with some of the strategies discussed in the next chapter.

15 *Reaching a Broader Audience*

Publicity might not seem terribly relevant to tutoring. After all, you agreed to tutor, not to advertise. But if you're staffing a drop-in center, and if you're going to have anyone to tutor, publicity is important. Publicizing the program also gives you a chance to share insights into writing with a broad audience, an activity that certainly furthers your goals as a writing tutor or teacher.

Students need, first of all, to learn that there is a tutoring program. They also need to learn what the program offers: not just proofreading but help with the whole process of writing, not just help for remedial writers but help for everyone. One tutor found a senior slinking into her room, fearful that someone would see her and know that she was seeking writing help. But the help was valuable, and the senior came again.

It can be difficult to persuade students that the program is not just remedial, that everyone can benefit from being tutored.

> I think that some upperclassmen feel that having a problem writing a college paper is supposed to only be a freshman phenomenon. But it isn't. I'm a perfect example for this because I, too, get writer's block or have particular grammar problems. I feel that it is imperative that we make students realize that even though a particular student is a dean's list student and gets straight A's, she shouldn't feel as if it's below her to go to someone when she does have an occasional problem, for example, generating ideas.
>
> Further, a second opinion about one's paper—especially when done by a tutor who is experienced at helping others write—can be valuable. A second reader, I've found, can be more unbiased about a piece of writing. Probably the worst thing I have to do to one of my papers is to revise and improve it after the rough draft. I frequently feel that the words or ideas came too hard to just cut them out, even if they don't really fit. However, having a keen reader, like a tutor, can, I feel,

help a student improve her writing and papers regardless of her level. (M. F. Withum)

It is thus important for publicity to stress that everyone can benefit from being tutored—it is important to educate people that writing well is not just a matter of inspiration or of getting all of one's semicolons right. One step in the right direction is for tutors and teachers themselves to be tutored regularly.

As for reaching people who could benefit from tutoring, the best way of publicizing the program is by word of mouth. But there are other ways as well—especially important if your program is new.

One is to hold workshops. At the beginning of the fall semester one could hold workshops in survival skills. We do so in conjunction with the residence hall staff.

> The academic skills workshop proved to be very successful, and I was extremely pleased both with my performance and with the participation of the group. The students seemed very interested in what I had planned, and they asked intelligent, thought-provoking questions. . . . At first I didn't think I could handle it, but since I have some vague aspiration of becoming a teacher, I thought this would be a wonderful challenge to test my ability and self-confidence in front of a group. I started off a bit shaky and tended to look at my notes a lot, but as I started talking I relaxed and felt comfortable. It almost felt natural being in front of a group in a sort of teacher-student interaction. I admit it was somewhat of an ego trip for me in that I was supposedly "the authority" and they were learning . . . from me. I often wonder if that is one of the intrinsic rewards of being a teacher, tutor, etc.—that one of the motivations behind becoming involved in something like tutoring is the boost in ego one feels when "helping" someone else. Not that this is bad—sharing yourself and your talents with others is wonderful—if it is not for selfish reasons. . . .
>
> Anyways, to get back to the workshop—I had a lot of fun planning it. My format went something like this: I began talking about writing papers, and asked about the background in writing people had, and if they felt jittery about their first paper at Wheaton. Many girls responded by sharing their thoughts about first-paper panic. It was a good way to start things off and created a relaxed, comfortable atmosphere. I then . . . stressed that organization is the backbone of a good paper (or any paper). The ranking exercises were very helpful as well [the first exercise in chap. 6, "Evaluating Writing"] and there was much discussion among small groups. This not only got them thinking

about the material, but it also allowed them to share their ideas and get to know one another better. Plagiarism was a sticky topic because many couldn't quite understand all the rules and regulations and they asked some questions. (Diane Ciarletta)

One could also hold special workshops on particular problems, such as avoiding plagiarism or preparing for standardized tests like law boards and graduate record exams. One can invite students to have lunch with a comma or to lunch on essay exams.

If students don't come to the workshops, perhaps you can bring the workshops to the students—by visiting classes. If you don't already work with writing classes, you can visit them—or other classes—and announce the program. Or, better yet, you can conduct a short workshop on a common problem for the class. These classroom visits also keep other instructors informed of what you do.

In addition, keep in touch with other people who advise students with academic difficulties. Just as you may refer students to specialists in reading or learning disabilities or English as a second language, encourage these specialists to refer students to you. And don't forget students who advise other students—dormitory residents, big sisters, preceptors, proctors, subject-matter tutors.

Flyers and campus mailings can inform people about the program—if they read their mail. So can posters. But demonstrations and personal contact are more effective. If you're a tutor, discussing a tutee's work with her teacher may help the tutee—and also the tutoring program. For the teacher will learn how helpful and responsible a tutor can be, and how a tutor doesn't just correct a student's paper, and will then refer more students.

It's important too to make announcements in the school newspaper and on the radio or television station. One can also offer a sampling of one's wares in these settings, by providing tips from tutors. (At the same time, one is educating students, the aim of a tutoring program.)

Beyond the school is still another audience. There's the community immediately outside. Should the school be providing services to the town or city (to improve town-gown relations, for instance)? Should local people be invited to drop in? Should the writing center set up a writing hotline?

A still broader arena is the national community of scholars.

Even if you're an undergraduate, you can share your experiences in professional journals like the *Writing Lab Newsletter,* the *Writing Center Journal,* and the *Writing Instructor.* You can also make presentations at regional and national conferences. And you can share not only your experiences in tutoring but your insights into the writing and tutoring processes. For working closely with a variety of writers can give you new insights and put you on the cutting edge of research in writing.

Appendixes

A   Ranking Grammatical Errors

In the discussion of grammatical errors in chapter 4, you were asked to find and rank the errors in a paragraph (p. 57). I'll first discuss the "errors" that I've found (giving one example of each type), then their possible rankings. Other people, I realize, would not only rank differently but consider different constructions errors. Here is the paragraph again, with numbers referring to errors:

> Being (1) picked on throughout my childhood by my older brother (2) I often aspired (3) I was (4) a male, (5) however (6) now that he and I have grown out of this stage I'm (7) very glad I am female. If I was living in an earlyer (8) century I'm not sure I would feel this (9). Having to unendingly (10) cook, clean, (11) and caring (12) for childs (13), (14) womens' (15) lives were very difficult. Men force (16) women too (17) work hard (18) than anyone should. But (19) now in late twentieth century (20) decades hopefully (21) women have the ability in (22) outdoing (23) men, which (24) is why I'm glad I am the (25) female.

1. "Being" should be "Having been."
2. "Brother" should be followed by a comma because the preceding is a long introductory clause or phrase. (The same principle would require placing a comma after "stage," later in the sentence, and probably after "century" in the next sentence.
3. "Aspired" is a diction problem: it could be replaced by "wished."
4. "Was" should be "were" (subjunctive), since it is part of a condition contrary to fact. (The same principle would require changing "was" to "were" in the second sentence.)
5. The comma should be a semicolon or possibly a period.
6. "However," as an extra element in a sentence, should be followed by a comma. (As in 2, the problem is a missing comma, but the reason for needing it is different.)

7. Some would consider contractions wrong in formal writing and would change "I'm" to "I am," here and elsewhere.
8. "Earlyer" should be spelled "earlier."
9. "This" is vague: it could be replaced by "so glad."
10. "Unendingly" splits the infinitive "to cook": the adverb could be moved before or after the infinitive.
11. Some might consider this comma unnecessary.
12. "Caring" is not parallel to—is not in the same form as—"cook" and "clean"; it should be "care."
13. "Childs" should be "children." (I'd consider this problem distinct from spelling problems—it's a matter of having the right ending on a plural noun.)
14. The initial phrase, "Having unendingly to cook, clean, and care for children," modifies the following noun: "lives." But it should modify "women." To make the phrase modify the right word, the second half of the sentence could be revised thus: "women had very difficult lives."
15. The apostrophe should precede the "s": "women's."
16. "Force" should be "forced." (I'd consider this problem distinct from spelling problems—it's a matter of having the right ending on the verb.)
17. "Too" should be "to." (17 might be classed with 8 as a spelling error, yet 17 differs in that it results from confusion of homonyms.)
18. "Hard" should be "harder."
19. Some feel that a sentence should never begin with a conjunction.
20. "Twentieth century" should be hyphenated when it is a two-word adjective followed by a noun: "twentieth-century decades."
21. Some consider "hopefully" an abomination, unless it modifies the verb of its clause: the sentence could instead read "women can hope to."
22, 23. "Ability in outdoing" should be "ability to outdo." (You may have counted this phrase as one construction.)
24. "Which" has a vague referent: "which is why" could be replaced by "and."
25. "The" should be eliminated.

Those are all the potential errors that I could find; perhaps you can find more. But be sure they are actual errors, not just stylistic preferences. If I were writing this paragraph myself, I'd do more than correct errors: I'd rethink the paragraph's optimism, reorganize, add detail, revise stylistically. If I were tinkering with the style in the last sentence I might revise it thus: "But now women can even outdo men, and I'm glad I'm a woman." With a student, however, I'd raise questions about stylistic matters (e.g., whether "in late twentieth-century decades" is necessary) only if outright errors were under control.

Now for rankings. I'll give you my own ranking—I'm well aware that others have different ones. But my choices at least give you something to start with. I'll start at the bottom, with "errors" of marginal importance. First, there are those that I frequently commit myself, as you may have noticed: using contractions (7), following the penultimate item in a series with a comma (11), beginning a sentence with a conjunction (19). I don't consider them errors, although a contraction might seem out of place in very formal writing.

Next are those "errors" that I generally avoid but recognize as increasingly acceptable in contemporary prose: ignoring the subjunctive (4), splitting the infinitive (10), failing to hyphenate (20), and throwing in "hopefully" (21). I'd talk about these matters only with students whose writing was nearly error-free, and I'd stress that these constructions are increasingly acceptable but some instructors are annoyed by them.

That still leaves a lot. Instead of giving you a rigid hierarchy, though, let me suggest some general principles. First, errors that obscure the meaning are probably more important than those that are simply incorrect—and thus some problems with faulty pronoun reference and diction may receive priority. Second, recurring errors are more important to tackle than isolated ones (this sample paragraph is so short and is such an artificial hodgepodge, though, that it's difficult to find clear patterns of recurring errors). Third, I'm inclined to give high priority to sentence-structure problems, such as the comma splice or run-on (5), and many other instructors do too (some automatically fail a student for committing three comma splices), but I'm no longer sure that these errors are more important than other errors of punctuation. Fourth, I find myself giving lower priority to errors that "good" writers tend to commit, such as comma errors (2) or dangling modifiers (14), but again I'm beginning to question this proclivity. Finally, I try not to place as high a priority as many do on errors that reflect dialect interference and perhaps class status, like the problems with word endings, marking singular or plural (13) and tense (16). But you should be aware that many readers will be strongly affected by such errors.

And how would I tutor the hypothetical student who presented me with such a paragraph? If we decided to focus on sentence-level errors, I'd try to get a larger sample of writing, to find more patterns. I'd ask the student to proofread the paragraph and then show me the revised version so that I could see what she corrected on her own. I'd ask her to read the paragraph aloud to me, to find out what she'd recognize as an error and what she'd silently correct. (If she silently corrected anything, I'd then focus on whether she could see the difference between what she said and what she wrote.) And in case the paragraph is a fluke, I'd ask the student more about her topic; after she'd thought about it some more, or possibly changed to a topic that interested her more, I'd ask her to write another paragraph, to find out if she continued committing so many errors. In any case, I'd hesitate to plunge in and start working on individual errors in such a small sample, without more context.

B   Answers to Exercises

Chapter 3

Exercise: Paragraph Organization (Pauline Meehan, p. 43)

Sentences 3 and 5 are unnecessary. The order of the rest is 4, 7, 2, 1, 8, 6. The exercise is based on a paragraph in Paul Roberts' *Understanding English*, reprinted in John C. Hodges and Mary E. Whitten's *Harbrace College Handbook,* 8th ed. (New York: Harcourt Brace Jovanovich, 1977), p. 327.

Exercise: Introductory Paragraphs (Nancy Solaas, pp. 43–44)

Although this exercise allows for flexibility as you write your introductory paragraphs, there are certain pieces of information that you probably should not include.

I: 3, 5, and 7 should not be included. They are either too specific or, in the case of 5 and 7, unrelated to the history of music. 3 is too specific because it mentions a particular composer—though you could refer to the Impressionistic period in your introduction.

II: 3 and 4 should probably not be included, as they are topics that fit under 5. You will probably want to save them for the body of your paper. Item 6 could fit under 5 too.

Chapter 4

Exercise: Spelling (M. F. Withum, p. 63)

1. absence
2. conscience
3. criticized (American spelling)
4. desperate
5. eligible, excellent, exercise
6. government
7. Grammar
8. hierarchy
9. instructor, grievances
10. license, laboratory

11. leisure, mortgage
12. neighbor, neither, noticeable
13. pneumonia
14. professor, privileged
15. questionnaire, rehearsal
16. restaurant, separate
17. schedule
18. Tuesday, Wednesday

Exercise: Spelling: I-before-E (p. 64)

The following words need to be corrected:

shriek
weird
receipt
chandelier
ceiling

Neither
height
seized
field

C   Comments on Sample Essays

Chapter 6

1. Aliosha and Miranda (pp. 94–97)

The student who wrote this paper could be commended for including excellent detail, for incorporating quotations well, for coming up with some good insights (such as Miranda's hating dolls because her grandmother treats her like one), for doing some good freewriting preliminary to writing a well-structured paper. But her major problem is inappropriate structure—she has relied on the structure in her sources (she retells the stories) instead of developing a structure suitable for her analysis, suitable for comparison and contrast.

> Obviously, the assignment was a comparison and contrast paper on the two stories. The author wasted much of the paper by relating a summary of both stories. . . . The most important thing to do is to make some concrete comparisons and contrasts between the stories and illustrate these with quotes and examples. The details of the story will come out through this anyway. The author here doesn't really make her comparisons until the last paragraph, and here she mainly states her basic ideas, forcing the reader to do most of the thinking. . . . She would have done better if she had devoted most of the paper to the comparisons instead of the summaries. (Cathy Halgas)

As Cathy indicates, the author expects too much of the reader, assuming that he'll make connections that she has only implied. At the same time, paradoxically, the author expects too little, assuming that the reader needs a plot summary. Possibly the writer doesn't have a good sense of who her reader is—and perhaps she could be encouraged to think of her reader as her teacher plus her classmates, people who are familiar with the stories and therefore don't need to hear the plot, but who want to know her analysis of the stories.

Another tutor, recognizing that the paper includes too much plot recall, suggests a strategy for starting to solve the problem.

> I think I would tell this student to do a little brainstorming—maybe have her . . . write down a list of similarities and differences between the two stories—the characters, theme, setting, etc. I would also, after she had done this, [ask her to] start relating her points—seeing if there were any connections, strong contrasts, etc. (Laura Guadagno)

Once the student has developed such a list, she might work on treeing her ideas, developing a structure that looks more like the second tree shown here and less like the first.

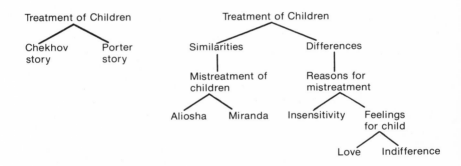

Then, once the student worked on restructuring the paper, she could work on remaining problems, such as transitions.

> I think this restructuring and paring down of the paper would make the argument much clearer and stronger but would also help eliminate some of the other errors. . . . If the ideas in the essay were made more obvious and if the structure of the paper were turned into a means to point out the connections of these ideas, I think the need for transitions may become more obvious. And with much of the extraneous material gone, the author may find it easier to put her sentences together with more style. (Terry Wood)

As Terry implies, the author has used rather short, repetitive, choppy sentences. Once she has worked out how to structure her paper, she might practice some sentence combining. She might also be sure to check spelling (e.g., "acquaintance," "confectionery," "interrupted," "presence," "fascinated," "buried," "burial"), punctuation, tense, and pronoun reference.

2. Take-Home Exam (pp. 97–99)

The first issue to address, in tutoring the student who wrote this essay, is the nature of take-home exams—and whether a student should receive tutoring help when working on one. Because different instructors have different expectations, you should, if the student is writing for someone else, find out from the instructor whether it's okay to tutor on this exam. Instructors who see a take-home as a paper with a controlled topic may consider tutoring permissible. Instructors who see it as more like an in-class exam may not. So first you need to decide whether you can in fact tutor the student.

It may also be useful to consider other aspects of take-home exams: the student may not know exactly what one is and how to take it. This essay may look more like a timed, in-class essay than an untimed one written outside class. And, in fact, the student may have felt that she had to write the take-home the way she would an in-class essay—not reviewing readings and notes once she received the question, timing herself so that she didn't spend more than an hour planning and writing the essay. If the instructor stipulated that she follow that approach—fine. But otherwise you might want to assure the student that, unless otherwise instructed, she can indeed look at her books and notes and should take the time to do so and to proofread.

Then you might turn to the essay itself. It incorporates some useful sociological insights that were probably covered in the course. But it has both overall and sentence-level weaknesses.

> The main problem with the take-home exam we had to evaluate was organization. The question was "What do you feel is the single gravest problem facing American cities today?" The student went on to list about four or five problems faced by cities, not one as specified. Although she did put a few of these under the general heading of "economics," the ideas were still disjointed, spread at various points throughout the paper. I could pick out her thoughts on the "grave problems facing cities today" but it took some time. She needed to group her ideas, organize them, rather than put them down as they came into her head (in *thirteen* paragraphs!).
>
> Another one of her big problems was simply that she didn't answer

the questions. As I mentioned before, she listed general problems, not just one as specified ("the *single* gravest problem"). In addition, I don't think she even addressed the questions of why she picked that problem and how she would proceed to deal with it (the exam called for an outline of steps). She basically just listed issues which she thought caused problems in cities in a very incoherent, unorganized fashion (which I can't understand because it was a take-home, not an in-class essay).

Besides organization and not addressing the questions correctly, the writer seems to have thrown in certain paragraphs, certain points that are out of place and probably have nothing to do with the question anyway. For example, the passages about money being the root of all evil and about why people live in cities. Furthermore, the paragraph stuck right in the middle of the paper stating that "This paper will attempt to touch on some of the other problems of the city, but looking closely at these you can see that the main problem relates to economics"—if she thought the main problem was economics and that all others stem from this, why didn't she say so in the first place?

Other minor, yet important problems:

1. spelling (government, relieve, etc.)
2. grammar
3. redundancy ("*just mere* symptoms")
4. transition (she jumps from economics to "When one thinks of poverty . . .")

My first steps in attacking this paper would be for her to tell me exactly what she thinks the gravest problem is, why, and how she would deal with it. We'd have to organize her ideas into a clear, cohesive, smooth-flowing essay. Then I'd tackle the spelling, grammar, and transition problems.

I think it would take quite awhile. (Leslie Aubin)

I would generally agree with Leslie's priorities: content and organization should take precedence over sentence-level errors like spelling and grammar. For one thing, once the student revises the essay to improve the content and organization, expanding on ideas and increasing specificity, she probably wouldn't have the same sentence-level problems.

On the other hand, the more I examine the essay, the more I find hints of what at first seemed missing in the student's response to the question—and she could solve some of her problems by expressing connections and significance more clearly. There may be some less-than-global fixing that she could do, such as improving transitions, that would improve the paper immensely. For instance, she does make some attempt at the end to discuss solutions: taxes, government regulation. But she could stress that these are in fact possible solutions and develop their implications more.

Or look at the paragraph beginning with "Automobiles, factories, powerplants and other sources pollute city air." If I stop to think, I may figure out that she's augmenting her previous references to pollution: the preceding paragraph indicates that physical problems include not just the substandard housing discussed in that paragraph but also pollution. Yet she could have helped me to recognize this connection immediately if she had begun with "Another physical problem is pollution."

Still another source of confusion appears in the second paragraph, where she notes how difficult it is "to single out economics as a main cause." The phrasing leads me to think she's dismissing economics and will focus on a different problem. Not until the fifth paragraph ("This paper will attempt . . .") do I realize that she is, in fact, focusing on economics. Thus in the second paragraph she was simply trying to acknowledge the difficulty of singling out any one cause, trying to acknowledge the complex interrelationships of the issues she's addressing, not dismissing economics as the central problem. I'd have found the paper much easier to follow if she'd replaced the second sentence of the paragraph with something like this: "It's true that it's difficult to single out the gravest problem, because there are so many problems and they are so complexly related. But economics is a central issue that has a wide-ranging impact."

Then, given my sense that seemingly unrelated paragraphs can potentially be related, I start to wonder if paragraphs that have struck me as irrelevant—such as the one on business slumps—could in fact be related. Maybe even the fourth paragraph, the one on money as the root of evil. But I doubt it. This paragraph seems to derive from another mode of discourse altogether, one that relies on the proverbial sayings of an oral culture. And building arguments from proverbs usually doesn't work in an academic essay.

As for sentence-level problems, Leslie does a good job of pointing to some of these. I might flesh out the "etc." in her list of spelling errors by adding "crises" and "receive." I might also point to a problem with apostrophes: "the cities biggest problem" and "todays cities." Some might point as well to a failure to include commas after the penultimate items in series, but I wouldn't consider that an error. I would, however, be concerned about imprecise diction: e.g., in what sense does poverty *"cause* a person's unwillingness or inability to work"; do overcrowded dwellings really *"consist of* a city's housing"; are social problems, precisely speaking, "inabilities"? But I'd delay attention to these sentence-level problems until others were solved. In fact, once the student had a better grasp of her topic, her awkward wording might disappear by itself.

Thus, the student might benefit from further thinking about the topic, the question, the interrelationships of parts. She might find it easier to convey the complexity of the topic if she took more of a stand. She could specify more what she means by the broad topic of "economics." And she might flesh out the short paragraphs by brainstorming for details and incorporating more of the specifics that were undoubtedly mentioned in class readings.

How would one tutor the student? Laura Guadagno would proceed as follows:

> I would suggest and stress the need to read over the professor's question several times. . . . I would then have her make a list of what the professor wants in the essay with the use of key words such as
>
> 1. single gravest problem in America
> 2. why?
> 3. how proceed to deal
>
> and then help her to discover how to synthesize the information she has studied in a loose organizational scheme that will adequately answer the question raised by the professor. I might also tell her that not only do essay exams . . . test a student's knowledge of the facts but also more importantly her ability to organize and present coherently an essay which will reflect her . . . interpretation and understanding of the material. . . .

I'd also ask questions to prod the student's thinking. What's the gravest problem facing cities? How can you make sure that I see that that's the gravest problem? How are these ideas related? How can you make sure that I see that that's how they're related? Can you think of an example?

3. In-Class Paragraph (p. 99)

First of all, how does one get to tutor a student on an in-class assignment? Let's assume that the student has not walked out of class to confer with you but is discussing the paragraph with you after her teacher (who may also be you) has seen it.

Then what? The author of this paragraph has managed to include all of the requisite items, but she has not done a good job of connecting them, of exploring their relationships. She simply devotes a sentence or two to each item, in the order given in the assignment, as if they comprised a laundry list.

> The student has included a lot of details in her essay, although she has failed to structure her essay in a logical, coherent way. Instead, poor use of tense and of punctuation gives the appearance that the student simply wrote down every fact that she knew about Elinor and Marianne's society and did not proofread her essay or . . . work on connecting those facts in an organized way that would best answer the question. I think that I would try to help this student by having her practice spending a few minutes . . . jotting down main ideas first and coming up with a loose organizational scheme. Her content is very good but the need for the student to analyze and set up preparation strategies is evident. (Laura Guadagno)

The student needed to think more, for instance, about how inheritance relates to marriage, instead of just tacking on several sentences on inheritance at the end.

Terry Wood similarly comments on the student's problems with organization and coherence.

> In reading paper number 3, in-class paragraph, I thought that the essay was written either by a student who had not anticipated that particular essay question or who hadn't had time enough to think about an answer or who hadn't studied much for the exam. I say this because the essay is full of ideas but they are not connected to the essay's topic sentence—"The society in which Elinor and Marianne lived consisted of many social rules." The writer of the essay points out some of the things about which there were clear rules to follow such as dating, marriage, and divorce. But she doesn't clearly point out, in all cases, what those rules are, and she never points out how these rules affected Elinor and Marianne. . . . Doing this would have alleviated a lot of the vague generalizations in the essay—e.g.,

> "Marriage was thought of as bringing together two houses"—and would have added richness, detail to the essay. It also would have better shown that the student had truly read the work and was not simply relating what she remembered from class discussion.
>
> . . . The writer would [likewise] need to include clear transitions between ideas, transitions which are now missing between the sentences in the essay.
>
> Also, . . . there are a number of spelling and grammatical errors, but I'm somewhat hesitant to point them out. These sorts of errors are easily made when writing an in-class essay and are somewhat unavoidable. In reading over some of my essay exams, I have seen an embarrassingly high number of careless spelling and even grammatical errors. In the rush of getting the ideas on paper in the allotted time, it's easy to become lax about sentence-level errors, and it's understandable.

Terry is right about occasional lapses in spelling or grammar on exams, but a large number of such errors can be distracting to the grader. Kris Leary, recognizing the basic problem with organization and development, goes on to catalogue some of the errors.

> Beginning with the very first sentence, I find errors in usage: "The Society *in* which Elinor and Marianne lived *in* . . ." doesn't make sense and is repetitive because of the use of two "in"'s where one would suffice.
>
> The author switches from the past to the present tense just about every sentence. This is extremely difficult and confusing to read, and makes the author sound as if she's not very educated and doesn't make a habit of proofreading.
>
> The fourth sentence contains a comma splice. The rest of the essay consists of short, choppy sentences that can be incorporated into longer sentences that flow better. This would entail some reorganization.

I might add that the student incorrectly uses a comma in the first sentence, incorrectly capitalizes "Society," needs a different verb for the second half of the "Divorce" sentence, misspells "gentlem*a*n," "rit*u*al," and "considered." Some of these errors are probably due to carelessness—and thus, in working with this student on sentence-level errors, I'd want to see what she could correct on her own as she rereads the paragraph.

The student also has a problem with diction and syntax, making her sentences awkward and vague. In the first sentence, for instance, it's not quite right to say that society *consisted* of certain rules. It may be governed by them, it may enforce them, but it doesn't exactly consist of them. It's hard too to know whether some diction problems result from a hasty choice of words or from fuzzy thinking. For example, is the writer really discussing something as rigid as rules—or would it be better to call them conventions? (Dating—she means courtship—certainly is governed by conventions, while marriage is governed by both conventions and laws.) As Terry Wood has pointed out, more thinking about the connections among items might reduce vagueness. But the student may have other problems with the language as well—as indeed this student had, for English is her second language. Many instructors will try to be tolerant of errors by such students in timed writing. And thus, in tutoring this student, I'd focus first on thinking and planning, on organizing and developing, and only later on grammatical, syntactical, and usage errors.

4. Discussion of the Crito (pp. 100–101)

This essay is pretty good; the classics teacher for whom the student wrote thought highly of it. It's difficult to respond to all of the instructions in two or three pages, but this essay does answer the questions, with some sophistication: the student even comes up with a present-day situation that might have given Socrates a moment's pause. She also has a sound organizational scheme and expresses herself clearly. If she'd been writing for a philosophy course, she might have needed to address the validity of the arguments more explicitly. And the informality of her style might have been less acceptable. But her implicit argumentation and informal style were suitable for her classics teacher.

The main weaknesses of the essay are sentence-level problems. Possibly the student simply needs to proofread, to read the essay aloud, in order to catch the errors. Further tutoring then depends on her responses, whether she needs just a reminder or needs work on overcoming entrenched errors.

In any case, here is a listing of the kinds of errors and problems that I noticed, in no particular order.

- *Punctuation*
    Commas: E.g., a better way of punctuating the last sentence of the third paragraph would be "To break it would be wrong and

consequently evil, and everyone knows one must never do evil." The student frequently uses commas in ways that might be considered borderline wrong—e.g., after "But" and "So."

Apostrophes: Three times she omits an apostrophe when "Socrates" is possessive.

End marks: She omits the final period of the essay and uses a period once when she should use a question mark.

- *Pronouns*

It's sometimes unclear, in the first paragraph and elsewhere, whether "he" refers to Socrates or to Crito. The writer also uses a vague "this" at the beginning of the third paragraph. And she switches between "one" and "you" in the fourth paragraph.

- *Parallelism*

To eliminate faulty parallelism from the second sentence she could write, "He came with the purpose of talking [or "He came to talk"] Socrates into escaping from Athens and avoiding the death sentence" or "He came with the purpose of talking Socrates into escaping from Athens to avoid the death sentence."

- *Spelling/Spacing*

"wherever" "enacted"

- *Diction/Phrasing*

"Jibe" might be considered a little informal.

"Could say nothing to argue it" (final paragraph) would be clearer if it read "could say nothing against it" or "could find no argument to refute him."

At the end of the first paragraph, I'd change "in convicting" to "to convict," "is right" to "would be right," and "in escaping" to "to escape."

- *Other*

The student could work on transitions between sentences, to improve flow and make it easier to see connections. For instance, I'd like to see a better transition between the second and third sentences of the third paragraph. Or perhaps the third sentence could be incorporated into the second as a subordinate clause ("since one has the right to live wherever one wants"). Similarly, I'd like to see the student clarify the connection between the two sentences in her conclusion.

There's a "seemed" in the middle of the fourth paragraph that I'd change to "seems."

I choose to consider "Either that or leave the state altogether" an appropriate fragment. For one thing, it's part of the invented dialogue, and certain kinds of fragments can make writing look colloquial.

Some people might also criticize the student's lack of documentation. Ideally, she would indeed include a footnote indicating the exact reference for her quotation in the third paragraph. But, assuming that she's using the edition that the class is using, and given that she indicates that the quotation is from the beginning of the *Crito*, her crime is not heinous.

In tutoring this student, I'd praise her for her analysis and presentation. Then I'd ask how she revises and proofreads—whether, for instance, she has tried reading the essay aloud. And if some errors seemed to be entrenched, such as those with commas or apostrophes, we'd go over some rules.

5. In-Class Essay (p. 101)

As with essay 3, let's assume that it's appropriate for the student to talk with you about this essay—that she hasn't walked out of an exam to take it to you. Then we can gauge the fundamental weakness of the essay: it's not mechanics or usage or organization (although those are weak) but thinking. The student needs to think more about her topic, to generate more ideas and scrutinize their connections.

In the first place, her answer to the question is a bit off target. What exactly is she describing that is typically American? Perhaps teen culture—but she never directly says that, and not everything that she discusses relates directly to teen culture. Instead, she seems to have invented her own question, something like "Discuss how something typically American differs from its counterpart in other countries."

But even if we grant her the topic that she seems to have chosen, her paper has problems. She claims, for instance, that American teens differ from teens elsewhere more than American adults differ from other adults. But does she support that claim? She talks, for instance, about American teens having greater access to cars. But, if that's the case, don't American adults have more access too? Is she perhaps getting at the issue of standard of living, an issue that affects both teenagers and adults?

Thus the writer first needs help in figuring out the question and finding a topic to focus on. She could write about teen culture, or perhaps family life and the frequency of broken homes. Then she could think of causes and implications, in order to write a cause-effect paper. Or she could think of descriptive details, in order to write a descriptive paper. I'd urge her to come up with specific examples and to avoid overgeneralizing: for instance, does she mean to imply that all American teenagers come from broken homes? And then I'd work on organizing whatever she came up with, rather than fiddling with the current paper.

Similarly, instead of working on sentence-level errors in the current paper, I'd wait to see the revision—though I'd mentally note the kinds of errors in the current paper (e.g., spelling, run-on sentence, punctuation, word choice) to see if they recur. And if they do, if they appear to be entrenched errors, I would eventually work on them.

6. Cheryl and I (pp. 102–3)

This essay is quite good—it is clearly organized and makes excellent use of detail. Most striking is its humor; the student is unusually skilled at sustaining a colloquial tone.

She could sustain the humor and colloquialism better, though. For one thing, some of the earlier humorous details are so good that the conclusion is a bit of a letdown. I don't quite see the point—or humor?—of setting goals if there are some that one wouldn't want to attain anyway. Perhaps she could also come up with a witty phrase or anecdote that would give the ending more punch.

She might work on transitions between sentences too. It's true that sometimes abruptness of transition may contribute to humor, as with the second sentence of the second paragraph ("My mother, by the way . . . "). But I think the paragraph would be easier to read and the humor just as effective if she put the sentence in parentheses. On the other hand, the digression in the third paragraph— the sentences that stray to thin adolescents and college eating habits—strikes me as less effective: it's harder to rationalize it as humorous abruptness or a colloquial aside. I'd like the writer either to find a better way of integrating these sentences or to eliminate them.

In general, the writer's weaknesses are a matter of polish. Sometimes she works too hard to underscore her conversational tone. She uses frequent underlining, for instance, but she doesn't need to. In almost all cases she could omit the underlining and still achieve the emphasis she wants. One can usually achieve emphasis through means other than underlining, such as positioning emphatic words in emphatic places in sentences, and the author is in fact skilled in crafting sentences for emphasis, without having to rely on italics.

She shows a similar uncertainty when she puts words like "stopped by" and "with child" and "rigged" in quotation marks. She seems to sense that these words are informal—but such informality is appropriate in an informal, conversational essay like hers, and the words are not out of place. They don't need quotation marks.

The author's sophistication in punctuating also hasn't quite kept pace with her sophistication in creating a conversational tone. In several places her tone would be well served by dashes: e.g., "Some of these goals—her weight, for example—I don't feel would be healthy—torturous, in fact—for me to try to attain," and "My awareness of Ms. Tiegs—we're not on a first name basis yet—intensified when I discovered that she was . . . ."

The author could also work on other aspects of punctuation. She should not, for instance, hyphenate her designations of feet and inches. She also needs to omit the comma in "I have always known of women, who were exceedingly thin as adolescents" (she needs a restrictive clause) and in the first sentence of the next paragraph; purists would also omit the comma after "nurse" in the second paragraph.

Other errors include spelling or typographical errors that she might be able to eliminate with more careful proofreading: twice she uses "women" instead of "woman"; she misspells "discrepancy," "fluctuating," and "exceedingly." She also occasionally misuses a pronoun: a vague "this," an appropriate "myself."

In addition, she could polish diction and phrasing. For instance, in her second sentence she could write, "Now when I say, 'came into my life,' I don't mean . . . ." Then, in the fourth sentence, does she mean several goals or one goal in particular? I'm also not convinced that "the cut of my jib, a sailing term" is fully effective. In the second paragraph, Katharine Hepburn might more accurately be said to represent rather than symbolize, and "as well as" should be something like "as did." Two sentences later she could omit the weak "in many aspects of life." In the last sentence of this paragraph she could omit "serves to." In the fourth sentence of the next paragraph she could omit "always," and in the seventh sentence I wonder if she means "height" instead of "age." In the last paragraph she could write, "Having a famous model approximately the same height as me has made my life . . ." (the "me" is not, strictly speaking, correct, but appropriate perhaps in conversational writing).

Finally, there are "errors" that seem acceptable in such a colloquial piece: two split infinitives and a misplaced "only."

In tutoring this student I would be enthusiastic about her skill in writing humorously and suggest that she might do some polishing to improve the humor. I'd also want to see how many errors she could correct if she proofread more carefully, perhaps by reading the essay aloud.

7. Application for a Legal Internship (pp. 103–4)

The student presents her background clearly, making effective use of headings, which are appropriate for this kind of writing. She also includes some effective details. But she could address her audience better and she could correct a few errors.

To see how she could address her audience better, compare the first paragraph of the application with the second paragraph under "Practical Experience." In the latter, she translates the skills she developed while working in the library into a quality that her prospective employer would appreciate: accuracy. What she has done here is far more effective than simply listing her experiences: she has presented her experiences so that her reader will immediately see how they relate to the internship.

Now look at the first paragraph. Here she stresses what a rare opportunity the internship would be, how much she would get out of it—not how much she could do for her employer. She fails to translate her interest into terms that the reader would immediately appreciate. Here and elsewhere in the application she could change the stress from what she herself would like to do to what she could do for the employer, and from what she has done to how her experiences would be valuable to her employer.

A similar principle applies—a similar insensitivity to the reader occurs—in the last two sentences of the section headed "Qualities and Skills." The last sentence is inappropriately telling the reader something that he already knows—the writer is preaching to him. The preceding sentence is more effective because it begins with "I also realize . . . ." Thus the writer is stating that she recognizes the value of dependability, instead of scolding the reader to follow through on promises. The "I also realize" makes a big difference. And, in fact, since the last sentence in the paragraph is effectively reiterating the preceding one, the writer could simply omit the last sentence.

Sometimes too she could better accommodate her reader by including more detail. Under "Academic Studies," for instance, she mentions the need to understand the legal principles of cases. She could make her statement more memorable if she gave an example—especially if the example related to a specialty of the firm to which she is applying.

She could also correct some errors. Twice in the first paragraph she uses relative clauses that do not immediately follow the words they modify (e.g., she could write, "experience that will be beneficial in the future"). In the same paragraph she uses faulty parallelism (she could write, "training in and exposure to"). She should capitalize the names of all the courses she mentions; some handbooks even advocate putting course titles in quotation marks. She could find a better word than "covered" in the first sentence under "Practical Experience." She could use a semicolon after "on order" in the next paragraph. She should correct "you better" to "you'd better" in the paragraph after that (if in fact she retained the sentence).

Selected Bibliography

This selected bibliography lists both works about writing and works about tutoring that I have found to be helpful. I have not included works that deal solely with the training of tutors.

A Bare-Essentials Reference Shelf

Bruffee, Kenneth A. *A Short Course in Writing: Practical Rhetoric for Composition Courses, Writing Workshops, and Tutor Training Programs.* 2d ed. Cambridge, Mass.: Winthrop, 1980.
    Bruffee's rhetoric not only includes sections on personal, argumentative, and research writing but also provides sample student essays. Most importantly, though, it discusses collaborative learning, including ways of using this approach in a course for peer tutors.
Chicago Manual of Style. 13th ed. Chicago: University of Chicago Press, 1982.
    This standard reference work provides information on a number of formats for documentation, plus information on mechanics and the publishing process.
Ehrlich, Eugene. *Punctuation, Capitalization, and Spelling.* Schaum's Outline Series. New York: McGraw-Hill, 1977.
    This workbook is one of many that provide lots of practice (much more than handbooks do) with, in this case, the mechanics of punctuation, capitalization, and spelling. The answers are at the back.
Elbow, Peter. *Writing with Power: Techniques for Mastering the Writing Process.* Oxford: Oxford University Press, 1981.
    Elbow, who has previously extolled the concept of freewriting, in *Writing Without Teachers* (London: Oxford University Press, 1973), here provides a gold mine of ideas for improving one's writing, including strategies for drafting and revising, for sharing writing with others, and for finding power and voice.
Epes, Mary; Kirkpatrick, Carolyn; and Southwell, Michael G. *The COMP-LAB Exercises: Self-Teaching Exercises for Basic Writing.* Englewood Cliffs, N.J.: Prentice-Hall, 1980.
    This workbook for basic writers includes not just fill-in-the-blank exercises but frequent work with complete units of discourse, such as paragraphs that need rewriting; such work bridges the gap between

211

most workbook exercises and a student's own writing. The exercises deal primarily with word endings, verb forms, and sentence construction.

Flower, Linda. *Problem-Solving Strategies for Writing.* 2d ed. New York: Harcourt Brace Jovanovich, 1985.

Drawing upon current research in writing, including her own, Flower suggests strategies for planning, generating ideas, organizing them, designing for a reader, revising, and editing. Most of her examples entail writing for the workplace.

Fowler, H. W. *A Dictionary of Modern English Usage.* 2d ed. Revised by Sir Ernest Gowers. New York: Oxford University Press, 1965.

Fowler's is the standard guide to usage, precision, clarity—arranged alphabetically. It provides British usage, however. You could also obtain an Americanized Fowler, such as Margaret Nicholson's *A Dictionary of American-English Usage: Based on Fowler's Modern English Usage* (New York: New American Library, 1956).

Gibaldi, Joseph, and Achtert, Walter S. *MLA Handbook for Writers of Research Papers.* 2d ed. New York: Modern Language Association, 1984.

This volume is a standard reference work on how to format footnotes and bibliographies, especially for papers in the humanities. It also includes some information on writing research papers, on mechanics, and on general formatting. The latest edition suggests a simplified approach to documenting sources, closer to what has been standard in the sciences.

Lanham, Richard A. *Revising Prose.* New York: Scribner, 1979.

Lanham's is a good book on style—on how to eliminate the turgidity of, for instance, what he calls "The Official Style" and "The School Style."

Mack, Karin, and Skjei, Eric. *Overcoming Writing Blocks.* Los Angeles: Tarcher, 1979.

Mack and Skjei provide a treasure trove of ideas for starting and continuing to write, from managing one's environment to programmed dawdling to constructive plagiarism (imitation) to creative juggling of several projects at once.

Maimon, Elaine P.; Belcher, Gerald L.; Hearn, Gail W.; Nodine, Barbara F.; and O'Connor, Finbarr W. *Writing in the Arts and Sciences.* Boston: Little, Brown, 1981.

This text not only provides useful information contained in many rhetorics (e.g., on prewriting, on library research) but is an excellent guide to the kinds of writing required throughout the curriculum.

Oliu, Walter E.; Brusaw, Charles T.; and Alred, Gerald J. *Writing That Works: How to Write Effectively on the Job.* 2d ed. New York: St. Martin, 1984.

In addition to prewriting, writing, and rewriting, this rhetoric gives good coverage of such practical matters as writing formal and informal reports, writing business correspondence, creating visual aids, making oral presentations. It also includes a brief handbook of rules.

Roget, Peter Mark; Roget, John Lewis; and Roget, Samuel Romilly. *Roget's Thesaurus of Synonyms and Antonyms*. New York: Galahad, 1972.

A thesaurus like this one can remind a writer of options when she's trying to find the right word. But it should be used with caution: some students use a thesaurus too much, aiming to impress their reader with inflated vocabulary over which they may have little control.

The Scribner-Bantam English Dictionary. Edited by Edwin B. Williams. New York: Scribner, 1977.

Other dictionaries would be fine, but it's probably a good idea to have a moderately large one like the *Scribner-Bantam*. Small paperback dictionaries often aren't complete enough. The *Scribner-Bantam* has the advantage of distinguishing among similar words and listing idioms (e.g., under "come": "come about," "come across," "come around," "come at," . . .).

Watkins, Floyd C., and Dillingham, William B. *Practical English Handbook*. 6th ed. Boston: Houghton Mifflin, 1982.

Other handbooks would do just as well. An advantage of this one, though, is that it is small and therefore perhaps less intimidating to students. A possible disadvantage is that the answers to exercises are only in an instructor's edition—and thus you need both a student edition and an instructor's edition if you are to work on exercises independently.

Other Useful Works about Writing

Theoretical and Empirical Works

Emig, Janet. *The Composing Processes of Twelfth Graders*. NCTE Research Report No. 13. Urbana, Ill.: National Council of Teachers of English, 1971.

Emig was one of the first to investigate writing as a process. The eight case studies in her monograph show the divergence of students' writing processes from the one implied in their product-oriented high-school instruction.

————."Writing as a Mode of Learning." *College Composition and Communication* 28 (1977): 122–28. Reprinted in *The Writing Teacher's Sourcebook*, edited by Gary Tate and Edward P. J. Corbett, pp. 69–78. New York: Oxford University Press, 1981.

Emig's is the classic essay on the value of writing—on how it reinforces or even constitutes learning.

Flower, Linda. "Writer-Based Prose: A Cognitive Basis for Problems in Writing." *College English* 41 (1979): 19–37. Reprinted in *The Writing Teacher's Sourcebook,* edited by Gary Tate and Edward P. J. Corbett, pp. 268–92. New York: Oxford University Press, 1981.

In this influential essay Flower distinguishes between writer- and reader-based prose: between prose that responds to the needs of the writer, reflecting the writer's process, and prose that responds to the needs of the reader, reflecting the writer's purpose. She discusses the uses of writer-based prose (e.g., for retrieving ideas or information) and how to transform it into reader-based prose.

Flower, Linda, and Hayes, John R. "The Cognition of Discovery: Defining a Rhetorical Problem." *College Composition and Communication* 31 (1980): 21–32.

This influential essay points out differences between the writing of novices and that of expert writers, including the extent to which expert writers develop a sense of audience.

Hirsch, E. D., Jr. *The Philosophy of Composition.* Chicago: University of Chicago Press, 1977.

This book by a well-known literary critic makes a case for relative readability as the benchmark for evaluating writing.

Hunt, Kellogg W. "A Synopsis of Clause-to-Sentence Length Factors." *English Journal* 54 (1955): 300, 305–9. Reprinted in *Rhetoric and Composition: A Sourcebook for Teachers,* edited by Richard L. Graves, pp. 110–17. Rochelle Park, N.J.: Hayden, 1976.

Hunt reports on an influential study of sentence maturity, a study that has been used to justify practice in sentence combining.

Kinneavy, James L. *A Theory of Discourse: The Aims of Discourse.* 1971. Reprint. New York: Norton, 1980.

In this pathbreaking scholarly tome, presumably a textbook, Kinneavy maps a typology for discourse, based on the communication triangle: reference discourse (reality), persuasive discourse (decoder), literary discourse (signal), expressive discourse (encoder). He discusses in detail the logic, organization, and style associated with each aim.

Kolln, Martha. "Closing the Books on Alchemy." *College Composition and Communication* 32 (1981): 139–51. Reprinted in *Rhetoric and Composition: A Sourcebook for Teachers and Writers,* edited by Richard L. Graves. 2d ed., pp. 292–303. Upper Montclair, N.J.: Boynton/Cook, 1984.

Responding to those who consider instruction in grammar ineffective in teaching writing and who would eliminate grammar from the curriculum, Kolln urges the value of grammar study—though she urges not so much memorizing rules and drilling as discussing choices in manipulating sentences.

Moffett, James. *Teaching the Universe of Discourse.* Boston: Houghton Mifflin, 1968.

Moffett has developed an influential typology of kinds and orders of discourse, including recording (what is happening), reporting (what happened), generalizing (what happens), and theorizing (what will happen). The typology suggests a sequence for teaching modes of discourse.

Perl, Sondra. "Understanding Composing." *College Composition and Communication* 31 (1980): 363–69. Reprinted in *Rhetoric and Composition: A Sourcebook for Teachers and Writers,* edited by Richard L. Graves. 2d ed., pp. 304–10. Upper Montclair, N.J.: Boynton/Cook, 1984.

Perl points out that the writing process is not linear, as traditional pedagogy implies, but recursive: writers constantly return to what they've already written and to their "felt sense" of the topic. Writers also engage in projective structuring, projecting the needs of the audience.

Rose, Mike. "Rigid Rules, Inflexible Plans, and the Stifling of Language: A Cognitivist Analysis of Writer's Block." *College Composition and Communication* 31 (1980): 389–401.

In this study of the writing processes of five effective and five blocked college students, Rose found that the blocked writers used rigid rules. The effective writers were more flexible.

Shaughnessy, Mina P. *Errors and Expectations: A Guide for the Teacher of Basic Writing.* New York: Oxford University Press, 1977.

In this pathbreaking book Shaughnessy categorizes difficulties in the work of basic writers—ranging from handwriting and punctuation to mediating between the abstract and the concrete—and discusses causes. Through examining how difficulties occur, she suggests ways of helping basic writers to improve.

Sommers, Nancy. "Revision Strategies of Student Writers and Experienced Adult Writers." *College Composition and Communication* 31 (1980): 378–88. Reprinted in *Rhetoric and Composition: A Sourcebook for Teachers and Writers,* edited by Richard L. Graves. 2d ed., pp. 328–37. Upper Montclair, N.J.: Boynton/Cook, 1984.

Sommers found that student writers are likely to consider revision merely a matter of tinkering with word choice. Experienced writers, however, are more willing to make global revisions, to reconceive the shape of their argument and the needs of the audience—to discover meaning.

Practical Works (Other than Rhetorics)

Adams, James L. *Conceptual Blockbusting: A Guide to Better Ideas.* 2d ed. New York: Norton, 1980.

Although not directly addressing the issue of writing, Adams provides a wealth of strategies and exercises for generating ideas. He focuses on overcoming perceptual, emotional, cultural, environmental, intellectual, and expressive blocks.

Christensen, Francis. "A Generative Rhetoric of the Sentence." In *Notes Toward a New Rhetoric,* 2d ed., edited by Bonniejean Christensen, pp. 23–44. New York: Harper and Row, 1978. Reprinted in *The Writing Teacher's Sourcebook,* edited by Gary Tate and Edward P. J. Corbett, pp. 353–67. New York: Oxford University Press, 1981.

Claiming that the modern English sentence is essentially cumulative (additive) rather than periodic, Christensen suggests an approach to teaching such sentences. He illustrates what he means by diagraming the levels of generality of sample sentences.

Cooper, Charles R. "An Outline for Writing Sentence-Combining Problems." *English Journal* 62 (1973): 96–102, 108. Reprinted in *Rhetoric and Composition: A Sourcebook for Teachers,* edited by Richard L. Graves, pp. 118–28. Rochelle Park, N.J.: Hayden, 1976. Reprinted in *The Writing Teacher's Sourcebook,* edited by Gary Tate and Edward P. J. Corbett, pp. 368–78. New York: Oxford University Press, 1981.

After discussing the justifications for sentence combining, Cooper provides an outline for a sequence of sentence-combining exercises.

Daiker, Donald A.; Kerek, Andrew; and Morenberg, Max. *The Writer's Options: Combining to Composing.* 2d ed. New York: Harper and Row, 1982.

Daiker and his coauthors offer lots of sentence-combining practice, including both controlled (e.g., prescribing a relative clause) and free. They also discuss how to judge sentences and develop paragraphs.

D'Eloia, Sarah. "The Uses—and Limits—of Grammar." *Journal of Basic Writing* 1 (1977): 1–20. Reprinted in *The Writing Teacher's Sourcebook,* edited by Gary Tate and Edward P. J. Corbett, pp. 225–43. New York: Oxford University Press, 1981.

D'Eloia discusses how to teach grammatical correctness to basic writers: she describes exercises that integrate grammar study and writing and also describes how to sequence instruction.

Dworsky, Nancy. "Appendix II: Writing as an Agon or How to Write an A Exam with a C's Worth of Knowledge." In *Free Writing! A Group Approach: Toward a New and Simple Method of Learning and Teaching Writing,* by Joseph Brown, Jean Colburn, Patricia Cumming, Nancy Dworsky, Peter Elbow, Sandy Kaye, Seth Racusen, Robert Rathbone, Steve Reuys, Lee Rudolph, Stewart Andrew Silling, Ken Skier, Gary Woods, and David Wray, pp. 176–82. Rochelle Park, N.J.: Hayden, 1977.

Dworsky's essay is a tongue-in-cheek (but disconcertingly insightful) discussion of how to outfox teachers on essay exams. It can spark heated discussion.

Eastman, Arthur M.; Blake, Caesar R.; English, Hubert M., Jr.; Hartman, Joan E.; Howes, Alan B.; Lenaghan, Robert T.; McNamara, Leo F.; and Rosier, James, eds. *The Norton Reader.* 6th ed. New York: Norton, 1984.

The Norton Reader is one of many anthologies of writing by professional writers. Students may benefit from reading model essays; you can also develop exercises keyed to passages in the reader.

Flower, Linda S., and Hayes, John R. "Problem-Solving Strategies and the Writing Process." *College English* 39 (1977): 449–61. Reprinted in *Rhetoric and Composition: A Sourcebook for Teachers and Writers,* edited by Richard L. Graves. 2d ed., pp. 269–82. Upper Montclair, N.J.: Boynton/Cook, 1984.

After explaining their problem-solving approach, Flower and Hayes suggest strategies for generating ideas, organizing them, and adapting to the needs of the reader: e.g., staging a scenario, nutshelling ideas, treeing them.

Foster, David. *A Primer for Writing Teachers: Theories, Theorists, Issues, Problems.* Upper Montclair, N.J.: Boynton/Cook, 1983.

In this primer Foster provides important background for writing teachers: on theories of discourse, language difference, testing, basic approaches to teaching a writing course. The book tends to be more theoretical than practical, and Foster frequently takes sides in the controversies he discusses.

Lindemann, Erika. *A Rhetoric for Writing Teachers.* New York: Oxford University Press, 1982.

Lindemann also provides useful background for beginning teachers: on prewriting, writing, rewriting, making assignments, designing courses. She summarizes recent research and theory in rhetoric, cognition, linguistics.

Paulston, Christina Bratt, and Bruder, Mary Newton. *Teaching English as a Second Language: Techniques and Procedures.* Cambridge, Mass.: Winthrop, 1976.

Paulston and Bruder offer a cornucopia of techniques for teaching English as a second language. They discuss speaking, listening, reading, and writing skills, and they devote additional chapters to grammar and pronunciation.

Podis, Leonard A. "Teaching Arrangement: Defining a More Practical Approach." *College Composition and Communication* 31 (1980): 197–204.

Podis explores ways of teaching organizational arrangement to students—making sure that the organization highlights the thesis, that likes are grouped with likes, and that the progression advances the thesis. He also outlines several patterns that students may find practical, unlike many patterns traditionally suggested in rhetorics.

Troyka, Lynn Quitman. *Structured Reading.* Englewood Cliffs, N.J.: Prentice-Hall, 1978.

If a student has trouble understanding any written material he's supposed to be writing about, Troyka's book may be useful. It offers advice on how to read, including SQ3R (Survey, Question, Read, Recite, Review), and also provides practice readings and exercises.

Rhetorics

The following is just a sampling of the many rhetoric texts that may be useful for your students (see also the books by Bruffee, Elbow, Flower, Maimon, and Oliu in the first section of the bibliography). Those included here generally offer a process approach to writing.

Berthoff, Ann E. *Forming/Thinking/Writing: The Composing Imagination.*
Montclair, N.J.: Boynton/Cook, 1982.
Berthoff draws frequently on philosophy in her organic approach to
writing. She stresses that writing is composing—the making of
meaning.

Brannon, Lil; Knight, Melinda; and Neverow-Turk, Vara. *Writers Writing.*
Montclair, N.J.: Boynton/Cook, 1982.
Brannon and her coauthors reinforce their focus on process by providing multiple drafts written by students and professionals. They discuss how writers discover by writing and how to get and use others'
perspectives on a draft. Most of the examples are of personal or creative writing.

Dawe, Charles W., and Dornan, Edward A. *One to One: Resources for Conference-Centered Writing.* 2d ed. Boston: Little, Brown, 1984.
After outlining the process of writing, Dawe and Dornan provide a
series of assignments through which students can work on their own,
in frequent consultation with a teacher or tutor. The assignments
generally call for personal experience. The text also includes a discussion of keeping a journal and a reference section for editing skills.

Hall, Donald. *Writing Well.* 3d ed. Boston: Little, Brown, 1979.
This rhetoric offers something for everyone: a section on the writing
process, a section on the units of writing (words, sentences, paragraphs), a section on modes of writing (e.g., exposition, narration,
criticism, research), and a handbook section. The chapter on words is
particularly useful.

Hashimoto, Irvin Y.; Kroll, Barry M.; and Shafer, John C. *Strategies for
Academic Writing: A Guide for College Students.* Ann Arbor: University of Michigan Press, 1982.
This text presents a sequence of examples and exercises for deciding
on an initial plan, developing and arranging, introducing and concluding, and making an expository essay coherent. The chapter on
arrangement is especially helpful.

Irmscher, William F. *The Holt Guide to English.* 3d ed. New York: Holt,
Rinehart and Winston, 1981.
Irmscher's potpourri includes discussions of audience, invention,
order and logic, paragraphs, sentences, words, style, revising, proofreading, writing on literary topics, writing reference papers, writing
business letters, the history and structure of English. In chapter 3 he
explains the pentad, a way of generating ideas—the technique is
based on work by Kenneth Burke.

Lauer, Janice M.; Montague, Gene; Lunsford, Andrea; and Emig, Janet.
Four Worlds of Writing. New York: Harper and Row, 1981.
Lauer and her coauthors coach the student through the process of
writing eight papers in four realms: self-expression, persuasion, college exposition, working-world exposition. The book concludes with a
section devoted to editing and sentence combining.

McCrimmon, James M. *Writing with a Purpose*. 8th ed. Revised by Joseph F. Trimmer and Nancy I. Sommers. Boston: Houghton Mifflin, 1984.
This popular text now includes discussion of prewriting, writing, and rewriting; of paragraphs, sentences, diction, and tone; of such genres as the essay examination, the critical essay, the research paper, and the business letter; of grammar and usage.

Macrorie, Ken. *Telling Writing*. Rev. ed. Rochelle Park, N.J.: Hayden, 1976.
Anticipating Peter Elbow's ideas on freewriting and on sharing writing with others, Macrorie provides many ideas for freeing up one's writing. He generally encourages personal and creative writing.

Strenski, Ellen, and Manfred, Madge. *The Research Paper Workbook*. New York: Longman, 1981.
Strenski and Manfred do a fine job of leading the student through the process of writing a research paper, whether the student is using first-hand information or library sources, one source or many.

Van Nostrand, A. D.; Knoblauch, C. H.; and Pettigrew, Joan. *The Process of Writing: Discovery and Control*. 2d ed. Boston: Houghton Mifflin, 1982.
Van Nostrand and his coauthors discuss how to develop an organizing idea, find evidence for it, accommodate the reader, forecast in an introduction, make the statement coherent, develop a conclusion.

Young, Richard E.; Becker, Alton L.; and Pike, Kenneth L. *Rhetoric: Discovery and Change*. New York: Harcourt, Brace and World, 1970.
One of the earliest texts to teach writing as a process, *Rhetoric* is particularly noteworthy for its particle/wave/field scheme for structuring prewriting.

Other Useful Works about Tutoring and Teaching

Amigone, Grace Ritz. "Writing Lab Tutors: Hidden Messages That Matter." *Writing Center Journal* 2, no. 2 (1982): 24–29.
Amigone outlines important nonverbal cues that tutors should be conscious of, including eye contact, posture, gesture.

Arbur, Rosemarie. "The Student-Teacher Conference." *College Composition and Communication* 28 (1977): 338–42.
Drawing upon guidelines for social workers, Arbur outlines the elements of a successful student-teacher conference, including engagement, problem exploration, agreement to work together, task assignment.

Argyle, Michael. "Social Skills Theory." In *Children as Teachers: Theory and Research on Tutoring,* edited by Vernon L. Allen, pp. 57–73. New York: Academic Press, 1976.
Argyle discusses nonverbal communication in the context of social skills theory.

Arkin, Marian. *Tutoring ESL Students: A Guide for Tutors (and Teachers) in the Subject Areas*. New York: Longman, 1982.

This brief volume is meant to accompany Arkin and Shollar's *The Tutor Book*. It focuses on problems that ESL students (students for whom English is a second language) have in listening, speaking, reading, and writing. The book is not meant for tutors who specialize in ESL but for general tutors who occasionally have an ESL student.

Arkin, Marian, and Shollar, Barbara. *The Tutor Book*. New York: Longman, 1982.

In this handbook for tutors in all disciplines, Arkin and Shollar discuss the principles of tutoring and such issues as tutoring the handicapped, tutoring adults, and tutoring in multicultural settings. They also include illuminating essays by other writers.

————. *The Writing Tutor*. New York: Longman, 1982.

In this brief volume meant to accompany *The Tutor Book,* Arkin and Shollar run through strategies for prewriting, writing, rewriting, and perfecting mechanics.

Beaven, Mary H. "Individualized Goal Setting, Self-Evaluation, and Peer Evaluation." In *Evaluating Writing: Describing, Measuring, Judging,* edited by Charles R. Cooper and Lee Odell, pp. 135–56. [Urbana, Ill.]: National Council of Teachers of English, 1977.

Beaven discusses three ways in which teachers can respond to writing and foster individual growth. The first is to set goals based on the individual student's needs; the second, to involve the student in evaluation by asking him to respond to questions on his strengths and weaknesses; the third, to create peer editing groups that respond to questions about each member's writing.

Brannon, Lil. "On Becoming a More Effective Tutor." In *Tutoring Writing: A Sourcebook for Writing Labs,* edited by Muriel Harris, pp. 105–10. Glenview, Ill.: Scott, Foresman, 1982.

In an essay addressed more to trainers of tutors than to tutors, Brannon outlines the roles a tutor can play. She stresses being sensitive to tutees' perceptions and responses and also balancing sociability and direction.

Bruffee, Kenneth A. "The Brooklyn Plan: Attaining Intellectual Growth through Peer-Group Tutoring." *Liberal Education* 64 (1978): 447–68.

In addition to providing a theoretical framework for peer tutoring and explaining the pathbreaking program he has developed at Brooklyn College, Bruffee points out that peer tutors should be the social equals of their tutees, not authoritarian "'little teachers,' puppets of the academic regime."

Carnicelli, Thomas A. "The Writing Conference: A One-to-One Conversation." In *Eight Approaches to Teaching Composition,* edited by Timothy R. Donovan and Ben W. McClelland, pp. 101–31. Urbana, Ill.: National Council of Teachers of English, 1980.

In this fine overview of writing conferences, Carnicelli provides a rationale for the conference method and guidelines for the teacher's role. He also includes transcripts of a successful and a less successful conference.

Clark, Beverly Lyon, and Dollase, Richard. "Whose Tower Is It? Training Peer Tutors of Writing." Wisconsin Council of Teachers of English, Service Bulletin, forthcoming (1985).

In addition to outlining a course for training peer writing tutors, Clark and Dollase suggest a model for tutoring sessions.

Clark, Cheryl, and Sherwood, Phyllis A. "A Tutoring Dialogue: From Workshop to Session." *Writing Center Journal* 1, no. 2 (1981): 26–32.

Clark and Sherwood discuss the importance to tutors of knowing some principles of learning and of developing interpersonal skills and tutoring strategies.

Danish, Steven J., and Hauer, Allen L. *Helping Skills: A Basic Training Program.* 1973. Reprint. New York: Human Sciences, 1977.

In a workbook format, Danish and Hauer address issues relevant to any kind of counselor, issues such as understanding one's motivation for wanting to help others and using effective verbal and nonverbal behavior.

Duke, Charles R. "The Student-Centered Conference and the Writing Process." *English Journal* 64, no. 9 (1975): 44–47.

Duke discusses how to approach conferences with students. Particularly helpful is a discussion of techniques used by counselors and psychologists, including focusing, clarifying, and offering acceptance and reassurance.

Dukes, Thomas. "The Writing Lab as Crisis Center: Suggestions for the Interview." *Writing Lab Newsletter* 5, no. 9 (1981): 4–6.

Borrowing techniques used by Crisis Center personnel, Dukes urges the value of working through a tutee's negative feelings before focusing on his writing.

Elbow, Peter. "Embracing Contraries in the Teaching Process." *College English* 45 (1983): 327–39.

Elbow points to a conflict at the heart of teaching: commitment to knowledge and society versus commitment to students. He suggests that one way to balance the two is to alternate consciously between the roles of judge and helper, instead of just muddling along, half committed to both.

Fassler, Barbara. "The Red Pen Revisited: Teaching Composition Through Student Conferences." *College English* 40 (1978): 186–90.

Fassler advocates responding to student writing not with the traditional red pen but in conference. She also offers guidelines for conducting conferences.

Fisher, Lester A., and Murray, Donald M. "Perhaps the Professor Should Cut Class." *College English* 35 (1973): 169–73.

In describing a writing class in which students have weekly conferences with the teacher (instead of meeting together as a group),

Fisher and Murray suggest strategies for conducting conferences. The article also outlines the benefits of such conferences.

Garrison, Roger H. "One-to-One: Tutorial Instruction in Freshman Composition." *New Directions for Community Colleges* 2, no. 1 (1974): 55–84.

In this influential article Garrison advocates a workshop/tutorial approach to the teaching of composition: the teacher has brief conferences with individual students during class meetings. Such instruction can be individualized, can address the entire writing process, and can be self-paced.

Goldsby, Jackie. *Peer Tutoring in Basic Writing: A Tutor's Journal.* Classroom Research Study No. 4. Berkeley: University of California, Bay Area Writing Project, 1981.

Goldsby's monograph is the journal she kept during a semester as a peer tutor, a journal in which she sensitively appraises her successes and failures in regular tutoring with four students.

Harris, Muriel. "Individualized Diagnosis: Searching for Causes, Not Symptoms of Writing Deficiencies." *College English* 40 (1978): 318–23. Reprinted in *Tutoring Writing: A Sourcebook for Writing Labs*, edited by Muriel Harris, pp. 53–59. Glenview, Ill.: Scott, Foresman, 1982.

Harris discusses preliminary questions that tutors can ask, ranging from whether the student thinks writing well will be important in future work to what she wants to learn, in order to ascertain her attitudes, apprehensions, hostilities.

———. "Modeling: A Process Method of Teaching." *College English* 45 (1983): 74–84.

Harris suggests two strategies for helping students in conference: one is to ask the student to compose aloud in front of the instructor (using a thinking-aloud protocol current in writing research); the other is for the instructor to compose aloud in front of the student, modeling desirable behaviors.

Hawkins, Thom. "Intimacy and Audience: The Relationship Between Revision and the Social Dimension of Peer Tutoring." *College English* 42 (1980): 64–69. Reprinted in *Tutoring Writing: A Sourcebook for Writing Labs,* edited by Muriel Harris, pp. 27–31. Glenview, Ill.: Scott, Foresman, 1982.

Hawkins discusses the dual role of the peer tutor: both instructor (superior) and friend (equal). The latter role enables the tutee to learn about the academic audience in an unthreatening way.

Herman, Jerry. *The Tutor and the Writing Student: A Case Study.* Curriculum Publication No. 6. Berkeley: University of California, Bay Area Writing Project, 1979.

Herman provides a brief case study of a basic writer working through six drafts of a paper; he also includes a transcript of the final tutoring session.

Hunt, Doug. "Diagnosis for the Writing Lab." In *Tutoring Writing: A Sourcebook for Writing Labs,* edited by Muriel Harris, pp. 66–73. Glenview, Ill.: Scott, Foresman, 1982.

Hunt discusses how to diagnose a student's writing problems, both formally through objective tests and analytic grading and informally through questions that probe for attitude, skills, potential.

Irmscher, William F. *Teaching Expository Writing.* New York: Holt, Rinehart and Winston, 1979.

Irmscher gives a sound overview of the process of writing and how to teach it. He includes representative projects—on prewriting, structure, words, mechanics, style—for classroom teachers.

Jacobs, Suzanne E., and Karliner, Adela B. "Helping Writers to Think: The Effect of Speech Roles in Individual Conferences on the Quality of Thought in Student Writing." *College English* 38 (1977): 489–505.

In discussing two partial transcripts of conferences with students, one of which led to successful revision while the other did not, Jacobs and Karliner point out how the instructor needs to learn not to dominate discussion.

Jacoby, Jay. "Shall We Talk to Them in 'English': The Contributions of Sociolinguistics to Training Writing Center Personnel." *Writing Center Journal* 4, no. 1 (1983): 1–14.

Jacoby discusses the interpersonal skills that tutors need, especially what they can learn from ethnographic and sociolinguistic studies of teaching and learning.

Judy, Stephen N., and Judy, Susan J. *The English Teacher's Handbook: Ideas and Resources for Teaching English.* Cambridge, Mass.: Winthrop, 1979.

Ostensibly for teachers of English at all levels, the Judys' book especially addresses the needs of middle- and high-school teachers. Their discussions of reading, writing, and language study stress the need for active student participation and variety. They discuss alternatives to traditional grading and how to individualize instruction, deal with the public, and use media. Also noteworthy are their creative Dear Abby and panel discussion sections, and their appendixes listing resources, including freebies.

Lichtenstein, Gary. "Ethics of Peer Tutoring in Writing." *Writing Center Journal* 4, no. 1 (1983): 29–34.

What Lichtenstein, a peer tutor, means by "ethics" is "principles": he discusses six principles for peer tutoring, including gaining trust and facilitating the process of writing without interfering with it.

Murray, Donald M. "The Listening Eye: Reflections on the Writing Conference." *College English* 41 (1979): 13–18. Reprinted in *Rhetoric and Composition: A Sourcebook for Teachers and Writers,* edited by Richard L. Graves. 2d ed., pp. 263–68. Upper Montclair, N.J.: Boynton/Cook, 1984.

Murray offers personal reflections on teaching writing through conference—on teaching the full process of writing, on listening, on expecting the student to take control.

———. *A Writer Teaches Writing: A Practical Method of Teaching Composition*. Boston: Houghton Mifflin, 1968.

In this early volume, addressed to teachers at all levels, Murray encourages the teacher to attend to ordering and rewriting as well as writing, to diagnose and coach rather than dictate, to confer frequently with individual students, to encourage students to teach one another and themselves. He includes frequent advice and quotations from professional writers, including facsimiles of pages revised by famous authors.

Neman, Beth. *Teaching Students to Write*. Columbus: Merrill, 1980.

Neman suggests a number of sound approaches to teaching the process of writing, including creative writing, and grounds them in relevant research. Especially useful are her transcriptions of taped classes.

North, Stephen. "Writing Center Diagnosis: The Composing Profile." In *Tutoring Writing: A Sourcebook for Writing Labs,* edited by Muriel Harris, pp. 42–52. Glenview, Ill.: Scott, Foresman, 1982.

North offers guidelines for learning about a student's composing process at the beginning of a series of conferences. He provides a chart for noting salient features.

Reigstad, Thomas J., and McAndrew, Donald A. *Training Tutors for Writing Conferences*. Theory and Research into Practice. Urbana, Ill.: Educational Resources Information Center and National Council of Teachers of English, 1984.

After discussing the theory and research underpinning collaborative learning and peer tutoring, Reigstad and McAndrew outline a course for training peer tutors. In discussing both the composing and the tutoring processes they suggest tutoring priorities, steps in tutoring, and three different tutoring styles. They also include forms, handouts, and an outline of a course for training tutors.

Roberts, Patricia. "A Peer Tutor Assesses her Teaching Ability." In *Improving Writing Skills,* edited by Thom Hawkins and Phyllis Brooks. New Directions for College Learning Assistance, No. 3, pp. 39–40. San Francisco: Jossey-Bass, 1981.

Roberts, a peer tutor, touches on such topics as suggesting instead of prescribing solutions, learning together with a tutee, fostering the tutee's sense of personal worth.

Sarbin, Theodore R. "Cross-Age Tutoring and Social Identity." In *Children as Teachers: Theory and Research on Tutoring,* edited by Vernon L. Allen, pp. 27–40. New York: Academic Press, 1976.

In examining the roles played by tutors, Sarbin stresses the importance of caring, which is characteristic of what social psychologists call an ascribed relationship.

Schaier, Barbara T., ed. *Critical Issues in Tutoring.* [New York]: Networks, Bronx Community College, n.d.
In addition to providing overviews of a number of tutoring programs and also sample handouts, this volume includes some suggestions for diagnosing a tutee's problems and for interacting with tutees.

Simmons, Jo An McGuire. "The One-to-One Method of Teaching Composition." *College Composition and Communication* 35 (1984): 222–29.
Building on the work of Roger Garrison, Simmons discusses the assumptions behind teaching writing through conferences, the advantages and disadvantages, and also the mechanics.

Spear, Karen I. "Empathy and Re-vision." In *Revising: New Essays for Teachers of Writing,* edited by Ronald A. Sudol, pp. 156–62. Urbana, Ill.: Educational Resources Information Center and National Council of Teachers of English, 1982.
Drawing upon the psychological therapist's notion of empathy, Spear argues that communicating empathy with a student—e.g., through paraphrasing—enhances the student's re-vision of a piece of writing.

Steward, Joyce S., and Croft, Mary K. *The Writing Laboratory: Organization, Management, and Methods.* Glenview, Ill.: Scott, Foresman, 1982.
One of the four chapters in this volume is devoted to conference teaching—in particular, how to conduct different kinds of conferences, as illustrated in two transcripts.

Walvoord, Barbara E. Fassler. *Helping Students Write Well: A Guide for Teachers in All Disciplines.* New York: Modern Language Association, 1982.
In this guide for teaching writing across the curriculum, Walvoord discusses the value of writing, how to incorporate it in a course, how to coach a student through the process of focusing and organizing, how to respond to error. She includes a brief discussion of conferences, frequent samples of writing, and a particularly good chapter on style.

Wiener, Harvey S. *The Writing Room: A Resource Book for Teachers of English.* With an Annotated Bibliography on Basic Writing by Ted Sheckels. New York: Oxford University Press, 1981.
Wiener's volume, addressed to beginning teachers of basic writing, discusses how to teach the paragraph and also sentence-level skills, how to organize the class, how to test and respond to writing, how to use support services. The annotated bibliography is also helpful.

DATE DUE